# A Blossom Like No Other

Ci Poems : —

Pages 6, 9 (ci means lyrics for a melody)
11/12/13/14/34 →

37 — Chinese literary tradition writers
borrow each others thoughts + styles

— not plagurism!
incorporate into own work

(40/41)          — a validation for my approach!
55/57/72/73/80

# A BLOSSOM LIKE NO OTHER
## LI QINGZHAO

*Wei Djao*

Ginger Post Inc.
Toronto Ontario Canada

Ginger Post Incorporated
Toronto Ontario Canada

Translations of Li Qingzhao's writings by Wei Djao.
Maps of Northern Song and Southern Song by Wei Djao.
Portrait of Li Qingzhao by Wei Djao.

Djao, Wei, 1943-
    A blossom like no other : Li Qingzhao / Wei
Djao. -- 1st paper ed.
Includes bibliographical references and index.

    1. Li, Qingzhao, 1084-ca. 1156.  2. Poets, Chinese--Song dynasty, 960-1279--Biography.  3. Women poets, Chinese--Biography.  I. Title.  II. Title: Li Qingzhao.

PL2682.Z5D43 2010          895.1'142          C2009-906764-1

ISBN 978-0-9813251-1-8
ISBN Agency/Agence ISBN
Library & Archives Canada/Bibliotheque & Archives Canada
555, boul. de la Cite, Gatineau, Qc K1A 0N4

Chinese calligraphy:  Irene Chu

**To Tony**

# Contents

Map of Northern Song  xi

Map of Southern Song  xii

Portrait of Li Qingzhao by Wei Djao  xiii

Preface  xv

1  Introduction: Poet's Blossom  1

    The Blossom  1

    Chinese Names and Romanization  3

    Chinese Calendar and the System of Reckoning Age  5

    Ethnicity in China  6

    *Ci* Form of Poetry  6

    Works Collected and Preserved  13

    Overview of the Book  16

2  Early Life  18

    Her Name  18

    Song Dynasty  20

    Father and the Scholar-Official Class  23

    Mother  27

    Ancestral Town and Early Years  30

    Early Writings  34

        *Ci*  34

        *Shi*  40

3  Marriage  51

    Zhao Mingcheng  51

*Ci* of the Newly Wed   55

**Political Turmoil: Factional Strife**   57

Background – the New Laws   57

Reformers and Conservatives   60

Zhao Tingzhi   63

**Last Years in the Capital**   70

**4   Years in the Province   76**

**Retreat to Qingzhou**   76

**Collectors and Editors**   82

***Ci*, Anecdotes and Relics**   84

**Essay on *Ci***   92

**Manuscript: *Jin Shi Lu***   95

**Reinstatement of Zhao Mingcheng**   98

**Desolation**   102

**5   Moving South   114**

**Jin Invasion**   114

**Nanjing Sojourn**   120

**Leaving Nanjing**   130

**Moving Inland**   134

**Li Qingzhao and the Collection**   142

**6   Second Marriage and Divorce   156**

**Mystery of Second Marriage**   157

**Divorce**   159

**Controversy about Remarriage**   165

**7   Later Years   178**

**Poems in Honour of the Envoys**   178

Hangzhou 1133 – 1134   181

The Year in Jinhua   185

*Historical Record of Emperor Zhe Zong's Reign*   192

Qin Kuai   195

Back in Hangzhou   199

Final Years   203

   Visit to Mi Youren   204

   "A Slow Sad Melody"   204

   Wine and Intoxication   210

   Final Events   211

   Date of Death   213

8   Legacy of Li Qingzhao   215

Her Legacy:  An Open Letter from Li Qingzhao   215

My Character   215

The Collection   217

*Ci* and Other Writings   220

Appendix A   Selected Writings of Li Qingzhao in Chinese   225

Appendix B   Chronology of Chinese History   234

References   237

Index   243

About the Author   250

# Northern Song 960 - 1127 CE

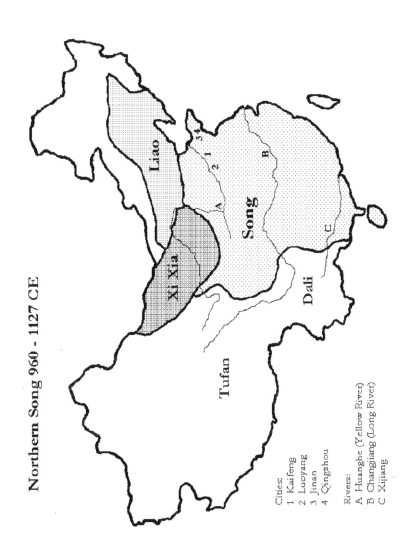

Cities:
1 Kaifeng
2 Luoyang
3 Jinan
4 Qingzhou

Rivers:
A Huanghe (Yellow River)
B Changjiang (Long River)
C Xijiang

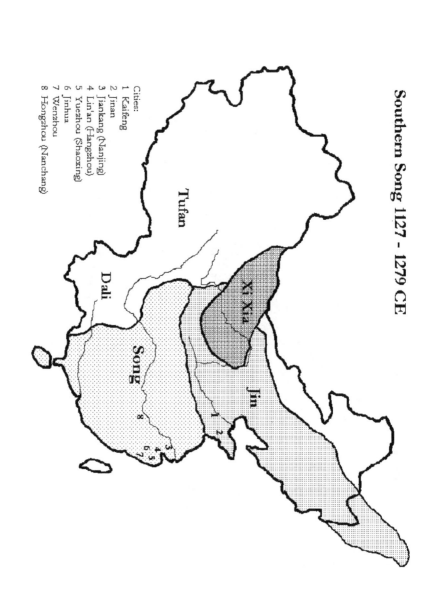

Southern Song 1127 - 1279 CE

Cities:
1 Kaifeng
2 Jinan
3 Jiankang (Nanjing)
4 Lin'an (Hangzhou)
5 Yuezhou (Shaoxing)
6 Jinhua
7 Wenzhou
8 Hongzhou (Nanchang)

Tufan

Dali

Xi Xia

Song

Jin

Li Qingzhao

by Wei Djao

# Preface

My mother Yen Shu-Jen was born on 23<sup>rd</sup> September 1910, a year before the last imperial dynasty of China was swept away by a revolution. This major political development and other social changes in Chinese society were reflected in how she was educated. She had tutors and received a private education at home. She became well versed in the teachings of the classical philosophers, history, essays by the ancient scholars, poetry in a variety of genres, and some novels. Like other youngsters getting an education in China, she spent hours practising calligraphy. She eventually excelled in the *shou jin shu* (瘦金書) style which was developed by Emperor Song Hui Zong (宋徽宗) through whose reign Li Qingzhao had the misfortune to live.

Love stories, such as the *Romance of the Western Chamber* (西廂記), were considered to have a corrupting influence on young people and, therefore, forbidden by her elders. Given the Chinese four-poster bed that had thick curtains on all sides, my mother would take a flashlight and the banned book to bed to read.

An accomplished young woman in the literati tradition was expected to play music. My mother did not learn to play any Chinese instruments. Instead her father arranged to have violin lessons for her. I think she was an indifferent violinist at best as I did not ever see that musical instrument in her presence. But later as a mother she saw to it that all her daughters would receive piano lessons.

When she was in her late teens, her father sent her to the prestigious McTyeire School for girls (中西女子中學)* in Shanghai, founded and run by American women missionaries, famous for teaching Chinese girls Western etiquette and deportment, and above all, a proficient knowledge of the English language. Although her home was in Shanghai, she was a boarder at school and spent some of the happiest years of her life there. Her school mates became her lifelong friends.

A photograph of her taken with her sister-in-law in the 1920s shows her in short hair and wearing a beaded vest with a high collar over a blouse, a mid-calf skirt, and Mary Jane shoes with one-and-half inch heels. That must have been the fashionable attire in the Western style in Shanghai at that time. This picture is symbolic of her life and the Shanghai society at that time: Chinese but with many American and European trappings.

My mother never graduated from McTyeire. She was 24 *sui* when she completed five out of the six years of secondary education. Her father thought that she should get married at that advanced age. She married my father, Djao Sing-Ming, who was her cousin's friend and fellow graduate from the University of Shanghai.

My siblings and I left Shanghai for Hong Kong in 1952, my parents having gone there a few years earlier. My fourth sister and I, the youngest girls in the family, did not even know the English alphabet at that time and English was a required subject in all the schools in Hong Kong. For half an academic year our mother kept us at home. She taught us English in the morning and classical Chinese in the afternoon. On many days after the lessons, she would leave us to practise English grammar and memorize classical Chinese essays while she did one of her favourite pastime activities: visiting with her former neighbours from Shanghai, seeing her best friend Lena Chen Miao, or window-shopping in a department store.

It was a rather easy-going term but it turned out to be one of the most meaningful and influential learning experiences I had in my life. Years later I realized that my love of Chinese literature, history and philosophy began in those few months when I was home-schooled. Although I became a social scientist and taught sociology, social policy and later Global/Asian Studies, in the final years as a full-time professor I managed to teach courses in Chinese history, literature or philosophy every year. I greatly enjoyed the opportunity and was happy that some of the knowledge I received from my mother was passed on to others.

I do not think that in those first months in Hong Kong my mother taught us Li Qingzhao's poems as they would be deemed too sad, too adult or too deep for us in the pre-teen years. But a couple of years later I found Li Qingzhao's *ci* among my mother's own reading materials. Those poems would have resonated with her as she too endured much loss in migrating south.

My mother composed some *ci* in the last years of her life. But they were lost forever in our family's global migration.

In the summer when I was 14 years old, I read the novel *Dream of the Red Mansions* (紅樓夢) by Cao Xueqin for the first time. It was wonderful having my mother around as I would throw out questions about the any of the over 200 characters, phrases or customs mentioned in the novel and she was the walking reference book who answered my questions.

My mother was a good seamstress.   She taught me how to embroider, knit and crochet. After our relocation to Hong Kong, in order to economize, she learned dress design and dressmaking. She sewed most of our Western-style dresses including school uniforms, but a tailor from Shanghai would make our Chinese dresses.

While in Hong Kong she got a recipe from her best friend and baked an orange cake on two or three occasions. I can still produce an orange cake if necessary. But my mother was not into cooking. I don't recall ever eating a meal cooked by her. Her daughters, sink or swim, had to learn cooking from other sources. I think she preferred reading to cooking.

When her daughters were all learning English in regular school, my mother enrolled in some English courses to develop further her proficiency in that language.

My mother would not have regarded herself as clever or learned. She probably thought of herself as less capable than her sisters-in-law or other relatives. Those who did not know her said that she was weak and pampered, like a flower grown in a hothouse. That is not my view. My mother raised five daughters and a mentally challenged son under circumstances not of her choosing. If that did not demonstrate strength of character, tell me what it was!

It will be the 100$^{th}$ anniversary of my mother's birth next year. But she only lived 50 years. Aside from the devastating grief of a daughter on the death of her mother that I felt, I lost a friend and a mentor. Throughout my adult life I have always lamented that I could not ask her about Chinese words, literature, philosophy and history, or whatever, including the life and writings of Li Qingzhao, that I happen to be concerned with at any time. Writing this book is my way of commemorating my mother and expressing my gratitude to her for having given me life, taught me, and enriched my existence.

My intellectual debts are impossible to repay as ideas and advice of my friends were so generously given. Nonetheless, I want to thank publicly those who rendered invaluable assistance in the writing and producing of the book. My deep gratitude goes to Godfrey Lee. I approached him, a *ci* and *shi* composer, for help as I needed to explain *ci* albeit briefly as a special genre of Chinese poetry. He helped me with that and then went on to read the entire manuscript, through several iterations, over every word and every detail, despite his very demanding schedule as the Director of Marine Engineering of a large American shipbuilding company. He caught numerous errors, not only in spelling or syntax, but also in content and in the translation of Li Qingzhao's poems. With his knowledge of Chinese literature and history, he saved me from many possible embarrassments.

A very warm "Thank You" goes to my sister Irene Chu for her calligraphy on the book cover. Marcia Barton, Leslie Padorr, my Aunt Winnie Lee, and Cousin Stephanie Chao also read the manuscript and gave insightful comments. From their wealth of knowledge Professors Helen Wu, Howard Xie, and Dora Choi Po-King provided me with important advice and suggestions about various issues related to Chinese literature and language. I would like to take the opportunity to thank Robert Rodbourne for the inspiration to write the concluding the chapter in the style that I did. With her expertise in drawing comic strips, my sister Yvonne Fung helped me immensely in creating the electronic maps. Lian Chan rendered indispensable services in the course of my research for and production of the book.

I finished a first draft of the book manuscript just before I began the 96-hour program in learning the Yan Xin Life Science and Technology. The program helped me through the tedious and apparently endless process of proofreading and revision; the challenging tasks of creating an index, the maps and a portrait of Li Qingzhao; and the vexations of producing the book. Learning and practising the basics of Yan Xin qigong, I found that I was able to concentrate better and procrastinate less. My sincere gratitude to Dr. Yan!

Again, without the unfailing, loving support and encouragement from Tony and Liso, this book would not have happened. Thank you!

Wei Djao
Toronto, autumn 2009

*McTyeire School was renamed No. 3 High School after Liberation in 1949

# 1 Introduction: Poet's Blossom

Li Qingzhao (李清照) was born in China over 900 years ago. Why is she significant to the English-reading public in the twenty-first century? The readers could only answer the question for themselves by the end of the book. But from the short explanation of the title of the book in the next section they may find a few essential aspects of her character which formed the compelling basis for writing this book.

In this Introductory chapter, after the section about the title of the book, there will be a discussion of several aspects of Chinese culture meant to assist the reader in understanding the context and the background of Li Qingzhao's life and works. The cultural issues are: first, the Chinese names and their Romanization; second, the Chinese calendar and the Chinese system of counting age; and third, ethnicity in China. Readers who are familiar with such topics can skip these three sections.

After the three sections about Chinese culture, there will be a discussion of the form of *ci* (詞) poetry for which Li Qingzhao is best known today. It will be followed by information about her works as collected and preserved through the centuries. The final section of this chapter is an overview of the book.

## The Blossom

Women in different cultures throughout time have been compared to the flower. Their beauty, graceful poise, delicate stature or sensibility is often described in terms of the delightful appeal afforded by the shape, colour, fragrance or attractiveness of a flower. Poems and songs with a floral motif are thus composed in tribute to women. However, since the second half of the twentieth century, it has been popular in some circles to shun from such comparisons as the focus on the physical beauty and delicacy of women, as an exquisite flower, is seen at times as demeaning to women. Comparing women to flowers seems to stress the bodily aspects of women. This all too often is associated with the exploitation of women with explicit or subtle allusions to the reproductive structure of both the woman and the flower. Against such a backdrop, some women and men across the globe in the twenty-first century feel that comparing women to blossoms as ignoring or negating other qualities of womanhood such as intelligence, strength, creativity and various talents. There is, therefore, a reluctance to employ the floral metaphor in regards to women.

The title of this book is not meant as a reversion to the less than flattering perception and description of women. Rather the metaphor not only emphasizes Li Qingzhao's beauty of mind and body, but draws us to some other common characteristics shared by her and the flowers. With what some critics would call traces of narcissism, she described herself, her thoughts and moods in her poetry where a variety of flowers appeared. They included plum blossoms, chrysanthemums, peony, begonia, lotus, pear and almond blossoms, osmanthus (cassia), the banana palm and many others. She praised the floral beauty and lamented its transience as thousands of other writers, in different cultures, have done since time immemorial. But her intense love of nature and particularly the flowers took her into a multi-faceted appreciation as if they were her intimate friends. She delighted in the flora whatever the season, whether they were the browning lotus leaves in autumn or the vigorous begonia that had been drenched by a summer shower. She saw herself and other women in them. For example, she teased her husband and dared him to say whether she or the flower was prettier.[1] On another occasion, she had become thin like the slender yellow chrysanthemums as a way of saying how much she missed her absent husband.[2] In her old age she compared her loneliness to the remaining plum blossoms on the branch.[3] The wilted chrysanthemum petals scattered on the ground, ignored by all, accentuated her own solitude.[4]

In Li Qingzhao's eyes the flowers like women were not frail or insipid. She saw in various blossoms beauty and fun, sorrow and loneliness, and strength and nobility of character. In particular she loved the plum blossom about which she wrote most frequently. In one poem written in her youth, she rejoiced in beholding the plum

---

[1] "The Abridged Version of Magnolia Blossom" in Chapter 3.
[2] "Inebriated in the Shadow of Flowers" in Chapter 4.
[3] "Telling Heartfelt Sentiments" in Chapter 5.
[4] "A Slow Sad Melody" in Chapter 7.

blossoms which appeared in all its splendour deep in winter.  In their very subtle fragrance and sparkling beauty on snow-laden branches in the moonlight she also felt hope and strength because they could withstand the bitter cold and snow to herald the coming of spring. Prophetically perhaps she was anticipating her future life:  she would weather much bitter cold later, but throughout her life she held up the beauty and strength of her character and of her mind like the plum blossom.  Indeed "this blossom is like no other" (see her *ci* to the tune of "The Fisherman's Pride" in Chapter 2).  Li Qingzhao ennobled the beauty, the fragrance and the elegance of the floral metaphor for all women to savour and enjoy with pride.

Li Qingzhao's brilliant and versatile talents have been rarely matched by anyone, male or female, over time or across space.  Her works, with genuine hallmarks of the only kind of immortality she probably would care to have, continue to delight the hearts and stimulate the minds of all who read them.  She was valiant in handling misfortunes.  But essentially she was a Chinese woman who lived in a specific period of time.  She had some unique advantages, but she was brought up like thousands of other girls of her class.  She walked in the footsteps of her mother, stepmother, and mother-in-law.  She kept company with her kinswomen who would forever remain nameless.  Her many talents blossomed under the nurturing guidance of a very literary family.  But it was by her strength of character, stamina and courage that she put her abilities and talents to such use that her extant writings still reflect the history and sentiments of a whole era.

Despite gaps in the present state of knowledge about her life and her writings, this book will add some human dimensions to her name and life.  My purpose for writing it is that the English-reading public will come to appreciate Li Qingzhao and her splendour while dispelling the stereotypes about past and contemporary Chinese women so popular in the global mass media.

## Chinese Names and Romanization

In referring to a person's name in China, the family name always comes first.  Chinese names used in this book will always begin with

the family name.  Most family names consist of a single character.[5]
However, there are a small number of family names that have two
characters, for example, Ouyang, Sima, Gongsun and Zhuge.
Personal names can consist of one or two characters.  During the
Song dynasty (宋朝 960 – 1279 CE), the conventional nomenclature
among the scholar-official gentry class was that the personal name
(*ming* 名) often would consist of one or two characters which friends
and colleagues out of respect would not normally use in addressing
the person.  The scholar would also have a courtesy name (*zi* 字),
usually consisting of two characters, which would be used by friends.
A scholar would often have a sobriquet or a style name (*hao* 號) which
could consist of two to four characters and which would often express
an aspect of the person's character, favourite activity or special
location.

As far as we know, Li Qingzhao did not have a courtesy name,
the *zi*, as it was not customary for women to have it.  She gave herself
the *hao* of Yi'an Jushi (易安居士 meaning the easily contented
inhabitant.  See Chapter 4 for further details).  She used this *hao*, or
simply Yi'an in her works.  She and her works would also be referred
to as Li Yi'an in the scholars' writings of Song and Yuan dynasties,
including the official history of the Song dynasty.

Due to the small number of Chinese family names for a very
large population, full names will be used most of the time in this book
in order to prevent any confusion. The person may only be referred to
by the family name if he/she is mentioned in the same paragraph.

The process of rendering the pronunciation of Chinese proper
nouns – names of people and places – into the Latin alphabet, which
is used in English, is called Romanization.  There have been many
ways and systems of Romanizing Chinese names.  The system
followed in China and the United Nations today is the *pinyin* (拼音)
system, which among all the Romanization systems used in the 19th
and 20th centuries provides the most accurate pronunciation in the
standard spoken Chinese known as  Putonghua (普通話 meaning the
common speech) or Mandarin.  The *pinyin* system will be used
throughout this book.

---

[5] A written word in Chinese is referred to as a character in English.  See
section on the *ci* form of poetry later in this chapter for more details about
the Chinese language.

# Chinese Calendar and the System of Reckoning Age

The measure word for a person's age in Chinese culture is *sui* (歲). It is usually translated into English as "year." However, the way of counting the years in a person's age is different in China. In the Chinese system of reckoning age, an infant is one *sui* at birth. One's age then increases by one *sui* at every Chinese New Year. Thus after the baby's first New Year, it is two *sui*. The baby is three *sui* after the second New Year, and so forth. In Li Qingzhao own writings, she would indicate her age in terms of *sui*. Most Chinese biographers and literary critics of Li Qingzhao use the Chinese *sui* in writing about her life or the age of those close to her. The Chinese convention will be followed in this book and whenever the age of any person is mentioned it refers to the *sui*.

The Chinese calendar dates back over 4,000 years. It has undergone many changes enabling more accurate calculations. It is essentially based on the lunar cycle but is also bound to the solar year. There are names for the years, months, days and hours, using a combination of ten characters known as the "heavenly stems" and twelve others known as the "earthly branches"[6] (Bai 2002:58). In the Song times, the month was usually given by number while the year was presented in terms of the reign title of the Emperor, for example, "the third year of *Jianyan* (建炎)."[7] That year was 1129 CE in the Gregorian calendar. *Jianyan* was one of the reign titles of Emperor Song Gao Zong (宋高宗) as the emperors of the Song dynasty changed their reign titles from time to time.

To facilitate reading of this book, the year has been converted to the Common Era (CE) or Before the Common Era (BCE) based on the Gregorian calendar. However, the year in the Chinese calendar

---

[6] The ten characters known as "heavenly stem" (*tiangan* 天干) are *jia* 甲, *yi* 乙, *bing* 丙, *ding* 丁, *wu* 戊, *ji* 己, *geng* 庚, *xin* 辛, *ren* 壬, *gui* 癸. The twelve characters of the "earthly branch" (*dizhi* 地支) are *zi* 子, *chou* 丑, *yin* 寅, *mao* 卯, *chen* 辰, *si* 巳, *wu* 午, *wei* 未, *shen* 申, *you* 酉, *xu* 戌, *hai* 亥.

[7] The reign period title is the name given to the reign when a new emperor ascended the throne. In the Song dynasty, it was not uncommon for emperors to change the title of their reign and they, therefore, had several reign period names or reign titles.

begins on the second new moon after the winter solstice. This means that the first month in the Chinese calendar is approximately a month later than the first month in the Gregorian calendar, and so forth. For example, if some incident is described as happening in the "second month" of the *wushen* (戊申) year, which was the second year of *Jianyan* of Emperor Song Gao Zong's reign, it would actually have taken place in March of 1128. As it is awkward to use two calendars in presenting the chronology in Li Qingzhao's life, the time of most events will be given in terms of the season, as in the early spring or late summer, of a year in the Common Era. In some cases when the month is actually given, it will be stated as a numbered month in the Chinese calendar, for example, "ninth month in the Chinese calendar" while the year will also be provided in the narrative.

## Ethnicity in China

China is a multiethnic society as it was in Li Qingzhao's time. Today there are 56 officially recognized ethnic groups in China. The most numerous group is the Han (漢), comprising about 90 percent of the total population.

Some ethnic groups trace their ancestry to places outside of China. The ancestors of the Hui, for example, were Arabs and Persians who came to China mainly as traders. Others groups invaded and conquered China, such as the Mongols and the Manchu. Some groups became Sinicized while others retained their separate identities and cultures. All ethnic groups, with the exception of the Hui, have their own language; the Hui use the Han Chinese language.

What is generally regarded as Chinese – people, language and customs, etc. – is usually that of the Han Chinese. Li Qingzhao wrote in the Han language. Unless otherwise stated, the word "Chinese" in this book refers to the Han Chinese.

## *Ci* Form of Poetry

Li Qingzhao used a variety of genres. In her own life time and the decades immediately following, she was best known for her *shi* poems

(詩), a more widely used form of poetry, and essays (*wen*文). But in the centuries since then she is most revered for her *ci* which is a specific form of poetry. Since Li Qingzhao is best known in the world as a *ci* poet and many of her *ci* will be discussed in this book, a cursory explanation of this particular form of Chinese poetry may be helpful to some readers.[8]

Chinese is a monosyllabic language. This means that each word has only one syllable. For example, in English, the word "cat" is monosyllabic whereas "table" has two syllables. In Chinese, "cat," "table" and most other words are monosyllabic. However, there are terms in the Chinese language that are made up of two or more characters, each of which separately has its own meaning. For example, the flower peony is *mudan* (牡丹). But *mu* by itself means "male," used especially in ancient times to describe male animals while the word *dan* by itself means the colour red. Nonetheless, while *mudan* has two syllables each of the words (*mu* and *dan*) that make up the term is monosyllabic.

In the written language, most words in Chinese writing are pictographs, ideographs, or some combinations of them. A word may also contain a signifier that suggests its pronunciation or meaning. Insofar as the written Chinese is not a phonic but a pictorial script, each written word is referred to as a character in English.

The monosyllabic nature of the Chinese word or character is important in this discussion of Chinese poetry. The meter in poetry is governed by the number of syllables in a line, which in the Chinese language, whether in the case of a *shi* or *ci,* is the same as the number of characters.

The most ancient anthology of poems in China, and in fact in the world, is the *Book of Poetry* (詩經), which contains 305 poems. The oldest pieces in the collection were composed in the Shang dynasty (商朝) which lasted from between 16th and 11th centuries BCE[9]. The

---

[8] The development of Chinese poetry and the essential characteristics of *ci* presented in this section, unless indicated by other reference citations, are based on the unpublished manuscript on Chinese poetry by Godfrey Lee (also known as Li Mengxuan) who is a *ci* and *shi* poet.

[9] When a dynasty is mentioned for the first time in this book, its years according to the Common Era (CE) or Before the Common Era (BCE) will immediately follow. The dating of various dynasties in this book follows the

most recent pieces were from the time of Kong Fuzi (孔夫子 551 – 479 BCE)[10] who according to tradition was an editor of the book. Most of the *shi* in the *Book of Poetry* have four characters in each line. In later centuries *shi* with uniform five-character lines or seven-character lines became more popular.

During the long Zhou dynasty (周朝 11th century – 256 BCE) and the very short Qin dynasty (秦朝 221 – 206 BCE) lyrics that could be set to music and accompanied by instruments were called *shi*. In the Han dynasty (漢朝 206 BCE – 220 CE)[11], Emperor Han Wu Di (漢武帝 the fifth emperor of the Western Han dynasty) established the Office of Music, known as the *yuefu* (樂府). It was responsible for many musical poems which were called song lyrics of the Office of Music, *yuefu geci* (樂府歌辭). Eventually such musical poems were simply referred to as *yuefu*. On the other hand, *shi* became the non-musical poetry.

By the Tang dynasty (唐朝 618 – 907 CE) poets were mainly concerned with *shi*. The ancient *yuefu* melodies of the Han dynasty were long lost. Even when some *shi* were composed in imitation of the style of the *yuefu* poems, they were really not *yuefu* as there was no music to accompany them.

Meanwhile, *shi* since the Han dynasty developed in such a way that the lines of a poem would uniformly consist of five characters in each line, or uniformly of seven characters in each line (Hu 1966:16). In other words, by the Tang time, the vast majority of poems would

---

chronology provided by Fan (1996). A complete chronology of major Chinese dynasties is given in Appendix B.

[10] Kong Fuzi, more commonly known in English by the Latinized name of Confucius, was a philosopher and teacher who lived during a period when there was nominally a king of the Zhou dynasty in China but the heads of many subordinate states were vying for hegemony. His humanist approach in political and social philosophy emphasizes harmonious relationships and qualities such as filial piety, loyalty, perseverance, learning and rituals. It has had a profound influence on Chinese culture up to the present not only in China and but also in Chinese communities around the world. See Fung (1964) and Djao (2003).

[11] The Han dynasty consisted of the Western Han dynasty (西漢 206 BCE – 24 CE) dynasty and the Eastern Han dynasty (東漢 25 – 220 CE).

have all lines with five syllables in each line or all lines with seven syllables in each line. With such a fixed number of syllables in each and every line, there would be unavoidable monotony in any attempt to sing or set a poem to music. While the Tang *shi* were very concise and expressive of the writers' purpose and sentiments, the uniform number of syllables in all lines of every *shi* would diminish its musicality if anyone tried to sing the *shi*.

Thus in the Tang dynasty a new form of poetry developed. Poets began to compose verses with lines of uneven length, that is, the number of characters or syllables would vary from line to line resulting in poems that have long and short lines. This new type of poems with uneven lines was then set to music. Later in the Northern Song dynasty (北宋 960 – 1127 CE),[12] poets began to call these musical poems *yuefu* again, reclaiming the proper name for this new genre of literature. These new *yuefu* poems were in fact *ci*. Li Qingzhao was born into this age of the revival of musical poetry.

There was another impetus to revive musical poetry. It originated in popular songs of the Tang dynasty during which China's contact with its neighbours on all sides was frequent and active. The Chinese and other peoples, from Japan in the east to regions beyond Lake Balkhash in the west, and from Mongolia and Siberia in the north to the islands of the South China Sea, travelled and intermingled. The famous Silk Road established since the Han dynasty, was a busy thoroughfare as goods, ideas and the arts flowed between China and the Western Regions, which included the present day Indian subcontinent, Central Asia, and lands further west such as Iran and Arabia. In fact the Li imperial family of the Tang dynasty was of mixed Chinese and Turkic ancestry. Along with the luxury goods, foods, religions, fashions and many other items of interest introduced to the Chinese through the Silk Road were popular songs (Ayling & MacKintosh 1969:xvii). Originally the melodies would have foreign words. In time the Chinese liked the music so much that they would write their own lyrics to fit the musical tunes from the Western Regions. The new lyrics sung to imported foreign melodies came to be known as *ci*. The word *ci* actually means lyrics for a melody.

---

[12] The Song dynasty (960 – 1279 CE) is divided by historians into Northern Song period (960 – 1127 CE) and the Southern Song period (1127 – 1279 CE). The reasons will be discussed in Chapter 2.

Not all the *ci* tunes were imported.   Some *ci* were written to traditional folk melodies. Many poets, musicians, and even courtesans also composed original music for *ci*.   For example, according to a legend, the envoy of a kingdom in the Western Regions presented several beautiful ladies to the Tang court.   They were dazzlingly stunning with their hair piled high and crowned with gold ornaments. They appeared as if Bodhisattvas had dropped down to earth.   The court musicians were so impressed that they composed a tune in their honour and entitled it "Bodhisattvas' Headdress" (菩薩蠻).   This melody was very popular even into later generations.   Many poets including Li Qingzhao wrote *ci* to this tune.   Of course many *ci* poets from the Tang to the Song dynasties, including the famous Liu Yong (柳永) and Li Qingzhao, were also accomplished musicians who composed music for their own *ci*.

There were five notes (*wu yin* 五音) in Chinese music: *gong* (宮), *shang* (商), *jiao* (角), *zhi* (徵), and *yu* (羽).   They would correspond respectively to *do, re, mi, sol* and *la* in the Western musical scale.   There were 12 standards (*shi er lü* 十二律) which established the correct pitch of each musical note.   This was done by means of the different lengths of the windpipe of the tuning reeds.   Each standard had the five basic notes.   Consequently there were half, quarter, one-third and two-third tones in Chinese music.

Virtually none of the popular tunes of the Tang and Song periods survived to the present.   Only the tunes of one *ci* poet Jiang Kui (姜夔) of the Southern Song dynasty (南宋 1127 – 1279 CE) have come down through the centuries. But they were undeciphered until they were decoded and transcribed into staff notations by some Chinese scholars in the 20th century.   Lawrence Picken later found that the tunes were most likely "four-squares," meaning that although the lines of lyrics had irregular number of Chinese characters, the musical lines "were composed to a rhythmic measure of eight beats" (Ayling & MacKintosh 1969:xvii).   At that time the tunes were mostly sung one musical note to one character or one syllable.   However, a tune might have notes of different time-values, such as the equivalent of the minim (half note) or the quaver (eighth note) in Western music.   As a result there would be an irregular number of notes and, therefore, of syllables or characters in the lines of the poem.   Nonetheless, the rhythm was still regular.   Syllables or characters would be sung to notes of different lengths in different lines.   An example of the combination of regular musical rhythm with irregular line-length of the lyrics is suggested by Ayling and MacKintosh (1969:xviii):

Daisy, Daisy,
Give me your answer, do.
I'm half crazy all for the love of you.
It won't be a stylish marriage,
I can't afford a carriage.
But you'd look sweet upon the seat
Of a bicycle built for two.

Similar to the popular American song quoted above, in those lines of a *ci* where there were many syllables or characters, the notes would be shorter (Ayling & MacKintosh, 1969:xviii). As there were longer and shorter notes in different musical lines, the number of words or characters could also vary from line to line. As a matter of fact, when it first emerged as poetry the *ci* was referred to as verses of long-and-short lines.

The original song of a *ci*, in addition to having a set number of words in each line and its own rhyme scheme, would also have a specific tone pattern. This is due to the peculiarity of oral Chinese as a tonal language, with each spoken word having a fixed tone. The tone refers to the pitch at which a word is pronounced. For example the sound of "yan" can mean very different things and written as quite different characters – smoke 煙, speech or words 言, eye 眼, or swallow 燕, – depending on the pitch at which it is pronounced. In a sense the Chinese language itself is musical.[13] The *ci* poet must pay attention not only to the notes of the tune and rhyming but also to the tones of the words. The musicality of *ci* was very important to Li Qingzhao as she would expound in an essay on the theory of ci. (This essay will be discussed in Chapter 4).

In composing a *ci* the poet could compose a melody and the words for it, or use an existing tune by following the number of words in each line, the rhyme scheme and the tone pattern set in the original song (Hu, 1966:16-21). As *ci* became increasingly popular in the Five Dynasties and Ten Kingdoms period (五代十國 907 – 979 CE) and

---

[13] For further explanation of the tone patterns in the oral Chinese language, refer to any Chinese language textbooks for beginners.

Northern Song period, scholars often chose to use existing songs [14].

By the Northern Song period, *ci* acquired the following characteristics by which contemporary *ci* are still judged:

1. *Ci* could be set to music and sung.

2. Lines in a *ci* have varying number of characters or syllables, in accordance with the number of the musical notes.

3. All *ci* of the same tune have a similar but not necessarily identical structure. This means that sometimes *ci* of the same tune may have different number of characters. Some tunes could be repeated, giving rise to stanzas.

4. The tones of each character and the rhyme used in any *ci* must follow the prescribed tone pattern and the rhyme scheme of a particular tune used.

5. A wider variety of rhymes is allowed in *ci* than in *shi*, but the rules of rhyming are stricter in the former.

6. The words used in *shi* are usually more solemn, almost stately, often dealing with public and political issues. Those in *ci* on the other hand are more elegant and graceful for the purpose of expressing personal feelings.

There are 700 – 800 *ci* tune models in all (Hu 1966:17). Over time as the melodies of the Tang and Song dynasties were also forgotten or lost, *ci* are read rather than sung today. As only the tone patterns and rhyme patterns for composing the lyrics remained, *ci* writing came to be known as filling in the words of the lyrics to the tune while the poet often has little or no idea what the original music sounded like. However, the *ci* composers, even down to the present, must strive to live up to the *ci* characteristics, except the first one, listed above.

Furthermore, the *ci* poets must be aware of the general mood and theme of the original tune. For example, the tune "Waves Washing Away Sand" (浪淘沙) originally expressed aroused impassioned feelings implying a sense of justice and indignation. This tune would be appropriate for recalling the past and expressing concern for the present. But the poet using this tune most likely would not have anything to say about waves or sand in the *ci*. On the other hand, the

---

[14] Between the Tang and the Song dynasties, there were about fifty years of disunity and fragmentation within China. There were in quick succession five dynasties in the north and ten kingdoms in the south.

tune "Butterflies Love Flowers" (蝶戀花) would denote gentleness and elegance, suitable for expressing personal emotions or describing the landscape. Again, a poet's lyrics would not be about butterflies or flowers, but the theme and mood of the *ci* must fit the atmosphere or the aura of the original tune. The lack of congruence in mood between the *ci* and the original tune could cause embarrassment to the poet.

Various writers could and still do write *ci* to the same tune, and all those *ci* would bear the title of the same tune. Most *ci* are referred to by the tune titles, although *ci* may have individual titles as Li Qingzhao did with some of hers. One author could of course write many *ci* to the same tune, as Li Qingzhao did with some tunes. If two or more *ci* were written to the same tune, unless they have individual titles, they are differentiated from each other by the words in the first line. Li Qingzhao's *ci* in this book will be referred to as "To the tune of (the name of a particular tune)," followed by the individual title if any.

## Works Collected and Preserved

Prior to any discussion of Li Qingzhao's writings, it is necessary to describe briefly what is known about the literary legacy she left behind.

Few of Li Qingzhao's works are extant today. The "Records of Arts and Literature" section in the *Song Shi* (宋史 1986:659), the official history of the Song dynasty, lists by her style name (*hao*), Yi'an Jushi, seven volumes of *Yi'an Jushi Wenji* (易安居士文集 *Collected Essays of Yi'an Jushi*) and another six volumes of *Yi'an Ci* (易安詞). The former would consist of her prose and *shi*. Writers of Song and Yuan dynasties who lived closest to her time mentioned 12 or 13 volumes of her works entitled *Li Yi'an Ji* (李易安集 *Collected Works of Li Yi'an*) (Wang 1979:292). It should be emphasized that in the century immediately following her death, she was known and respected first and foremost in literary circles for her *shi* and prose. Zhu Bian (朱弁), a Song writer, said this of her: "She excelled in writing (literary pursuits). Her *shi* was particularly superior." Chao Buzhi (晁補之 1053 – 1110 CE) even regarded her as a *shidafu* (士大夫)" (Wang 1979:208). Chao was a well known scholar whom Li Qingzhao most certainly met in person when she was an adolescent and again later in life (Chen 1995), and *shidafu* was a title only a man could attain after years of assiduous study and passing the civil service examinations. Zhao Yanwei (趙彥衛), also of the Song dynasty, commented that the ink of her writings had hardly dried before people would clamour to have it distributed (quoted in Wang 1979:208). Zhu Xi (朱熹 1130 – 1200 CE), a conservative and influential philosopher of the Southern Song period who promoted the suppression of women ideology, nevertheless admitted that the only two capable women of letters "in the current dynasty were Li Yi'an and Madam Wei (魏夫人)" (Wang 1979: 293).   He then went on to cite several verses from Li Qingzhao's *shi*.

Scholars put greater emphasis on *shi* and prose than on *ci* as the prevailing outlook at that time was that these two genres were part of the mainstream literature.  *Ci,* on the other hand, was something that adorned moments of song and dance in halls of entertainment or private residences.  Even when the status of *ci* was raised and accepted as a legitimate genre employed by more and more scholars including high ranking officials, it was still regarded mainly as a vehicle for expressing personal sentiments and not for discussing weighty matters of the state. Nevertheless, it was also noticed by Zhao Yanwei that her *ci* enjoyed great popularity and had already been published (Liu 1990:114).  At about the same time, different scholars mentioned in their memoirs and records one collection of *ci* by Li Qingzhao entitled *Shu Yu Ji* (漱玉集 *Pure Jade Collection*).  Other writers later mentioned superb calligraphy and paintings by her (Wang 1979:208-209; Yu 1995:12-13).  However, none of this survived to this day.

In the Ming dynasty (明朝 1368 – 1644 CE), the scholar Yang Shen (楊慎) recorded in 1551 that in his efforts to compile an anthology of *ci*, he attempted to find the *ci* collection *Shu Yu Ji* but to no avail (Liu 1990:114).  Towards the end of the Ming dynasty, Mao Jin (毛晉) produced a collection entitled *Shu Yu Ci* (漱玉詞 *Pure Jade Ci*), which was not the original *Shu Yu Ji* mentioned in the Song records. Mao claimed that his collection dated from 1370 in the early Ming period.  However, this collection contained only 17 *ci*.  Later Mao produced another version of *Shu Yu Ci* which contained 49 *ci*.  This collection was copied by hand and not printed. As a result few people knew about it let alone saw it.  Even Wang Xuechu 王學初 (also known as Wang Zhongwen 王仲聞), who was an eminent 20th century scholar and authority on Li Qingzhao and her works, thought that *Shu Yu Ci* was last seen at the end of the Qing dynasty (清朝 1644 – 1911

CE). Although throughout the Ming and Qing periods, interest in Li Qingzhao's works mounted and scholars tried to collect her works from various sources (Wang 1979:292-302; Xu 2002:1-2) far fewer pieces of *shi* and prose were found than her *ci*.

In more recent years a contemporary Li Qingzhao scholar Xu Peijun (徐培均) on a visit to Japan was given a photocopy of Mao's later hand copied version of *Shu Yu Ci* that is kept in Tokyo. It contains 49 of Li Qingzhao's *ci*. Xu was also given a copy of Li Qingzhao's *ci* entitled the *Shu Yu Ci Hui Chao* (漱玉詞彙鈔) that was edited by two Qing dynasty scholars in 1830 during the Qing dynasty (1644 – 1911 CE) and that is now kept in Tokyo. It has 51 *ci*. Furthermore, Xu notes that the Shanghai Library has a version of *Shu Yu Ci* from 1830 which contains 38 *ci*, six *shi*, six essays and an appendix of four anecdotes (Xu 2002:2-3).

Among Li Qingzhao's extant works today, there are about 50 *ci*, about 14 *shi*, some fragmentary verses, and five or six essays (Xu 2002:1; Liu 1990:115; see also Zhu, Sun, and Rong 1984; Hou and Lü 1985; Chen 1995; Sun 2004). The numbers are imprecise because there is uncertainty about the authenticity of some of her writings as her Yi'an style was copied by numerous later *ci* writers. Debate continues and so does research as to what Li Qingzhao wrote or did not write. However, all the *ci*, *shi* and essays discussed in this book are generally accepted as coming from Li Qingzhao's hand.

In her *ci*, Li Qingzhao would sometimes use the word *ren* 人, meaning people or person, to denote herself. She rarely used first person pronouns "I," "we," "my," or "our" at all in her *ci*. The first person pronouns would appear in the translation of her *ci* in this book only when there is no other way of making the meaning clear.

In this book, the placement of selected pieces of Li Qingzhao's *ci* at various periods of her life reflects my interpretation of her poetry, the events in her life, and the history of the Song dynasty. My interpretation is influenced to a large extent by the evidence and discussions of past and present experts on Li Qingzhao. Undoubtedly many critics would disagree with the chronological order of her *ci* presented here. Except for a couple of pieces, there is no certainty as to when any of her *ci* were composed; thus other interpretations are welcome.

## Overview of the Book

In the rest of the book, Chapter 2 is about her family background and early life, together with some *shi* and *ci* thought to have been written before her marriage. Chapter 3 covers the time from her marriage to Zhao Mingcheng (趙明誠), courtesy name Zhao Defu (趙德甫), at the age of 18 *sui* to the time when she and her husband retired to Qingzhou (青州) in their ancestral province of Shandong (山東省). Chapter 4 is about those years of seclusion in Qingzhou when the couple was able to devote most of their time and material resources to scholarly activities. Chapter 5 describes the major upheavals in her personal life and in the political conditions of the Song dynasty. Zhao Mingcheng was assigned to new posts while the political deterioration of the Northern Song court ended in its demise. Li Qingzhao along with many other officials and their families became exiles in the southern part of China where Zhao Mingcheng died. She was then 46 *sui*. Chapter 6 is about her controversial second marriage and divorce. Chapter 7 is about her final years. The last chapter will be an assessment of Li Qingzhao's legacy, in her own voice: her character, *ci*, and worldview including some thoughts on the art collection to which she and her husband Zhao Mingcheng devoted so much of their life.

Throughout the book, a conscious effort is made to include the time and place of her life, that is the Song dynasty and its shrinking domains. The happiness and pleasures she savoured, and the sadness and anguish she experienced could only be fully understood against the backdrop of that dynasty.

Each translated *shi* and *ci* presented in this book will be followed immediately by the original Chinese in traditional characters (*fantizi* 繁體字, more accurately, the "complex form of characters").[15] Some of Li

---

[15] *Fantizi*, the so-called traditional characters, refers to the forms of the written Chinese words that have been in use more or less since the Han dynasty. Some traditional characters run into more than 20 strokes. However, over the centuries a certain degree of simplification of characters was always practised in the calligraphic style known as the "grass script" (草書 *caoshu*) as scribes needed to write very fast. Since the founding of the People's Republic of China in 1949, simplification of the characters was systematized and promoted. Along with other educational reforms the adoption of the simplified characters, *jiantizi*, in China has yielded amazing

Qingzhao's other works mentioned, quoted or discussed in the book but not translated will also appear in Appendix A in traditional characters. Appendix B is a chronology of the major dynasties of China.

When proper nouns and Chinese words appear for the first time in the book, they will be followed by the traditional characters. Chinese words and terms, such as *ci, shi, shidafu* and *sui*, are italicized throughout the book. The index lists all proper nouns and special terms with their original Chinese characters in simplified characters (*jiantizi* 簡體字).

---

results such that the vast majority of people born after 1949 can read and write. *Jiantizi* is used in China while *fantizi* is used in Taiwan, Hong Kong and Macao. It is the former that is usually taught now at educational institutions in the West where Chinese language classes are offered.

# 2 Early Life

## Her Name

There is no record of Li Qingzhao's exact birth date. The most commonly, but not unanimously, accepted view is that she was born in the seventh year of the *Yuanfeng* (元豐) reign periodof the Emperor Song Shen Zong (宋神宗 r. 1067-85 CE).[1] That was the year 1084 CE in the Gregorian calendar (Huang 1974; Wang 1979; and Yu 1995).[2] Her biography is not included in the official history of the Song dynasty, the *Song Shi*. However, she is briefly mentioned in the biography of her father Li Gefei (李格非) in the *Song Shi*, without the dates of her birth or death, as follows: "(Li has a) daughter Qingzhao, particularly renowned for her *shi* and essay in her time. She was married to Zhao Tingzhi's (趙挺之) son Mingcheng. She gave herself the *hao* of Yi'an Jushi" (*Song Shi* 1986:487). Li Qingzhao's *hao*, the style name, means "the easily contented inhabitant" which will be further explained in Chapter 4.

In imperial China, the official history of a dynasty was written by some appointed officials in the succeeding one. The format of the official history was established by Sima Qian (司馬遷 145 – 90 BCE) who wrote the first general Chinese history, *Shi Ji* (史記 often

---

[1] Emperors in this book are referred to by the title Emperor followed by the name of the dynasty and the honorific title given to each emperor posthumously. Thus "Emperor Song Shen Zong" means an emperor in the Song dynasty who was given the posthumous title of Shen Zong. Each emperor would have his own surname, which in the case of the imperial family of the Song dynasty was Zhao (趙). Each emperor would also have a personal name. Emperor Song Shen Zong's personal name was Xu (頊). But in pre-republican China, a person's name was always regarded with respect and not generally used by his associates, and certainly not by his subordinates. It was no exception in the case of emperors. Hence emperors were usually not called by their personal names but by the title of their reign period or by the posthumous title.

[2] An alternative but less accepted view is that Li Qingzhao was born in 1081 (see Deng 2005:2). The chronology followed in this book is based on 1084 as her year of birth.

translated as *Historical Records*), in the Western Han dynasty. This magnum opus encompasses 3,000 years of history from the legendary Yellow Emperor (Huang Di 黃帝), to the author's own time. Half a million words in length, it contains 130 sections, of which 70 are biographies of eminent people. While the general history gives a detailed account of political events, economy, geography, social conditions, and literature of each era, every biography is a concise yet vivid description of the person. *Shi Ji* became the model of all subsequent history writing in which biography of eminent people in each dynasty was an integral feature of any official dynastic history (Sima 1996). Both Li Qingzhao's father Li Gefei and father-in-law Zhao Tingzhi were important enough to have their biography included in the official *Song Shi*, the former for his scholarship and the latter for being a prime minister.

The family name Li is an ancient one. According to tradition, the philosopher Lao Zi (老子 585 – 500 BCE, meaning the old master) was surnamed Li; he was the alleged author of the book *Lao Zi (老子)* popularly known as *Dao De Jing (道德經* see note 6 of this Chapter), which has been translated into many languages and is widely read around the world. The imperial family of the Tang dynasty had the same surname. Perhaps one of the most famous personages by this name was the Tang dynasty poet Li Bai (李白 701 – 762 CE). By Li Qingzhao's time, people with that family name were numerous and spread all over China.

Naming in Chinese culture has always been an important event. In theory any character or a combination of two characters can be the personal name. But those who give names to others or themselves usually give the matter very serious thought. A personal name is to denote some noble, idealistic or praiseworthy aspect of the person's character. At the very least it should be propitious, acting as a good omen in the person's life. The two characters in her personal name, Qingzhao, were most likely selected by her parents, especially her father. They had significant meanings and posed ideals which she could pursue in life. The character *qing* means "clean," "clear" or "pure." The character *zhao* as a noun means a picture or an image. As a verb it means to illuminate, to shine, to light up, to reflect or to mirror. Taken together, *qingzhao* would mean to illuminate clearly and to reflect with purity. As she was born into a very literate and literary family, it could be safely ventured that the parental expectations were that she would always write to illuminate with clarity and with a purity of purpose unsullied by whatever sordidness that might surround her. In life and most certainly through her writings she lived up to those expectations. She illuminated the deepest recesses of her heart, baring her joy and pleasure, sorrow and anguish for all to see whenever she chose to do it. But with unmatched fortitude she fearlessly shone a spotlight on disastrous political situations of the time while the high officials retreated into the corners of silent blindness.

Thus she lived, and this is the tale of her life.

## Song Dynasty

The Song Dynasty was indeed one of the most magnificent periods in Chinese history. But it was also one of the most tragic. It was a time when scholarship was honoured and all forms of arts flourished. It was during the Song that the class of literati truly came to its own. But it was also a dynasty which saw inept rulers, rampant corruption and national humiliation unprecedented among the major dynasties. The dynasty was founded in 960 by one Zhao Kuangyin (趙匡胤) known in history as Emperor Song Tai Zu (宋太祖) who launched the unification of China after over five decades of warlords establishing their short periods of rule in quick succession. In fact after the overthrow of the Tang dynasty in 907, there were five dynasties in the north and ten kingdoms in the south. This was the period of disunity known as the Five Dynasties and Ten Kingdoms in Chinese history. Zhao was an officer of the palace guard of the Later Zhou, the last of the five dynasties in the north. He led a mutiny against the weak boy king. His fellow officers, so it was alleged, came to him and draped a yellow robe over him. The yellow robe was an imperial symbol and thus Zhao was proclaimed an emperor.

Emperor Song Tai Zu established the capital of the Song kingdom in Bianliang (汴梁 the present day Kaifeng 開封 in Henan province 河南省). It was often called the Bianjing (汴京 meaning the Bian capital) which is the name that will be used in this book.

As he essentially came to power by means of a coup d'etat, Emperor Song Tai Zu was fearful that an ambitious soldier might one day topple him and assume the imperial mantel. In an ingenuous manner he solved what he considered a major problem. He held a banquet for all his senior military officers and offered them retirement in the provinces with substantial estates and riches. He then centralized all military, political and financial power in his own hand. This would prove quite disastrous for the Song emperors later as not many of his successors were as capable, conscientious and responsible as he was. Without well trained and trustworthy army leaders that the imperial court could rely upon, throughout the Song dynasty China was militarily unable to deal with invaders at its north and western borders.

Although a military leader, Emperor Song Tai Zu had a profound respect for scholarship. He thought that able ministers who could assist the emperor, himself or his descendants, would best be chosen from among the scholars. The selection process was through the civil service examinations. While the examination system had already been in existence for about a thousand years by then, in previous dynasties, high ranking ministers would usually come from the emperors' own family, the aristocracy with military background or scions of the rich, powerful land-holding clans. However, the examination system was reformed in the Song period in such a way that any scholar by dint of diligence and dedication to learning could pass a series of examinations and thus rise in the civil service. In fact there was a preference for promoting the sons of commoner families, often from the poorer members of the land-owning class, at the expense of those from families of the emperor, the empress, the aristocracy, the senior ministers or the wealthy landlords. This was to ensure that no one family or clan could form a power block that would pose as a threat to the central power which nominally resided in the emperor. The early emperors of the Song dynasty went to such length as disqualifying the successful candidates of the civil service examinations who happened to be scions of senior ministers' families to prevent the formation of any power cliques (Zhuge 2004:7-9).

It was into these circumstances, that is, the suppression of military leaders and promotion of commoner scholars, that the families of Li Qingzhao's parents and their social circle of friends and acquaintances were born (Zhuge 2004:3–11; Huo 1997:61-66).

In literature, the Song dynasty scholars promoted a return to the simple classical style of essay writing, a trend begun in the Tang dynasty. However, it was the *ci* form of poetry that was the crowning glory of Song literary development. As described in Chapter 1, people simply loved the popular musical poems. At first it was just entertainment, and the lyrics were mostly about romantic love between young men and women. But from the time of the Five Dynasties and Ten Kingdoms period to the early Northern Song, that is approximately the $10^{th}$ century, *ci* was raised to the status of high art, to the point that it became the defining feature of Song literature. This can be seen in the explosion of *ci* compositions during the Song dynasty. During the whole of the Tang dynasty and the Five Dynasties and Ten Kingdoms period, there were only about 170 *ci* composers and their extant works total about 2,500 pieces. In the Song dynasty, Northern and Southern, the works of over 1,430 *ci* poets have been preserved, with an astonishing total of more than 20,500 extant pieces (Chen and Wang 2001:i).

The rise of *ci* to such a height was in no small measure due to the creative push by women. Of all social classes – from queens, through the daughters of the scholar-official class, to the prostitutes – women composed superb and unforgettable *ci*. Altogether the works of 107 Song women have been preserved (Zhao & Li 2003:149). Li Qingzhao is the best known among them but she was certainly not alone as a female *ci* poet.

Despite many outstanding and upright civil and military officials, luminous men and women of letters, artists and scientists who remain cherished folk heroes to the present, the Song dynasty is also remembered for the enormous humiliation that it had to endure. It is divided by historians into two periods, the Northern and Southern Song. During the Northern Song period, China was unified but there were smaller non-Han kingdoms in the north and northwest. One of them was Liao (遼) consisting of semi-nomadic but also Sinicized Qidan (契丹) people who were of the Mongolian stock, and the other was Xixia (西夏) of the Tibetan-speaking Tangut ethnic group. There was also another multi-ethnic kingdom in the southwest called Dali (大理) the rulers of which claimed to be of Han ancestry. The kingdom of Jin (金) was founded in 1115 CE by the Nüzhen (女真) ethnic group in the northeast. It destroyed Liao of which it was a vassal state previously. It then proceeded to invade Song and sacked Bianjing in 1127. Emperor Song Hui Zong (宋徽宗) and his son Emperor Song Qin Zong (宋欽宗) in whose favour the former abdicated the previous year, together with their consorts and concubines, sons and daughters, and other retainers, were taken captive to the northeast. They were never to return to China. With the occupation of northern half of China by the Jin, another son of Song Hui Song, who was not in Bianjing at the time of its destruction, escaped to the south and set up court later that year in Jiankang (建康 today's Nanjing 南京 in Jiangsu province 江蘇省) and eventually in Lin'an (臨安), the present day city of Hangzhou (杭州 in Zhejiang province 浙江省)and thus began what is now referred to as the Southern Song dynasty. He became known in history as Emperor Song Gao Zong. Southern Song was eventually destroyed by the Mongols under the leadership of Kublai Khan (忽必烈) who conquered all of China in 1279.

Li Qingzhao was born in the Northern Song period and died in the Southern Song. She like many of her class fled the Jin invasion and became an exile in the region south of the Changjiang (長江 meaning the Long River) also known as Yangzi River (揚子江). She suffered the loss of family, home and country keenly and immortalized her utter sense of sorrow in her poetry. But her life began under much happier circumstances.

## Father and the Scholar-Official Class

Li Qingzhao's father Li Gefei, courtesy name Li Wenshu (李文叔), was such a renowned scholar that his biography was included in the official history of the Song dynasty. He is described as bright and precocious. He passed the highest civil service examination and attained the rank of *jinshi* (進士)[3] in 1076 during the reign of Emperor Song Shen Zong. In the early Song period, following the standards and practice set in the previous Tang dynasty, the literary forms emphasized in the civil service examination were *shi* poetry and the poetic essay *fu* (賦). But Li Gefei emphasized essays in the style of ancient writers and concentrated on the classical traditions, dating back to the time of Kong Fuzi and other philosophers. He wrote over 100,000 words of commentaries and exposition on the classics which unfortunately were lost. His only extant writings are a few poems and a treatise on the famous gardens in Luoyang (洛陽 in

---

[3] *Jinshi* is the highest rank attainable in the civil service examinations. Holders of such a rank were assigned important official positions.

Henan province) where he was an official (Yu 1995:7-8).

Li Gefei began his career as a provincial education officer and examination official in Jizhou (冀州 in present day Hebei province 河北省) and rose to the rank of the highest administrator in the imperial university in the capital. As an official he was conscientious and incorruptible. When he was a professor in the city of Yunzhou (鄆州 in present day Shandong province), his superior sought to supplement his meagre salary with a secondary position. He refused the offer (*Song Shi* 1986:487).

As a scholar of classics, he was intolerant of charlatans who preyed on the ignorance and gullibility of the people. While he was an administrator in another province, there was a daoist priest who in Li Gefei's view was deceiving people with his fortune-telling. Li Gefei met the priest on the road one day and ordered his men to pull the priest from his cart and punish him with a severe lashing. Li Gefei then deported and banned the priest from his administrative domain (*Song Shi* 1986:487).[4]

In 1091 when Li Gefei was a professor at the Imperial University in Bianjing, Emperor Song Zhe Zong (宋哲宗) visited the university and composed poems along with the professors and students. Li was

---

[4] Daoist religion is quite different from daoist philosophy. The latter is a philosophical tradition that traces its origin to Lao Zi, allegedly an older contemporary of Kong Fuzi, and to Zhuang Zi (莊子 circa 369 – 286 BCE) who lived in the latter part of the Warring States period (戰國時代 475-221 BCE). The philosophy of Lao Zi was first classified as the Dao De Jia (道德家), "The School of the Way and its Power" (Fung 1964:31) by the Western Han court historian and librarian Sima Tan (司馬談 d. 110 BCE, father of Sima Qian) as the book *Dao De Jing* (also known as the *Lao Zi*) was thought to be a record of Lao Zi's teachings. This school of philosophy came to be known simply as the Dao Jia, or in English as the daoist school of philosophy. Daoist religion began in the Han dynasty. Its belief system and rituals had origins in shamanism dating back to the neolithic period, a pantheon of gods and goddesses native to China, practices and knowledge of medicine men and women, Buddhist liturgy, veneration of Huang Di (the Yellow Emperor considered by the Chinese as their ancestor) and a few terms from daoist philosophy. Daoist religion was and still is a folk religion with no unified theology or centralized hierarchical organization. As Fung (1964, 1991) points out the daoist philosophy and daoist religion are not only different, but their essential teachings are even contradictory.

entrusted with the task of compiling the poems into a book.  He wrote a preface for it (Yu 1995:25).

As a man of letters, Li Gefei maintained that an essay must flow from genuine sentiments.  There would be only empty words without honesty and sincerity.  He held up literary giants of the past as writing from the heart (*Song Shi* 1986:487).  This kind of literary critique and standards must have been the foundation of Li Qingzhao's upbringing and education from her earliest days.

Li Qingzhao's father Li Gefei in many ways epitomized the ideal scholar-official.  Many years later after her migration to the south, Li Qingzhao wrote a poem in honour of a high official.  In it she described both her father and paternal grandfather as neither attaining senior positions nor striving for wealth.  Instead they achieved unblemished and highly respected reputation as upright and dedicated scholar-officials. They would congregate with other scholars to engage in passionate discussions of national and political issues of the day (Wang 1979:109-111).

Li Qingzhao's forebears were like many scholars of the Song dynasty who were from the commoner background, but were dedicated to the ideals of learning and leadership in political affairs. They were well versed in the philosophical traditions, especially the *ru* school (儒家) based on the teachings of Kong Fuzi and Meng Zi (孟子) on the one hand, and the daoist school founded on the ideas and worldviews of Lao Zi and Zhuang Zi on the other.  They were also skilled essayists and poets.  In addition, long years of education would also mean developing more than a nodding acquaintance with all the arts:  music, calligraphy, painting and the chess game *weiqi* (圍棋)[5]. The arts were always seen as means of developing one's character and the cultivation of one's inner self, an indispensable aspect of being an upright and impartial public servant.

There were indeed other scholar-officials like Li Gefei who not only devoted their life to public service but were also renowned writers, artists and calligraphers.  From modest or even poor family backgrounds they reached literary and artistic heights because the political and cultural milieu fostered by the first emperor of the Song

---

[5] *Weiqi* is the game in which two opponents using black and white pieces respectively try to encircle each other's position.  It is a game that is easy to learn but hard to master.

dynasty, Song Tai Zu, was favourable to them and their development.

Despite the threat of attack by neighbouring peoples or actual skirmishes along China's northern borders, the first century of the Song period saw relative peace in a unified country.  With the emphasis on civil administration rather military endeavours, the economy prospered.  Towns and cities increased in number and expanded.  Crafts and industries developed.  Markets sprang up.  In the cities there were numerous restaurants, hotels, and entertainment venues, which greatly facilitated the travels of scholars going to the provincial or national capital for examinations and of officials sent to various postings.  Commerce thrived, locally, regionally, and internationally.  For the first time in human history, paper money came into use during the Song dynasty.  In the coastal cities there were ships to and from Japan and Korea to the northeast; all the countries in the present Southeast Asia such as Vietnam, Malaysia, Indonesia, Cambodia, Thailand and Myanmar; the entire Indian subcontinent including the islands; and Iran, Arabia and even Africa to the west.

Technological development further promoted the formation of the new class of commoner scholar-officials.  At the same time, the emerging class of scholar-officials without origins in the aristocracy spurred the development of certain technologies.  During the Song dynasty coal production increased greatly to meet the demands of the city dwellers, especially in the capital Bianjing.  The ancient Chinese invention of gunpowder was used in rocket-powered arrows and piston flamethrowers against the Liao invaders (*Chinese History* 1988:114).  Although the magnetic property of the lodestone was known in China since the Warring States period (戰國時代 475 – 221 BCE, part of the Zhou dynasty), it was in the Northern Song period that the mariner's compass in the form of a magnetic needle was used in navigation to lands in the South China Sea and to Korea (Lin 1987:157-161).  Goods from different countries brought back to China found their way to the homes of the scholar-officials.

Above all, it was the breakthrough in printing, from using the wood block to printing with movable type, in the Northern Song time that was of the greatest benefit to the scholars.  Concomitant with the literati cultural milieu, the invention of the printing press was of utmost importance to the spread of the written word and to learning.  Back in the time of the Sui dynasty (隋朝 581 – 618 CE), wood block printing was already invented. It came into widespread use during the Tang dynasty during which the world's earliest extant printed book, the Buddhist scripture *Diamond Sutra* (金剛經), was produced bearing the date of 868 CE. In the Northern Song dynasty, a commoner by the name of Bi Sheng (畢升) invented movable type printing. He made clay types, one for each character. They were hardened by fire. The clay types of characters were arranged on iron plates, one for every page, according to the content of the book. When the printing was finished, the clay types could be reused (Xing 1987:383-391). Such technological development acted as an impetus to literary creations as the authors knew that their writings could be printed at low cost. Dissemination of scholarly works from expositions on the classics to poetry to scientific treatises was rapid and efficient, making the literati popular, famous and accessible. The widespread use of the printing press beginning in the Northern Song period helped to foster the commoner scholar-official class and enabled some children of even the lower classes to be educated.

Given the social conditions set up by the founder of the Song dynasty Emperor Song Tai Zu to promote the civil service, the formation of the social class of scholar-officials was a matter of course. The literati families intermingled and intermarried with one another, and together established a certain lifestyle. This lifestyle in turn spawned or fostered the growth of urban centres with restaurants, inns, entertainment particularly song and dance, silk weaving and embroidery, wine making, construction, printing of course, and a variety of other crafts and industries. As has been discussed in the previous chapter, music and songs were inextricably linked to the development of *ci*. While Li Qingzhao was very much a lover of nature who delighted in the beauty of the flora and scenes of nature, snippets of city life found their way into her verses as will be shown in the later chapters.

## Mother

In the Northern Song period, with the rise of the commoner scholar-official class, the female children of many literati families were remarkably well educated. Li Qingzhao's mother was one such woman.

There is a widespread view that women in patriarchal Chinese society were relentlessly oppressed and victimized. Elsewhere I have discussed the discrepancy between the real culture and the ideal culture concerning Chinese women, and proposed to look at their real life as opposed to stereotypes about them (Djao 2003). Suffice it to emphasize here that although there was gender inequality in the long history of China, the position of women was not uniformly degraded. How they regarded themselves or how they were treated by others depends on, among many factors, their social classes, locale, and the individual's particular circumstances. Nonetheless, at the end of the neolithic period (approximately 5000 years ago), with the ascendancy and triumph of patriarchy over matrilineal clan communities as an organizing principle in both the family and society at large there were increasingly severe measures aimed at the suppression of women. They were brought to bear ideologically and materially to limit the freedom, honour and independence of women, especially regarding their role in political affairs.

Yet despite men's attempts at subordinating the position of women and confining their activity to the home, through the ages women in some aspects of their life or during some periods in their life were or tried to be agents of their own destiny. The best known examples of this agency came from some empresses of various dynasties who as widows ruled through their young sons and who then were reluctant or refused to give up power when their sons came of age. The lives and deeds of the empress dowagers are known because they were recorded in history. Not surprisingly, the patriarchal scholar-officials were fierce opponents and detractors of empresses and consorts who were thought to meddle in state affairs. Folklores and some tombstone inscriptions of the commoner women (Ebrey 1993), still largely belonging to the upper echelons of society, also give some glimpses into their times and their conduct. But generally the lower the women's positions in the social hierarchy, the less likely would their lives and agency be recorded.

In the Northern Song period, some women like their predecessors in earlier dynasties, were able to exercise some free choice in the selection of a husband. It was not uncommon for widows to remarry. The widowed sister of the founder Emperor Song Tai Zu married a second time ( Zhao and Li 2003:170; Gao, Xu and Zhang 1991342; Ma 1971:44).

Furthermore, some women of the rising commoner scholar-official class at that time were not simply literate; they were in fact remarkably literary. According to the biography of Li Gefei in the official history of the Song dynasty, his wife was the granddaughter of Wang Gongchen (王拱辰). This grandfather was famous because at the age of 19 *sui* he was the top student known as the *zhuangyuan* (狀元) to pass the highest civil service examination in his year, the youngest ever to attain that honour. He was a senior minister in the reign of Emperor Song Ren Zong (宋仁宗 r. 1022-63). In Li Gefei's biography, no personal name is given to Wang Gongchen's granddaughter, as is the case regarding most women in official histories. However, the biographer did mention that Li's wife, nee Wang, "was also skilled in literary composition" (*Song Shi* 1989:487).

Despite the official historical record of Ms. Wang as the wife of Li Qingzhao's father, there is debate about the identity of Li Qingzhao's mother. A Song writer, Zhuang Chuo (莊綽) claimed that Li Gefei was the grandson-in-law of Wang Zhun (王準) whose son Wang Gui (王珪) was a prime minister during the *Yuanfeng* reign period of Emperor Song Shen Zong and was known from childhood as an excellent essayist. Since Zhuang Chuo was a contemporary of Li Qingzhao, the opinion of the 20th century Li Qingzhao expert Wang Xuechu (1979) is that Li Qingzhao's mother was most likely the granddaughter of Wang Zhun. Furthermore, the inscription on the burial tablet of Wang Gui states that his eldest daughter, who died early, was married to Professor Li Gefei (Xu 2009:398-399). This view of her mother's lineage – daughter of the prime minister Wang Gui and granddaughter of Wang Zhun – is held by most literary critics and biographers of Li Qingzhao today as it seems to have the most supporting evidence.

Chen Zumei (陳祖美 2001:6–80; 1995:41), a present day Li Qingzhao scholar who has published several books and articles on her, further opines the following sequence of events: Ms. Wang, the daughter of the prime minister Wang Gui, died soon after giving birth to Li Qingzhao. The Ms. Wang mentioned in Li Gefei's biography, Wang Gongchen's granddaughter, was Li Qingzhao's stepmother whom Li Gefei married about eight years after the birth of Li Qingzhao. The stepmother bore a son, the younger half brother by the name of Li Hang (李迒). Li Qingzhao did mention a younger brother in her writings later.

Zhuge Yibing (諸葛憶兵 2004), a 21ˢᵗ century biographer of Li Qingzhao and her husband Zhao Mingcheng, holds a different view. He thinks that it would be highly unlikely for a scholar like Li Gefei in the Song times to remain a widower for seven or eight years. Furthermore, there is a total absence of anything remotely suggesting what must be a tremendous loss and sorrow of a motherless child in Li Qingzhao's writings.    Zhuge, therefore, argues that Wang Gongchen's granddaughter was Li Qingzhao's mother.

Regardless of which Mrs. Li nee Wang was Li Qingzhao's birth mother, they both came from literati families.    That Wang Gongchen's granddaughter is described in her husband's biography in the official Song history as an accomplished writer suggests that she probably provided a positive model to Li Qingzhao and literary instruction in Li Qingzhao's early education.    Li Qingzhao was no doubt taught deportment, etiquette, needlework and other proper rules of conduct befitting a young woman of her class.    But her education encompassed much more.    She learned a variety of literary forms, and how to exercise the freedom of expressing herself and being herself (Yu and Shu, 1999:250-253).    Insofar as Li Qingzhao's mother or stepmother and Li Qingzhao herself were recognized by male scholars living close to their time as established writers speaks not only of their accomplishments but also to the fact that some daughters of the scholar-official class were educated, and sometimes very well educated.    An educated mother or stepmother who was fond of writing most probably encouraged Li Qingzhao's love of learning and writing.

## Ancestral Town and Early Years

Most literary critics in the past, including Wang Xuechu, thought that Li Qingzhao was born in the city of Jinan (濟南) of Shandong province.    However, from excavations carried out in the twentieth century, a tablet bearing an inscription written by Li Qingzhao's father states that he was from Xiujiang (綉江). This would put his ancestral hometown in today's Mingshui (明水), in the county of Zhangqiu (章丘).    The gazette of the county appears to confirm that he was from Mingshui.    However, Jinan in the Song dynasty was comprised of Zhangqiu and five other counties.    It would not be entirely incorrect to say that Li Qingzhao's family hailed from Jinan (Liu 1990:7).

Mingzhui in Zhangqiu county is very scenic. It is surrounded by gentle hills. It is known for its many springs which feed the streams, rivers and lakes, and bestowed on the town its name Mingshui meaning "bright water." Although situated in northern China, its climate is mild. The surrounding countryside could produce rice and fish, like the region south of Changjiang, the Long River. The local people regard it as a bright pearl (Chen 2001:1–2). To the southwest of the county is the site of the famous Longshan (龍山) neolithic culture (Zhuge 2004:2-3) which produced the exquisite translucent black pottery more than five thousand years ago.

Very little is known about Li Qingzhao's early life. It is mainly from her largely autobiographical essay "*Jin Shi Lu* Hou Xu" ("金石錄後序") meaning "Postscript to the *Jin Shi Lu*" (henceforth referred to as the "Postscript") that we know of the main events of her life. *Jin Shi Lu* (金石錄 often translated as *Inscriptions on Bronzes and Stones*) is a book about the inscriptions on ancient bronze vessels and stone tablets that her husband Zhao Mingcheng wrote in collaboration with Li Qingzhao; she edited it for publication several years after his death and thus wrote the postscript. However she is silent in that essay about her life before marriage. In fact we only know about the year of her birth from the age and year of her marriage mentioned in the "Postscript."

There is much speculation about her birthplace. Although she is quite proud of her father and grandfather being scholars of Shandong province in a later *shi*, there is no record that she was actually born in the ancestral town of Mingshui or even in Shandong. After her father attained the *jinshi* status in 1076, he was an official in the provinces or in the capital. She was most likely born in the capital Bianjing (Xu 1990:4) and for the most part grew up there, with some time spent in the provinces where her father was assigned as an official. She was in Bianjing in 1089 at the age of six *sui* when her father bought a house by a luxuriant bamboo grove in the capital (Yu 1995: 22-23). But insofar as the Li family's ancestral town was Mingshui, she would have been to the town and Shandong province to visit family, to attend funerals, or to sweep the tombs of the ancestors.[6]

---

[6] The phrase "to sweep the tombs" refers to looking after tombs of the departed family members. Chinese today still visit their ancestors' graves

A different opinion is that she was born in Mingshui, grew up there, and did not go to the Bianjing until she was about 16 *sui* (Chen 1995). Her father was only a junior official at the time of her birth and his salary would not be sufficient to move the family to his various postings (Zhuge 2003:12). If that were the case, she would have been separated from her father, if not both parents, during much of the time during the first 15 or 16 years of her life. Given her vast and deep knowledge of history, the classics, poetry and the arts, it would be difficult to imagine who else could have laid such a solid educational foundation for her in her formative years besides her parents, especially her father.

On the other hand, if Li Qingzhao did indeed grow up in Mingshui while her father was away on official postings, and remained there until she joined her father in the capital Bianjing when she was 16 *sui*, her teacher could have been the renowned scholar Chao Buzhi. Chen (1995:130) argues that Chao Buzhi would have been, according to the custom for officials at that time, on the three-year bereavement leave in mourning for his mother in his ancestral town in Shandong province while Li Qingzhao was growing up in Mingshui. He could have easily visited Li Qingzhao before she moved to the capital. This could have led to Chao's high esteem of her as a *shidafu* which meant in imperial China a court scholar-official who would in all cases be male. However, even if he were a mentor when she was about 14 – 15 *sui*, there could not have been enough time for her to be so well versed in the classics, history and poetry. Her education would have begun much earlier. It was possible that Chao Buzhi visited Li Qingzhao while she was an adolescent in her ancestral town and in Bianjing. She would have more time for a sustained scholarly interaction with him in her 20s (see Chapter 4).

Li Qingzhao most likely grew up in comfortable but modest surroundings. Her father as a middle level official during her childhood would have provided more than mere necessities but not too much luxury. Li Qingzhao in the "Postscript" describes her own family and that of her husband as poor. But that poverty must be

---

especially on the anniversaries of their death, the *Qingming* 清明 festival in the spring and the *Chongyang* 重陽 festival in the autumn when they would remove debris from around the grave sites, and make offerings of food, wine, incense and paper money to the deceased.

understood in relative terms. If her maternal grandfather was indeed the prime minister Wang Gui then Li Gefei's household would in fact be comparatively humble. But as a child or unmarried young woman Li Qingzhao would not have suffered privations. Later in her adult life she moved among the social and political elites of Song society.

As both her parents – whoever her mother or stepmother might be – were educated, Li Qingzhao undoubtedly would have received a sound education from her earliest years. She would be taught to read and write, play music, practice calligraphy and painting, and learn the chess game *weiqi*. Her education would include the art of composing poetry with attention to rhymes and tones. She would also be steeped in history and the classics including the teachings of ancient philosophers. Insofar as Li Qingzhao was such a well rounded person would certainly be due to her intelligence and her passion for learning. But aside from her natural ability and inclination, her excellence in so many areas – poetry including both *ci* and *shi*, essay, calligraphy, music, painting and games of fortune – must also be attributed to her particular home environment. As her father was known for his expertise in the classics and writing essays, her education in classical literature, philosophy and history would be rigorous and thorough. Her prodigious knowledge of history, philosophical traditions, and literature comes through in her frequent allusions to these sources. This could be seen in all her writings, particularly in her *shi* and essays where she expressed her views on current and historical events and personages. Her writings are full of references to people and events in literature or history, some of which were quite obscure. It would be difficult to imagine that her parents did not play a major role in her education.

The fact that she reached such literary heights must be at least in part due to a carefree and liberal home atmosphere. Her parents probably did not put limits on her love of learning or creative abilities. They instead most likely encouraged her to think independently and to speak her mind and heart. Her talent and achievement were recognized and admired by those who lived in her own time or shortly after when the cultural climate was increasingly conservative and repressive with regards to the status and ability of women. The Song dynasty writer Wang Zhuo (王灼) did not mince words in his criticism of her conduct in later life and of her *ci*, but had this to say about Li Qingzhao: "Even from an early age she was famous for her *shi*. Her ability and talent were brilliant and admirable, in the footsteps of the ancients. She was the most accomplished writer among women of the current dynasty" (quoted in Wang 1979:208).

The special qualities of her outstanding writings, especially her *ci*, will be discussed further in various chapters. What must be emphasized is that her works were valued from her own life time to the present because she expressed genuine feelings and depicted scenes, events and emotions with sincerity and honesty as her father Li Gefei would no doubt have instructed and encouraged her to do. There are indeed freshness in her phrases and simplicity of language that are entirely original. Such naturalness accentuates her candour and is her own hallmark of excellence. But the fact that she was able to be creative, to turn her own phrases, and to express her own thoughts must be, in no small measure, due to the home environment that nurtured her talent and fostered her independence in thought so that she would "illuminate clearly" with words, in accordance with her name.

## Early Writings

### *Ci*

Li Qingzhao personally dated only a few of her works. The year in which she wrote the few extant *shi* and essays could be fixed somewhat from their content. Very few of her *ci* could be dated in such a way as in most of them there are explicit allusions to historical events or literary texts, but rarely to the events of the day. Literary critics through the centuries since her death have divided her undated writings into early and later periods again based on the content. But there is no certainty as to when most of the *ci* were actually written. The *ci* thought to be written in her youth describe the conduct and reflect the mood of a young woman before marriage. However, they could have been written later in life as reminiscences of the carefree days in her parents' house.

If Li Qingzhao in the early years of her life lost her mother and grew up with a stepmother, there is nothing in Li Qingzhao's writings or those of her contemporaneous writers that gives any hint of such circumstances. A few *ci* that are considered to have been written in her youth or at least regarded as descriptions of her youth were happy poems. In a few short phrases, she would express her spontaneous love of nature and enjoyment of life. There is a vivaciousness that cannot be suppressed, but no hint at all of a sad or mournful childhood or adolescence. There would be melancholia and sorrow in her *ci* yet, but that would come later. The poems about her girlhood express an eagerness for life and a certain playfulness. With joy in her heart she sings with simplicity and striking vividness. One of her best known *ci* is about a boating experience, which could have taken place near her ancestral town Mingshui which is known for the clear spring water of its streams, ponds and lakes, or in Bianjing.

To the tune of "As in a Dream"[7]

Recall often lingering in the brook-side pavilion till dusk[8],
Intoxicated, forgetting the way home;
Delighted, tarrying, we slip into the boat.
Lost in the depth of the lotus patch,
Splash, row; splash, row!
Surprise the seagulls and egrets into flight.

如夢令

常 記 溪 亭 日 暮, 沈 醉 不 知 歸 路。 興 盡 晚 回 舟, 誤 入 藕 花 深 處。 爭 渡、 爭 渡, 驚 起 一 灘 鷗 鷺。

In this *ci*, the reader can taste the sweet carefree day Li Qingzhao and her companions spent outdoors, sharing in the joy of her outing, wine and rowing. In a few words she depicts the time and the settings of a pavilion by the brook, lotus blossoms and birds. But it is her mood that we feel the most: her pleasure in wine, a little wilfulness in

---

[7] Most literary critics today place this *ci* among Li Qingzhao's earliest extant works. Xu Peijun (2002), however, dates this piece to the time after her marriage when she was about 23.

[8] There was actually a placed named Brook-side Pavilion within the Jinan jurisdiction during the Song time.

lingering too long till it is dusk, and even having fun in getting lost and waking up the water fowl that have settled down for the night. This is a happy poem. A prevalent view in Chinese literature since the ancient times is that it is difficult to compose works of joy and happiness while verses of sorrow are easy to perfect as poetry lends itself to expressing sadness (Chen 1995:140). That Li Qingzhao could express her joy so simply and effectively attests to her remarkable talent.

There is another *ci* that describes the conduct and mood of a young woman who would perhaps be a year or so older than the girl in the previous *ci* and has an interest in who comes to call.

## To the tune of "Painted Lips"

Alighting from the swing
Too lazy to wipe her slender hands.
Frail blossoms in the gathering mist,
Light perspiration seeps through her thin dress.
A guest arriving she sees.
No time to put on shoes,
Slips away in stocking feet, hairpin falling.
Blushing, shy;
Turning her head at the door,
Savours the green plum fragrance in pretence.

## 點絳唇

蹴罷秋千, 起來慵整纖纖手。露濃花瘦, 薄汗輕衣透。見客人來, 襪剗金釵溜。和羞走, 倚門回首, 却把青梅嗅。

The sensuality in this *ci* is palpable: motion of the swing, perspiration on her skin, falling hairpin, peeping at the door and fragrance of the plums. What makes the *ci* so charming is the depiction of a girl who is curious about the visitor. She is shy and blushes, but she decides to have a look at the caller. Then she hides her curiosity by pretending to smell the plums.

It is conceivable that the guest is a suitor or a go-between on behalf of a suitor asking for her hand. Marriages were, of course, arranged by parents at that time. But adherence to this norm varied by degrees from region to region and from family to family (Zhao and Li 2003:170).    In a relatively permissive household such as Li Qingzhao's, her parents might have dropped some hints as to who might be calling that day.    They might even have solicited her preference or obtained some tacit consent from her in the choice of a husband.

In the *ci*, nonetheless, there is still that mischievous playfulness as in the previous one.    It is all so natural and spontaneous although this *ci* is a take-off from a *shi* composed by Han Wo (韓偓) in the late Tang dynasty.    That *shi* is about a young Imperial Concubine who after stepping off the swing smiles at a guest as she brushes aside the plum tree at the door.    However, Han Wo's piece is almost prosaic compared to the lively *ci* by Li Qingzhao (Zhuge 2004:36).

It should be pointed out that in the long Chinese literary tradition, writers would take phrases, ideas and themes from compositions of others, to improve on them or to incorporate them into their own pieces.    No citation of references was required unless the writers felt it necessary for special reasons.    It was not considered as plagiarism since the readers – if they were worthy to be called scholars – were expected to recognize the sources.    In fact, it was deemed an honour to the original authors when their phrases or ideas were copied or used in others' writings.    Li Qingzhao typically alludes to or uses ideas, descriptions and phrases of many authors in her writings.

One striking characteristic of Li Qingzhao's writings, and especially noticeable in her *ci*, is her facility in turning a phrase.    She would use ordinary words and phrases from everyday life and paint a vivid picture or strike a resonant chord with the reader.    She would even use thoughts and phrases from other writers, ancient and contemporary, as we have seen in the above *ci*.    But at her hand, words are not only amazingly refreshing and poignant but express original ideas.    She thus takes her readers to an entirely unexpected view of the land or glimpse into the heart.    It is no wonder that Zhao Yanwei of the Southern Song period heaps generous accolade on her in light of the popularity of her writings (see Chapter 1).    This is his comment about Li Qingzhao in its entirety:

> Ms. Li gave herself the *hao* of "Yi'an Jushi." She was the wife of Zhao Mingcheng, courtesy name Defu, and the daughter of Li Wenshu. She was most talented and

original. The ink of her writings had hardly dried before people would clamour to have it distributed. Her *ci* enjoy great popular acclaim, and have been published and widely circulated. Other writers have seldom met with such reception (quoted in Chu, Sun and Rong 1984:17).

Another *ci* that is usually considered to be among her early works is one in praise of the plum blossom mentioned in the Chapter 1. The Chinese, especially the literati, have had an abiding fondness of the plum blossom. It is a simple flower, with five petals, red or white or some hue in between. It begins to bud and bloom often in the depth of winter undeterred by the cold. Its simple elegance is thus compared to an upright, honest character that can withstand hardship and adversity. As the blossoms usually appear around the Chinese New Year, they also symbolize hope, heralding a new beginning with the coming of spring. After describing its exquisite beauty, Li Qingzhao invites the reader to share in a toast to the flower in moonlight because "this blossom is like no other."

To the tune of "The Fisherman's Pride"

Spring announces its arrival in the midst of snow.
The glistening alabaster boughs dotted with plum blossom
     buds,
Withstand cold.
Half revealing her fragrant face –
Oh, so enchanting!
Stands in the courtyard,
The beauty fair as jade newly bathed to be adorned.
Even nature plays favourites
Commanding a bright moon to illumine her exquisite splendour.
Let's raise our golden cups of new wine;
Don't decline in fear of inebriation:
This blossom is like no other!

漁家傲

雪裏已知春信至, 寒梅點綴瓊枝膩。香臉半開嬌旖旎。當庭際, 玉人
浴出新妝洗。造化可能偏有意, 故教明月玲瓏地。共賞金尊沈綠蟻,

莫辭醉, 此花不與群花比。

In celebrating the beauty and strength of the plum blossom Li Qingzhao is most likely depicting herself. She would not be referring to the physical beauty alone. Most certainly she is capturing also the character of the plum blossom: endurance and ability to display magnificence in the harsh cold. Like the blossom she would uphold her honesty and beauty of character in times of adversity. It seems that at an early age she is signalling to the world the high standards she has set for herself and that she would live up to them. It is not arrogance but self-confidence. It is her candid announcement of what she is and will always be.

Li Qingzhao in the literati tradition borrows phrases or metaphors coined by earlier writers. She also alludes to historical or mythical events. In this simple *ci*, she has seven allusions to sources ranging from the long poem *Li Sao* (離騷) by Qu Yuan (屈原circa 340 – 278 BCE) of the Chu kingdom (楚國) and the philosopher Zhuang Zi, both from the Warring States period, to Tang dynasty poets such as Du Fu (杜甫), Li Bai, and Bai Juyi (白居易). The beauty fair as jade rising from her bath to be adorned is the Imperial Concubine Yang Yuhuan (楊玉環貴妃)[9] as described by Bai Juyi in his famous narrative poem "The Everlasting Regret" ("Chang Hen Ge 長恨歌") about her and Emperor Tang Xuan Zong (唐玄宗). Their story will also be the topic of Li Qingzhao's *shi* which will be discussed in the next section. The references and allusions in this *ci* certainly show Li Qingzhao's familiarity with the philosophy and poetry of the ancients, yet they do not make her *ci* pedantic or contrived. It flows naturally and spontaneously. Nonetheless, in the opinion of some critics this *ci* shows that Li Qingzhao is not quite experienced in composition as in her later works. This piece is, therefore, considered to be written in her youth before her marriage (Xu 2002:8).

Written about the same period as the *ci* describing her experience of rowing into the lotus patch, the following *ci* is also about scenes around an unspecified lake. It could be in Mingshui or in Bianjing.

---

[9] Concubines of emperors were given different ranks. The Imperial Concubine was of the highest rank.

To the Tune of "Grievance Against the Lord"

A breeze over the lake stirs widening ripples.
It's late autumn,
Few flowers in bloom, barely fragrant.
Sparkling water and colourful hills snuggle up to people.
Endless words cannot describe their charm.
Lotus seeds have ripened and the leaves turned brown.
Dewdrops wash the reeds by the bank.
Gulls and egrets resting in the sandbar turn not their heads,
Offended that we leave so early.

怨王孫

湖上風來波浩渺, 秋已暮、紅稀香少。水光山色與人親, 說不盡、無
窮好。蓮子已成荷葉老, 清露洗蘋花汀草。眠沙鷗鷺不回頭, 似也
恨、人歸早。

The time is autumn when the lotus seeds have ripened.
Thousands of poets have written about this season, usually with a
tinge of sorrow or melancholy at the passing of the year. But there is
no sadness in this *ci*. The scenes are undoubtedly autumnal but she
still enjoys the beauty. She simply has intense love for nature (Liu
1985:8-10). While the playfulness in this *ci* is more subdued than in
the other pieces quoted above, it speaks of intimacy with nature. Yet
instead of saying that she is close to nature, she lends her voice to
nature. The lakes and hills press on people to be close to them (Xu
1990:75-77). Similarly, she does not say that she regrets leaving the
water fowl. Rather it is they that reproach people for leaving. This is
her unique lively style. As her father's daughter, she speaks her heart
with sincerity and simplicity.

## *Shi*

In her early life at least, Li Qingzhao held to the conventional view of
the time that *ci* and *shi* served different purposes. The latter was a
vehicle for analysis and opinions of political affairs or historical events
while *ci* was used to express intimate feelings and perceptions

especially in personal relationships (Liu 190:115). The *ci* discussed above certainly conform to this understanding of its purpose. Yet about the same time when she was supposed to have written those *ci* she also composed two *shi* which are entirely different in content aside from the obvious differences in genre. In the two *shi* entitled "Two poems on 'The Wuxi Ode in Praise of the (Tang) Restoration' to Rhyme with Zhang Wenqian" (浯溪中興頌詩和張文潛二首), she demonstrates a maturity of acumen that was so far beyond her years that literary critics through the centuries could not believe that a mere youth, and a female to boot, could have written those lines.[10] But the scholar Huang Shengzhang (黃盛璋 1974:146) after looking into corroborating evidence came to the conclusion in mid-20th century that they were written by Li Qingzhao around the year 1100 when she was 17 *sui*.

These two *shi* refer to events in the final years of Emperor Tang Xuan Zong in the mid-Tang period, more than 350 years before her time. The Tang dynasty, founded in 618, was a golden era in Chinese history with developments in all areas – economic, political, agricultural, and cultural – reaching magnificent heights. However, by the mid-eighth century there was political unrest leading to great turmoil throughout the land. Emperor Tang Xuan Zong ascended the throne in 712 when he was a boy. After he came of age, he was initially a ruler with a sense of responsibility, but in his 50s became infatuated with a sixteen-old girl, Yang Yuhuan, who was originally a concubine of his son. He took her and she eventually ascended to the rank of an Imperial Concubine.

From then on, as recounted by Bai Juyi in his narrative poem "The Everlasting Regret," Emperor Tang Xuan Zong neglected affairs of the state. He spent his time in debauchery, amusing Imperial Concubine Yang and himself. For example, she fancied the

---

[10] Zhang Wenqian (張文潛) was the courtesy name of Zhang Lei 張耒. According to some scholars Zhang's two poems cited here were actually written by Qin Guan (秦觀) who like Zhang was a student of Su Shi and was also exiled in the political strife between the Conservatives and the Reformers (Xu 2009:198-199).

fruit *lizhi*[11] of southern China. He had men riding day and night and risking lives of people and horses to bring it to the capital Chang'an (長安, meaning "everlasting peace," present day Xi'an city 西安 in Shaanxi province陝西省) in the north. Ambitious and insidious men took over the reins of power. The prime minister Li Linfu (李林甫) was vindictive and treacherous, abusing his power to cut down those who did not go along with his devious schemes. One year he failed all the candidates who sat for the civil service examination in the capital so that there would be no new recruits into public service.

Relatives of Imperial Concubine Yang occupied important positions. Her first cousin Yang Guozhong (楊國忠) became the prime minister in 752 after Li Linfu's death. Her three sisters were all given barony and enfeoffed. The power-hungry An Lushan (安祿山) who gained the trust of the emperor became Imperial Concubine Yang's adopted son and was appointed the military satrap of a large jurisdiction in northern and north-eastern China. Another powerful personage who was close to the emperor was the eunuch Gao Lishi (高力士) with whom even Li Linfu and An Lushan had to curry favour (Bai 2002:200-201; Huang 1992:99-103; Yu 1988:188-189).

The multilingual An Lushan, of mixed Turkish and Chinese ancestry, and Yang Guozhong were rivals and harboured deep antagonism towards each other. An Lushan and his high ranking general Shi Siming (史思明), together with most of his army were of Qidan or Turkish background, referred to by the Chinese at that time as the Hu people (胡人); Hu being a generic term for all non-Han ethnic groups. An Lushan staged a rebellion in 755. At first the emperor did not believe the news. But in the following year, after An Lushan proclaimed himself the Emperor of the Great Yan (大燕) and threatened to attack the capital, Emperor Tang Xuan Zong accompanied by his son the heir-apparent, the Imperial Concubine Yang and Yang Guozhong, fled westward. However, shortly after they left the capital, the soldiers protecting the royal party refused to advance further unless Imperial Concubine Yang and Yang Guozhong were put to death (Bai 2002:200-204).

---

[11] *Lizhi* (荔枝) is the fruit of a tree belonging to the soapberry family that is native to southern China. About three centimeters long and oval in shape, it has reddish brown scaly outer shell, white edible flesh, and a single seed about one centimeter in diameter.

The heir-apparent ascended the throne with the support of the eunuch Li Fuguo (李輔國). The new emperor is known in history as Emperor Tang Su Zong (唐肅宗). Under the capable leadership of military strategists Guo Ziyi (郭子儀), Li Mi (李泌) and Li Guangbi (李光弼), the rebellion was put down. In 757 An Lushan was killed by his son. The Tang army recovered Chang'an and Emperor Tang Xuan Zong was able to return to the capital. An Lushan's son in turn was killed two years later by An Lushan's former general Shi Siming. In 761 Shi Siming also was killed by his own son who hanged himself two years later as he faced certain defeat. Thus ended eight years of turmoil brought on by the An Lushan and Shi Siming rebellion and the Tang dynasty was restored (Bai 2002:202; Yu 1988:188).

This excursion into mid-Tang political history is necessary because the events were the topic of Li Qingzhao's two *shi* and the poems to which she refers in the title.

In 761, in the second year of Emperor Tang Su Zong's reign, the scholar Yuan Jie (元結) wrote an ode in praise of the restoration. The ode was later copied by the highly renowned calligrapher Yan Zhenqing (顏真卿) and his calligraphy was inscribed on the cliff side by a river in the present day Hunan province (湖南省). Yuan Jie had settled by this river as he was most impressed by the scenery and named it Wuxi (Hou and Lü 1985:209). This is the ode that Li Qingzhao commented on in her own poem composed when she was about 17 *sui*.

Although the ode was written to celebrate the restoration of Tang and the return of the two emperors to the capital, Yuan Jie did not fail to mention that he was personally involved in quashing the rebellion. He denounced the treacherous officials whose scheming and unbridled ambition led to the revolts. He had a personal grudge against one of those officials, Li Linfu, as Yuan had the misfortune of sitting for the civil service examination in the year when Li failed all candidates. In his ode Yuan had only praise for the two emperors; there was not the slightest reproach against them. But Emperor Tang Xuan Zong was essentially responsible for the havoc wreaked throughout the land because while he indulged in pleasures with his Imperial Concubine Yang he allowed the villainous officials to run amok (Chen 1995:170-171).

More than three centuries later, in the year 1100 CE, Zhang Wenqian, a scholar-official of the Northern Song period, wrote a *shi* about Yuan Jie's ode that was inscribed on the Wuxi cliff side when he visited the site. Zhang Wenqian was a student of Su Shi (蘇軾 1036 – 1101 CE), a very famous man of letters. Su and his followers at that time were demoted and banished from high offices due to the factional conflicts among the scholar-officials. They occupied minor positions in remote areas. The inscription on the Wuxi cliff about the flight of Emperor Tang Xuan Zong from the capital to the countryside reminded Zhang of his personal exile. Thus he wrote a poem about the events in the mid-Tang dynasty. In it, Zhang praised the loyal and upright Tang military strategist Guo Ziyi who was responsible for the victory over the rebels. The subtext was that loyal and righteous officials like himself and Su Shi were unjustly put to pasture and thus prevented from contributing to the present regime. It should be noted that Zhang put the blame on the Imperial Concubine Yang Yuhuan for the rebellion and turmoil in mid-Tang dynasty. Quite conveniently she was the scapegoat (Chen 1995:172). This was a popular patriarchal tenet among scholars which censured women, especially beautiful women, who meddled in state affairs and were, therefore, blamed for bringing calamity to the country.

Li Qingzhao's father Li Gefei was also a follower of Su Shi. In the year 1100 he was not yet demoted or banished. As he and Zhang Wenqian were close friends, the two families maintained contact. In a note in Zhang's collection of poems, he wrote that Li Gefei came to see him off in Fan Kou (樊口 in Hubei province by the Changjiang). It is, therefore, not surprising that Li Qingzhao would have access to Zhang's *shi* about the ode inscribed on the Wuxi cliffside. She then composed her two *shi* in rhyme with Zhang Wenqian's poems on the Wuxi ode (Chen 1995:171).

Two Poems on "The Wuxi Ode in Praise of the (Tang) Restoration" to Rhyme with Zhang Wenqian

Poem One

Fifty years of accomplishment swept by one lightning,[12]

---

[12] The emperor mentioned throughout these two poems was Emperor Tang Xuan Zong. He was on the throne for 40 some years. Li Qingzhao in the *shi* rounds up the number of years of his reign to 50.

Flowers and willows of Huaqing Palace[13] were overrun
By weeds as in the whole capital.
The emperor kept five stables and kennels
Of cocks, falcons and dogs for gambling and sport.
Dining and wining, he forgot he was aging.
Hu soldiers seemed to fall from heaven.
The untrustworthy Hu were indeed treacherous.
Hu rebel horsemen paraded in front of the palace gate;
So many imperial consorts and palace maids slain
That the earth was fragrant with their perfumes.
Why was the Tang army defeated in every battle?
Many were the guards and horses
That had perished while transporting *lizhi* from the south.
Merits and virtues of Yao and Shun[14] overarch as the sky,
No need to record them on some piddling tablet.
Inscriptions of heroic deeds are shallow,
They merely excite ghosts to scratch the rocky cliffs.
Ziyi and Guangbi[15] harboured no suspicion of each other;
Heavens felt misery should end, so people could feel joy.
The extinction of Xia should be a good lesson for Shang,[16]
Recorded history is still available for all to read today.
Don't you see:

---

[13] Huaqing Palace (華清宮) on the outskirts of the present day city of Xi'an was where Emperor Tang Xuan Zong and Yang Yuhuan lived in luxury and pursuit of pleasure.

[14] Yao (堯) and Shun (舜) were two legendary rulers of antiquity. They were virtuous and wise. Having the welfare of the people at heart, they did not establish dynasties but chose the best person, not anyone from their own families, to succeed themselves. These two have always been held up in Chinese history as model rulers.

[15] Guo Ziyi and Li Guangbi. See discussion above.

[16] Xia (夏) was the first dynasty in recorded Chinese history (21st – 16th centuries BCE). The last king of Xia dynasty, known for his debauchery, was killed by the founder of the Shang dynasty (also known as Yin 殷 dynasty).

Wily Zhang Yue[17] was always up to some scheme,
Yet even alive he was already betrayed by Yao Chong.

## Poem Two

Have you not heard
The amazing tale of the downfall and restoration of
    Emperor Xuan Zong?
But weeds now cover the tablet bearing
The inscribed ode in praise of the restoration.
It extols the achievements of Tang generals and officials,
But is silent about treason by wicked ministers.
Who instructed the Imperial Concubine to descend from
    heaven?
Heaven enfeoffed sisters with the baronies of Guo,
    Qin and Han.[18]
Drums and cymbals made noisy merriment for the emperor,
And the spring breeze dared not stir up dust.[19]
Unknown the names of strong lads and brave officers
Who perished in the An and Shi rebellion.
Baoweng Peak rises to pierce the sky
On it the emperor would have his reign title carved.[20]

---

[17] Zhang Yue (張說 667 – 730 CE) and Yao Chong (姚崇 660 – 721 CE) were ministers in Emperor Tang Xuan Zong's court.  They often backstabbed each other.

[18] Guo (虢), Qin (秦) and Han (韓) were names of fiefdoms bestowed on the three sisters of Yang Yuhuan.

[19] These two lines mean that while Emperor Tang Xuan Zong and his concubine Yang Yuhuan indulged themselves in the lap of luxury thus attaining a false sense of peace, a war was brewing to stir a dust storm.

[20] Upon his return from exile in Sichuan to the capital, Emperor Tang Xuan Zong would have liked to have the title of the prosperous period of his reign, Kaiyuan (開元), carved on the Baoweng Peak (抱甕峰) of the Hua Mountain (華山) range. But he was forced to abdicate in favour of his son Emperor Tang Su Zong.  He became a mere figure head, as is made clear in the next line.

Pitifully time moved power from his grasp.
The heart of the villain was deep as the gorge.[21]
From his exile ten thousand *li* away the emperor returned,[22]
But when would the gates of the South Palace once shut
      reopen?[23]
His son's filial devotion was vast as heaven,
Yet it called the officers' treachery good.[24]
Alas, Eunuch Gao could not warn him
That Fuguo held power with Empress Zhang;
Could only versify that the weeds in his exile
Fetched good price as a delicacy in the capital.

浯溪中興頌詩和張文潛二首

其一

五十年功如電掃，華清宮柳咸陽草。五坊供奉鬥雞兒，酒肉堆中不知
老。胡兵忽自天上來，逆胡亦是姦雄才。勤政樓前走胡馬，珠翠踏
盡香塵埃。何爲出戰輒披靡，傳置荔枝多馬死。堯功舜德本如天，
安用區區紀文字。著碑銘德真陋哉，迺令神鬼磨山崖。子儀光弼不
自猜，天心悔禍人心開。夏商有鑒當深戒，簡策汗青今具在。君不
見當時張說最多機，雖生已被姚崇賣。

---

21 The villain here refers to the eunuch Li Fuguo who hatched the abdication
scheme.

22 *Li* (里) is a unit of length measurement, about half a kilometer.

23 After his return from exile, Emperor Tang Xuan Zong was removed from
the south wing of the palace and put under house arrest. See explanation in
this chapter.

24 When under Li Fuguo's order Emperor Xuan Zong was moved from the
south wing to the west wing of the palace, he was frightened that he would
be killed and almost fell from his horse. His eunuch Gao Lishi shouted to
the "good" arresting officers to stay in their place. In these two lines, Li
Qingzhao is saying that Emperor Tang Su Zong might have filial devotion
to his father, but they became estranged from each other when villains were
in power.

其二

君不見驚人廢興傳天寶，中興碑上今生草。不知負國有姦雄，但說
成功尊國老。誰令妃子天上來，虢、秦、韓國皆天才。花桑羯鼓玉
方響，春風不敢生塵埃。姓名誰後知安、史，健兒猛將安眠死。去
天尺五抱甕峰，峰頭鑿出開元字。時移勢去真可哀，姦人心醜深如
崖。西蜀萬里尚能反，南內一閉何時開。可憐孝德如天大，反使將
軍稱好在。嗚呼，奴輩乃不能道：輔國用事張后尊，乃能念：春薺
長安作斤賣。

Li Qingzhao's two *shi* about the ode inscribed in Wuxi are elegant
and clear. She does not use flowery words. With her refreshing and
poignant words these two *shi* have artistic merit. However, the most
striking aspect about them is the depth of her analysis of historical
events in the Tang period and by extension of the current affairs of
her own time.

Li Qingzhao's analysis of the Tang events was more perceptive
than that by Zhang Wenqian or Yuan Jie on several points. First of all,
regarding the cause of the rebellion, Li Qingzhao puts the blame
squarely on Emperor Tang Xuan Zong's negligence of duty without
absolving treacherous officials and the Yang family of their share of
responsibility (Chen 1995:172).

Second, she points out that Yao and Shun are traditionally
revered in history because they were virtuous and meritorious rulers,
as great as the sky. Their deeds are remembered by people in their
hearts. There is no need for any inscriptions on stone, which after all
was overrun with weeds (Liu 1981:4; Chen 1995:173).

Thirdly, the rebellion was put down and the dynasty was restored
not by any particular great hero but because the conscientious leaders
like Guo Ziyi and Li Guangbi were united in their goal and action
(Chen 1995:173). There was not the undercurrent of jealousy,
suspicion, rivalry or back-stabbing between them, unlike two other
Tang high officials Zhang Yue and Yao Chong whose relationship
was a series of betrayals and personal vendettas.

The reference to the exemplary cordial relationship between Guo
Ziyi and Li Guangbi in the Tang period is a pointed comparison to
the then current events. In Li Qingzhao's own time, the reigning
Emperor Song Hui Zong was also given to the pursuit of pleasures.

He squandered precious resources on building a grandiose garden, leaving state affairs to incompetent, corrupt and selfish villains like Cai Jing (蔡京) and Tong Guan (童貫) (Liu 1981:2). The officials who could have run the country competently and efficiently were caught up in factional struggles to the death, neither side showing any willingness to compromise. In praising the cooperation between Guo Ziyi and Li Guangbi, Li Qingzhao is indirectly criticizing Zhang Wenqian's original poem in rhyme of which she was composing her own pieces. It is also a criticism of Zhang himself as he was caught up in the factious conflict (Zhuge 2004:21).

Finally, in her second poem, Li Qingzhao points to the suspicion and lack of harmony even between Emperor Tang Xuan Zong and his son. By the time the abdicated Emperor Xuan Zong returned to the capital, the new emperor Tang Su Zong was totally controlled by his eunuch Li Fuguo, who was in collusion with Empress Zhang (張皇后), just as Emperor Tang Xuan Zong relied on his power wielding eunuch Gao Lishi and the Imperial Concubine Yang. Fearing that Emperor Tang Xuan Zong might attempt a comeback, Li Fuguo had the abdicated emperor removed from the south wing of the palace which bordering on the street could give the old emperor access to his supporters. Thus Emperor Tang Xuan Zong was under house arrest in the west wing of the palace till his death (Liu 1981:6).

Gao Lishi meanwhile was exiled to the southwest where he wrote a *shi* in which he laments the fact that the vegetable *jicai* (薺菜) in his place of banishment was regarded as a weed which no one would gather but was valued and sold at a high price in the capital (Hou 1985:216). Gao Lishi returned to Chang'an only to see the old emperor and his heir die in quick succession.

In criticizing the Tang emperors in her two *shi*, Li Qingzhao was in fact raising a warning to the Song rulers. It appeared to her that they were not learning any lesson from the fall of the ancient Xia and Shang dynasties but were repeating the mistakes of the Tang emperors (Chen 1995:174; Hou and Lü 1985:217). She was able to put her finger on a fatal flaw in the Song political life, which was allowing factional strife within the officialdom to weaken and paralyze the government when every effort should be made to foster and promote cooperation among high officials in the face of internal popular dissatisfaction and external threat.

The two *shi* in rhyme with Zhang Wenqian's poem show that Li

Qingzhao was far more insightful in her understanding of historical and current political events than even some scholar-officials. She blamed the Tang emperors and their unscrupulous ministers as well as the Imperial Concubine Yang for the turmoil in mid-Tang and the subsequent decline of the Tang dynasty. She not only praised the trustworthy and capable Tang officials Guo Ziyi and Li Guangbi, but identified the key to their success: cooperation instead of mutual suspicion and back-stabbing. Zhang Wenqian in his original poem saw Imperial Concubine Yang as the only culprit and praised Guo Ziyi in the events during the Tang time without explicating the enormous damage to the body politic by factional conflict of which Zhang Wenqian was very much a part in the Song period.

The Song scholar Wang Zhuo probably had these two *shi* in mind when he wrote his comment about Li Qingzhao's fame for *shi* from an early age as has been quoted in "Early Life" section of this chapter.

In conclusion, we have few details about the early life of Li Qingzhao. In fact even today, there is some debate about the year of her birth. There is little confirmed information but much speculation regarding where she spent her childhood or who tutored her. However, the two *shi* written when she was 17 *sui* and a few *ci* thought to be written in her youth afford the reader a glimpse into her personality. On the eve of her marriage, she was already an accomplished writer, and her character was developed in such a way that she was prepared to meet many challenges in her adult life without sacrificing her integrity.

# 3 Marriage -

## Happiness and Political Turmoil

## Zhao Mingcheng

At 18 *sui*, in the year 1101 during the reign of Emperor Song Hui Zong, Li Qingzhao was married to Zhao Mingcheng who was then 21 *sui* and a student at the Imperial University in Bianjing. He was the youngest of three sons of Zhao Tingzhi and his wife surnamed Guo (郭). The senior Zhao was then the Minister of Interior while Li Qingzhao's own father Li Gefei was a senior official in the Ministry of Rites.

Zhao Mingcheng came from a family very similar to Li Qingzhao's. His father and grandfather were also scholar-officials. His father, Zhao Tingzhi, passed the highest level of the civil service examinations and attained the *jinshi* status in 1070, six years before Li Qingzhao's father Li Gefei. Like Li Gefei, the senior Zhao occupied a series of provincial positions before rising to senior ranks in the capital.

Zhao Mingcheng's mother came from a scholar-official family too. It was described by a scholar at that time that her father knew how to pick excellent husbands for his four daughters. Most of his sons-in-law and many of their descendants achieved literary fame or honourable official statuses. Zhao Mingcheng thus grew up in a very cultured environment in which scholarship was prized. He had two older brothers and two brothers-in-law who also held prominent positions (Huang 1974:133-134).

From his childhood Zhao Mingcheng was fond of learning. In the preface to his magnum opus *Jin Shi Lu*, of which Li Qingzhao was a collaborator and later editor, he acknowledges that from a tender age he likes to visit the leading scholars and enquire about inscriptions on ancient bronze vessels and stone tablets. Even then he would collect ancient books, bronze vessels, stone tablets, and rubbings of inscriptions. His inclination towards and ability in studying the ancient records was well nurtured in his home environment. Of the over 2000 inscriptions presented and discussed in his book, many came from the Zhao family collection as indicated in his book the *Jin Shi Lu*. According to Zhao Mingcheng's own account there were over 2000 rubbings of bronze and stone inscriptions in his father's house and some were ancient and had been in the family for a long time (Zhao 1991). When he was five *sui*, three well known scholars, including Huang Tingjian (黃庭堅), a renowned poet and calligrapher, came to the Zhao residence to admire some calligraphy. They witnessed a rich collection of ancient books, paintings and calligraphy (Huang 1974:137-138; Zhuge 2002:30).

When Zhao Mingcheng was nine *sui* (in the year 1089), his father Zhao Tingzhi was an official in a provincial city of Xuzhou (徐州 in Jiangsu province). Thirty-some years later, he recorded in the *Jin Shi Lu* that he obtained a Sui dynasty tablet with inscriptions there. Quite possibly that was the first piece in his own collection (Huang 1974:140).

In his tome Zhao Mingcheng also mentions that at 17 or 18 *sui* (around 1097) a scholar by the name of Chen Shidao (陳師道, also known as Chen Wuji 陳無己), wrote to him about a tablet bearing the signature of the famous Tang calligrapher Liu Gongquan (柳公權) although only the three characters of Liu's name were still discernible while the rest was rubbed quite smooth over the ages. Zhao Mingcheng was able to procure the tablet. Chen also sent him word about an erected tablet with an inscription that commemorated the repair of the mausoleum of the founder of the Han dynasty. Zhao Mingcheng began making enquiries and eventually obtained the tablet several years later (Huang 1974:144). It is interesting to note that Chen was an uncle, married to the sister of Zhao Mingcheng's mother. That an elder scholar would help Zhao Mingcheng in his hobby of collecting tablets and rubbings of inscriptions indicates that even at that age Zhao Mingcheng was already much respected by other scholars.

A year later, in 1098, an ancient royal jade seal was excavated in Xianyang (咸陽 near present day Xi'an). As Zhao Mingcheng's father was well connected in officialdom, the imperial librarian personally made an extra rubbing of the seal and gave it to Zhao Mingcheng (Zhuge 2004:30).

Thus we see that Zhao Mingcheng at the threshold of marriage was an earnest young man, dedicated to learning and already making a name for himself as a passionate collector of bronze and stone inscriptions.

The marriage of Li Qingzhao and Zhao Mingcheng according to custom was most certainly arranged by parents and brokered by a match-maker. Who was the go-between in the Zhao-Li union is not known. In a story told by a Yuan dynasty (元朝 1271 – 1368 CE) writer Yi Shizhen (伊世珍), at the time Zhao Tingzhi was considering the prospects of a wife for his youngest son, Zhao Mingcheng one day fell asleep during the day. When he woke up he could only remember a riddle consisting of twelve characters. Zhao Tingzhi interpreted the dream and explained that Zhao Mingcheng would be the husband of a female *ci* composer (quoted in Zhuge 2004:34-35).[1]

The conundrum posed in a dream was probably imagined by the Yuan period scholar or others who were fond of the high-achieving couple. But it would not be too far-fetched to think that Zhao Mingcheng asked for the hand of Li Qingzhao. The two young people most likely knew of each other. For a year before their marriage, both their fathers were officials in Bianjing. They were colleagues and, more significant, were both from Shandong province. People from the same locale while posted elsewhere together often sought each other's company. The two families would be acquainted with each other and a marriage between children of the two houses would be considered quite ideal. Li Qingzhao and Zhao Mingcheng might even have met each other in person (Zhuge 2004:35).

The most likely person who might have suggested the match to Li Qingzhao's father and then Zhao Mingcheng would be the latter's uncle by marriage, Chen Shidao. He was a follower of the highly respected scholar-official Su Shi as was Li Qingzhao's father Li Gefei. With common interest in classical learning and similar political views they would be close associates rather than mere acquaintances. As Li Qingzhao had already gained renown for her poetry from other scholars within their circle, Chen would most likely have known about her talents and quite possibly met her. Although Chen had deep feelings of antipathy towards Zhao Mingcheng's father Zhao Tingzhi who was also his own brother-in-law, he obviously liked Zhao Mingcheng and respected the young man's dedication to studying inscriptions. He could quite naturally have recommended Li

---

[1] The riddle consists of the following characters: 言與司合, 安上已脱, 芝芙草拔. It means: 詞女之夫.

Qingzhao to Zhao Mingcheng as a most suitable bride although he would not likely be the formal match-maker.

Years later, Li Qingzhao wrote the "Postscript" to her husband Zhao Mingcheng's *Jin Shi Lu*. By that time she was about 51 years of age (in 1134), Zhao Mingcheng was deceased for five years and the Northern Song was no more, vanquished by the invading Jin. The "Postscript" gave some important details of her life with Zhao Mingcheng. In her reminiscence, the early days of her marriage were happy and very much to her liking. She describes the Zhao and Li families as poor. But a more accurate description would be that the two families were not profusely wealthy and were indeed of commoner background. However, as Li Gefei and Zhao Tingzhi were relatively high-ranking officials by then, their salaries would not be at poverty level. On the other hand, even if their fathers might be comfortably well off, Zhao Mingcheng as a university student would still be dependent on his father for support. The point that Li Qingzhao seems to emphasize was that the Li and Zhao families had a tradition of modesty and frugality.

The "Postscript" gives a glimpse into the married life of Li Qingzhao and Zhao Mingcheng and how happy they were in their pursuit of learning through stone tablets, bronze vessels and other works of art. Zhao Mingcheng would take leave from the university on the first and the fifteenth days of each month. He would pawn his clothing for 500 copper coins. Then he and Li Qingzhao would go to the market at Xiang Guo Temple (相國寺) and buy rubbings of stone tablet inscriptions and fruit. The temple was originally built during the Northern Qi dynasty (北齊朝 550 – 577 CE) and rebuilt during the Tang and Northern Song dynasties. During Li Qingzhao's time, the temple compound was a busy market place five days every month. The different trades were allocated stalls in designated parts of the temple courtyards. A wide variety of wares was on display: household utensils, articles for personal hygiene, decorative materials, fruits, seasoned meats, saddles, straw mats, and so on. Behind the main pavilion were the vendors of books, paintings, calligraphy and antiques (Xu 2002:323). Once home, the young couple would thoroughly enjoy the new acquisitions. Their delight was such that they felt as carefree and happy as the ancients during the time of Ge Tian (葛天), a legendary king of antiquity who was such a good and wise ruler that his people were free and content.

Marriage to Zhao Mingcheng was a very important event in Li Qingzhao's life but not in the conventional, idealized view of a wife obeying and following the husband subserviently. Both Li Qingzhao and Zhao Mingcheng recognized from the start that their marriage was one between two kindred spirits devoted to scholarship and the arts. Their union was going to foster much creativity on both sides as well as a productive partnership. On a personal level, Li Qingzhao's outpour of strong emotions and passion in the *ci* with some exceptions were, or are interpreted by critics to be, singularly focused on Zhao Mingcheng. To her, *ci* was the poetic vehicle for expressing feelings and this she did superbly regarding a wide range of tender feelings about Zhao Mingcheng. To the extent Li Qingzhao was defined by her ci, her *ci* were inspired by her relationship with Zhao Mingcheng.

## *Ci* of the Newly Wed

In Li Qingzhao's *ci* that are thought to be written shortly after her marriage, we can still see the vivacious and fun-loving young woman. In the following *ci*, Li Qingzhao is comparing her beauty to that of a flower, more accurately she is teasing her lover to do so (Sun 2004: 54).

To the tune of "The Abridged Version of Magnolia Blossom"

From the flower vendor
I bought a budding spring blossom,
Freshly covered with morning dew,
Its lustre a hint of rosy cloud.
My lover may think that my face is no match for the flower.
With jade pins adorning my hair at temples
You, my lover, must decide which is prettier.

減字木蘭花

賣花擔上, 買得一枝春欲放。淚染輕勻, 猶帶彤霞曉露痕。怕郎猜道、奴面不如花面好。雲鬢斜簪, 徒要教郎比並看。

This *ci* is included in Mao Jin's collection *Shu Yu Ci*.  Some critics did not think that Li Qingzhao composed it because the lyrics were so simple and straightforward.  However, as Wang Xuechu (1979:71-72) points out, simplicity in expression cannot be the basis for refuting its authenticity.  The best supporting evidence that this *ci* came from Li Qingzhao is ironically provided by the Song scholar and a severe critic of Li Qingzhao, Wang Zhuo (mentioned in Chapter 2).  According to him, "Yi'an Jushi . . . in her long-short verses (that is, *ci*) can twist and turn new frivolous and easy phrases to express human feelings.  She wilfully includes obscenities from the street without any reservation or shame.    Since ancient times no gentlewoman of letters was so unmindful of her status" (quoted in Chen 1995:54, 127-8).

Li Qingzhao was certainly bold in writing about her conduct and intimate feelings, be it teasing her lover, stealing a look at a visitor while pretending to smell the plum, or, in another *ci*, inviting her lover to come again in moonlight.[2]  As *ci* developed out of songs sung in tea houses, restaurants, taverns and brothels, many lyrics were infused with sexual innuendos. But they were for the most part composed by male scholars and female entertainers or courtesans.  The literati of the gentry class by Li Qingzhao's time certainly had moved away from romantic love themes in their *ci* lyrics.  For a gentlewoman of her pedigree and social standing, Li Qingzhao was far too brazen, especially by the Southern Song times in which Wang Zhuo voiced his criticism.  Even during the Northern Song period when Li Qingzhao wrote these love *ci*, it was still not quite the norm for a woman to be so candid.  Nevertheless, through these *ci* Li Qingzhao reveals her fearlessness in being honest and often passionate, unfettered by conventions or the restrictions of feminine etiquette (Zhuge 2004:36). This was the free spirit nurtured by home environment coming to the fore.

In the first year of their marriage, Zhao Mingcheng as a student would live at the university and would come home only on the first and the fifteenth day of the month.  This meant that there were regular periods of separation.  Even though they were still in the same city, the brief and regular separation must be felt keenly by the newly weds.  A few *ci* that are thought to be among her early works speak of being alone with her wine and waking to the red begonia tossed by the

---

[2] See "<浣溪沙> - 閨情 Washing Brook Sand" in Chinese in Appendix A.

wind and drizzle over night. Without mentioning herself explicitly, she bemoans the scattered flowers. She feels lonesome but there is not the wrenching sorrow or misery that would appear in her later *ci*.

To the tune of "As in a Dream"

Light rain, gusty wind last night,
Deep slumber dispels not remaining effects of wine.
I ask the one rolling up the screen about the begonia.
The casual reply: "It is still the same."
Don't you know? Don't you know?
Green leaves are invigorated but the red flowers are less.

如夢令

昨夜雨疏風驟, 濃睡不消殘酒。試問捲簾人, 却道海棠依舊。知否、知否? 應是 綠肥紅瘦。

The last four characters in this *ci* "綠肥紅瘦" (*lü fei hong shou*) literally mean "green fat, red thin." Taken separately these four characters are ordinary words of everyday life. Yet they have been admired and praised by literary critics throughout the centuries. In Li Qingzhao's hand, the dull words are refreshingly alive. They evoke a rich visual image of abundant glossy green leaves enlivened by the rain and a few sparse red flowers left by the wind. They also depict her lonesome predicament in the midst of hustle and bustle or compared to her husband's active scholarly pursuit at the university. They show her creative use of words to convey subtle feelings and thoughts.

## Political Turmoil: Factional Strife

### Background – the New Laws

In the second year of her marriage, a political maelstrom would sweep both the Li and Zhao families into its vortex, pitting Li Gefei and Zhao Tingzhi against one another from opposing factions. The political turbulence was several decades in the making.

A century after its founding, the Song dynasty proceeded on a downward spiral towards extinction. The decline actually set in earlier and had its roots in the very political and social structures fashioned by the founder Emperor Song Tai Zu to centralize power (Bai 2002:235-252). The civil service bureaucracy with the recruitment of scholars expanded throughout the reign of his successors and even the military bureaucracy became inflated. Civil officials, sometimes even uneducated eunuchs, were appointed to lead military campaigns, with disastrous consequences. While there were a few honest and hardworking officials, political corruption became rampant.

With a weak defence against invaders, Song was constantly threatened by Liao in the north and Xi Xia in the Northwest, kingdoms set by two neighbouring ethno-cultural groups. Even before the unification of China by Emperor Song Tai Zu, during the period of Five Dynasties in northern China and Ten Kingdoms in the south, one of the dynasties in the north was established with help from Liao. The founder of this minor dynasty, known in history as the Later Jin (後晉 936 – 947 CE), acknowledged the Emperor of Liao, although several years his junior, as his father. But to ensure the continual support and protection from Liao, 16 districts in the border areas (in the present day Hebei and Shanxi provinces) were ceded to Liao. During the Song period, Liao continued to occupy the 16 districts. Song rulers were unable to reclaim those territories due to temerity, inept diplomacy or poorly organized military campaigns. The Song government in fact lost more lands. There were some dedicated and far-sighted ministers and generals with proposals and plans to resist the invaders and to recover lost territories, but the court was most often swayed by other officials who lacked the will and confidence to stand up and face the aggressive neighbours. The Song emperors were often incompetent and cowardly, and surrounded themselves with like-minded advisors. In order to pacify these two rising powers, Liao and Xixia, and particularly in fear that they would join forces in an attack against China, the Song government repeatedly agreed to pay them annual tributes of silver, silk and other precious items.

The small farmers or tenant farmers bore most of the tax burden. They paid in cash, in kind and in labour force. The last was corvee, practised through the different dynasties, whereby able bodied men were conscripted to work unpaid in public construction projects or military defence. Yet the rich class of landowners hardly paid any taxes at all as the levy was based on the size of the household rather than on landholdings. Meanwhile the government coffers were continually drained by the time Emperor Song Shen Zong ascended the throne in 1067.

Emperor Song Shen Zong was an earnest young man who tried to remedy the situation. Early in his reign he allowed the introduction of reform called the "New Laws" under the leadership of Wang Anshi (王安石 1021 – 1086 CE). The main reforms were:

1. The government would provide loans to the small or tenant farmers at the interest rate of 20 percent. The wealthy owners of large landholdings were typically charging 40 percent.

2. The government was to introduce tax reforms. The tax reform would abolish corvee, the conscription of farmers for unpaid labour in government construction projects. Corvee invariably disrupted the cycle of agricultural work while the gentry, the class of high officials and landlords, were exempt from it. In its place each family would pay a tax based on the size of landholdings. Land in the whole empire would, therefore, be surveyed.

3. The government would undertake substantial hydraulic projects to improve irrigation for small farmers and thus squash the monopoly of the large landlords over the distribution of water.

4. The government would also introduce commercial reforms to ensure the stability of commodity prices and prevent speculations by rich merchants.

5. There were going to be reforms in the organization of the army, military training, production of weapons, and provision of equipment and horses (Zhou, Yang and Wang 2002:127-134; Bai 2002:240-245).

All these reforms initiated by Wang Anshi would result in diminishing the power and privilege of the landed gentry while providing benefits to the small farmers as well as increasing revenues for the government. The conservative gentry class, especially the large landlords, were bitterly opposed to the reforms. Among them were families of the empress and empress dowager. The spokesmen for the gentry were the conservative officials both in the capital and the provinces. Two political factions quickly divided the officials: the Reformers referred to as the new party and the Conservatives collectively known as the old party.

Emperor Song Shen Zong wavered between retaining the

established economic, social and political structures as demanded by the Conservatives, and supporting the reforms, which he thought were necessary if the empire were to reverse the course of decline. The Conservatives in their fierce opposition also mustered the support of Emperor Shen Zong's mother and grandmother to lean on the emperor to put an end to the reforms. The New Laws were only implemented between 1070 and 1074 and not uniformly throughout the empire. But to the extent they were correctly carried out, there were benefits to the government coffers and to the small farmers (Bai 2002:241-242).

## Reformers and Conservatives

After Emperor Song Shen Zong's death in 1085 the Reformers and the Conservatives alternately were in power and controlled the government. When in power, they would suppress or even persecute their opponents. The scholar-officials found themselves on either side of the political struggles. Even within the ranks of the Reformers and Conservatives there were different factions. On the other hand, on a personal level, association and even friendship crossed party lines. For example, Wang Anshi the instigator of the New Laws and the esteemed Conservative Su Shi had genuine respect for each other as scholars. Before party struggles ripped their association totally apart, Huang Tingjian, a Conservative and a student of Su Shi, wrote a poem to wish *bon voyage* to Li Qingzhao's father-in-law Zhao Tingzhi, a Reformer (Huang 1974:137).

In Li Qingzhao's case, her father was a Conservative while her father-in-law was a leader among the second generation of Reformers. We do not know how these two elders of Li Qingzhao felt about each other personally but politics would put them in opposite camps with dire consequences. Li Qingzhao's father, Li Gefei, belonged to a faction of Conservatives led by Su Shi who together with his father and brother were known for their scholarly writings as the "Three Su." They supported the reforms in the early days but eventually became uncompromising opponents (Bai 2002:243).

As a scholar Su Shi is regarded even today as one of the brightest lights, if not the brightest, among the many literary luminaries of the Song dynasty. He was a stalwart advocate of the direct and simple classical style of prose. Su was also a *ci* enthusiast who preferred *ci* to *shi* poetry (Bai 2002:243).  His *ci* is known for breaking through the confines of utterances of tender feeling between young men and women and raising it to the status of a literary genre worthy of scholars.  He did this by using it as a means of discussing larger political and social issues.  In his *ci* as well in his prose, Su is intrepid, uninhibited and forthright.

As an undaunted spirit and a well admired writer, Su Shi attracted many students and followers most of whom were well respected for their own writings.  The best known among them – Huang Tingjian, Chao Buzhi, Zhang Lei (Zhang Wenqian), Qin Guan, Chen Shidao and, of course, Li Gefei – all had direct dealings with Li Qingzhao, Zhao Mingcheng or Zhao Tingzhi.  We have already seen the two *shi* poems that Li Qingzhao wrote in harmony with Zhang.  We have also seen the interest that Chen had in Zhao Mingcheng's hobby of collecting inscriptions.   Of importance here is the relationship between the Su faction and Zhao Tingzhi.  But first a few words about Li Gefei as a follower of Su.

Li Gefei's clear and forthright prose in the classical style was appreciated by Su.  In temperament and philosophy, Li Gefei was closer to Su Shi than to any of the other Conservative notables such as the Cheng brothers[3] with their heavily moralist philosophy of reason as the essence of the universe and their emphasis on the chastity of women.  In contradistinction, Su with his bold outlook and uninhibited style extolled the natural tendencies in people.  For instance, he argued that as people ate when they were hungry and drank when they were thirsty, the sexual attraction between men and women was also normal.  Li Gefei was a kindred spirit in this naturalist approach to life.  It was likely that this was the underlying principle in the liberal and permissive education and upbringing he bestowed on Li Qingzhao.  In any case, Li Gefei's political career

---

[3] Cheng Hao (程顥 1032-1085 CE ) and his brother Cheng Yi (程頤 1033-1107 CE) in the Northern Song period and Zhu Xi (1130-1200) of the Southern Song developed the philosophy which in English is known as "Neo-Confucianism."  The argued that "reason" was the essence of the universe, which existed before all things and with which people and all material things formed one inseparable whole (Bai 2002:303).  They developed and promoted the ideology of women's chastity (Gao et al. 1991:524), which will be discussed in Chapter 6.

followed closely the rise and fall of the Su faction of Conservatives (Zhuge 2004:14).

As an official, Su Shi was concerned about the welfare of people. He would try different measures to improve the lot of the common folks (Zhou, Yang and Wang 2002:162). Thus in the early days of the New Laws he was in favour of some political reforms. But he became disillusioned with the excesses that enveloped the hurried implementation of the New Laws in some places. He was even more disgusted with some scholar-official Reformers. One of them for whom he had unbridled contempt was Zhao Tingzhi, the future father-in-law of Li Qingzhao. As recorded in the official Song history *Song Shi* (1989:6424), when Zhao Tingzhi applied to be one of the assistant prime ministers Su objected unequivocally, the reason being that Zhao Tingzhi associated with untrustworthy characters and that nothing in his learning or conduct could recommend him for the appointment. It appeared that Su's dissatisfaction with the reforms was all let out through heaping scorn on Reformers such as Zhao Tingzhi who understandably felt the barbs of Su's aspersions very keenly. The seeds of enmity between the Su faction and Zhao Tingzhi were sown.

Su Shi's low opinion of Zhao Tingzhi was shared by his followers, especially Huang Tingjian and Chen Shidao. As has been mentioned above, Huang as a colleague once paid a visit to Zhao Tingzhi's house to view some paintings and antiques, so they had similar tastes as scholars. Nonetheless, Huang ridiculed Zhao Tingzhi's Shandong dialect accent and humiliated him in front of colleagues. Huang as a Conservative was opposed to Zhao Tingzhi's attempts at implementing commercial reforms at the local level and made Zhao Tingzhi's efforts the butt of his joke in correspondence with other officials (Huang 1974:139; Yu 1995:19).

Chen Shidao, as has also been mentioned above, was married to the sister of Zhao Tingzhi's wife. In his later years, Chen was quite poor. His wife borrowed some winter clothing from Zhao Tingzhi's house. Chen loathed Zhao Tingzhi so much that when he found out where the warm clothing came from, he refused to wear it. He got ill and died in the winter of the year in which Li Qingzhao and Zhao Mingcheng got married (Wang 1979:215).

Was Zhao Tingzhi such an unsavoury character that deserved this kind of unrelenting ridicule and contempt?

## Zhao Tingzhi

When Zhao Tingzhi passed the civil service examination and attained the status of *jinshi* in 1070, Wang Anshi was just beginning to promulgate the New Laws. As the reforms were bitterly opposed by the conservative scholar-officials who at the time filled all the important posts, Wang had no choice but to recruit supporters and functionaries who would carry out the reforms from the new graduates. Zhao Tingzhi, knowing how the wind was blowing then, quite possibly praised the reforms in his examination papers and was thus selected by the Reformers. Of those who joined the ranks of Reformers at that time some were undoubtedly opportunistic. These became trusted functionaries and gained promotion by dint of flattery and courting favour with the new party leaders. Many of these new recruits without convictions about any particular political philosophy would go with the flow and were of questionable integrity. All the same, Zhao Tingzhi and his fellow *jinshi* graduates became ardent promoters of reforms most of the time and would be involved in party struggles until the end of Northern Song (Zhuge 2004:27).

Although a Reformer, Zhao Tingzhi did not always adhere to the New Laws. After the death of Emperor Song Shen Zong, his son, the new Emperor Song Zhe Zong (r. 1085 – 1100), was too young to rule. The regency was held by the Empress Dowager Gao (高太皇太后), the new emperor's grandmother, and those years of regency were known as Yuan You (元祐) period, the first reign title of Emperor Song Zhe Zong. The Empress Dowager was a staunch supporter of the old party of Conservatives and detested the reforms. She also admired Su Shi. As Su's faction was very much favoured by the Empress Dowager Gao during the regency of the Yuan You years, it was often referred to as the Yuan You Party (元祐黨). However, the Conservatives who were in power conveniently used Zhao Tingzhi to suppress Su Shi's faction of Conservatives, leading to the demotion and banishment of Su and some of his followers. In other words, Zhao Tingzhi worked for the Conservatives and handled the Su faction with a vengeance and severe criticisms (Yu 1995:20-21). But political fortunes were reversed soon enough as not long after Zhao Tingzhi found himself among over 70 other Reformers who were dismissed from office (Chen 1995:252).

With the death of the Empress Dowager Gao and the end of

regency, Emperor Song Zhe Song reverted back to the New Laws and Zhao Tingzhi as a member of the new party was promoted frequently. Emperor Song Zhe Zong died in 1100 and was succeeded by his brother Emperor Song Hui Zong who continued to favour the Reformers. Zhao Tingzhi became a deputy prime minister in 1102. By then he was a close associate of Cai Jing who was inept and incompetent but a crafty politician. With Cai's recommendation, Emperor Song Hui Zong appointed Zhao Tingzhi as a co-prime minister with Cai in 1105[4]. However, the political partnership did not last long. After a few months, Zhao Tingzhi became disgusted with Cai's abuse of power and treacherous conduct. Zhao resigned from the co-premiership on the pretext of ill health.

Zhao Tingzhi was undoubtedly ambitious and opportunistic. During most of his political career he was able to rise in officialdom by supporting and implementing the reforms. But his commitment to the ideals of the New Laws was at best half-hearted as he also served the Conservatives when the opportunity presented itself as in the early Yuan You reign period of Emperor Song Zhe Zong.

On the other hand, Zhao Tingzhi was a capable and conscientious administrator. When he was a low-ranking official in the provinces, his supervisor was greedy and did not distribute the money that the new Emperor Song Zhe Zong had allocated as gratuity to the soldiers. The angry soldiers with clubs in hand marched into the government compound. All the other officials, from high to low, fled in fear. Only Zhao Tingzhi stayed behind to conduct government business. He looked into the matter and immediately distributed the money but punished the ringleaders who caused the disturbance. Thus he brought a volatile situation to a peaceful end (Huang 1984:137).

In the biography of Zhao Tingzhi in the *Song Shi* (1989:6424), it is also recorded that during a severe flooding, he personally went to inspect the disaster area and offered some useful suggestions for dealing with the situation. When he was an envoy to the Liao kingdom, he preserved the dignity of the Song state in diplomatic protocols. Furthermore, he broke up the partnership of co-

---

[4] At that time, the Song court followed the Tang dynasty system of collective premiership. There were, therefore, two prime ministers, the left and the right (Zhuge 2004:53-54).

premiership with Cai because he repudiated the latter's selfish and disloyal ways even though Cai was his patron. That was a courageous act, and a rather rare occurrence in officialdom (Chen 1995:248). Later as the prime minister he reversed Cai Jing's policy of ill-prepared military expeditions against Liao and tried to maintain peaceful relationship with China's neighbours as wars could only bring death to the people and soldiers.

Finally, on the personal and familial level, although Zhao Tingzhi was not pleased with his youngest son's admiration of writings by Su Shi and Huang Tingjian (Chen 1995:257-258), he allowed him to marry the daughter of another Su follower in an era when no marriage, especially one among the gentry, could have taken place without parental consent or blessing.

His deeds which forever spoiled Zhao Tingzhi's reputation revolved around his role as the henchman in banishing the Su faction of Conservatives including Li Qingzhao's father. In 1102, the second year of Li Qingzhao's marriage, the deputy prime minister Zhao Tingzhi executed the Reformers' order to purge again from officialdom the Yuan You Party members who were mostly Su Shi's followers. Lists of Conservatives were drawn up and one of them was even inscribed on a stone tablet which was then erected at a palace gate. Those on the lists could not live in the capital Bianjing. Moreover, they and their sons could not hold any official positions. Li Gefei's name appeared in two of the lists. He was dismissed from office and later that year exiled to Guangxi province (廣西省) in the southwest of the country (Xu 2009: 422).

There are two fragments of poetry allegedly written by Li Qingzhao during this period of political strife. One of them was recorded by Zhang Yan (張琰) in his preface to Li Gefei's treatise on the famous gardens of Loyang "*Loyang Ming Yuan Ji* Xu" ("洛陽名園記序"): "Let alone the human feelings between father and child 何況人間父子情" (quoted in Chu, Sun and Rong 1984:3-4). This line is obviously a part of a longer poem. Zhang added a commentary that Li Gefei's daughter, married to Zhao Mingcheng, addressed the verse to the deputy prime minister Zhao (that is, Zhao Tingzhi) in an attempt to save her father from banishment.

Decades later, Chao Gongwu (晁公武), a nephew of Chao Buzhi, quoted another line allegedly written by Li Qingzhao at the time of the purge and addressed to her father-in-law who was the deputy prime minister: "Very powerful and exceedingly arrogant (while) cold-hearted 炙手可熱心可寒" (quoted in Chu et al. 1984:10).[5] The rest of the poem of which this single line was a part was lost. This line, if indeed written by Li Qingzhao to Zhao Tingzhi, would be a strong criticism of her father-in-law. We know that Li Qingzhao could be bold and would not hesitate to speak her mind. On the other hand, she would also know her manners well enough not to be disrespectful to her husband's father and a deputy prime minister at that. Could it have been misquoted or taken out of context by a descendant of an ardent Su follower? It is a question that could not be answered unless more writings by Li Qingzhao are discovered.

What could be surmised is that in the second year of her marriage she was in a most delicate and untenable predicament. Her father was dismissed from office and banished from the capital where he had lived for the last fifteen or sixteen years. Until the ban was lifted a few years later, Li Qingzhao's younger brother who would be coming to the age for the civil service examinations could have no chance of becoming an official. In Chinese culture, at that time and even today, a married woman's family of origin is called *niangjia* (娘家) meaning the "mother family." It refers to the wife's kinsfolk. A prosperous and powerful *niangjia* would make the wife, especially a new bride, more respected and acceptable to the husband's family. It would usually guarantee better treatment by the in-laws. With the purge, Li Qingzhao's *niangjia* was in utter disgrace and she most likely would have felt the anguish of emotional and physical isolation.

From the above discussion one could see that Zhao Tingzhi certainly had some flaws but he was not as despicable as Su and his followers made him out to be. While the Reformers and Conservatives persecuted each other, the personal attacks between Zhao Tingzhi and Su's faction were started by the latter, often times

---

[5] This line literally means "(The one who roasts meat) has hot hands but cold hearts." The first part of the line about the hand being hot comes from a poem entitled "Li Ren Xin" (麗人行) written by the famous Tang dynasty poet Du Fu about Yang Guozhong, the clansman of the Imperial Concubine Yang Yuhuan (see Chapter 2). Yang Guozhong as a prime minister had supreme power. The phrase "the hot hand that roasts meat" became synonymous with being "very powerful and exceedingly arrogant" (*Concise English-Chinese Chinese-English Dictionary* 2001:II 613). Zhao Tingzhi was also a prime minister (Zhuge 2004:45).

with the former standing alone while facing a group of Su supporters (Chen 1995:251). But historians through the centuries, in deference to Su's stature as a writer, have been more inclined to take the view of the Su faction and hence a less objective assessment of Zhao Tingzhi's character. Thus Zhao Tingzhi in history has often been criticized for being cold-hearted towards Li Gefei to whom he was related by the marriage of their children and for not saving him from ruin and exile. However, Zhao Tingzhi was carrying out a policy that was made by a previous prime minister. If he did show favouritism towards Li Gefei, would he not then be criticized not only by his contemporaries but also by posterity for nepotism and, therefore, lacking in honesty and integrity? It was likely that he did his best to shield Li Gefei from the worst hardships and humiliation. In 1106, when Zhao Tingzhi was the prime minister, the Emperor began to pardon the Yuan You Party members. Li Gefei, Huang Tingjian and Chao Buzhi were among the first group to be pardoned (Xu 2002:428).

Years later in her "Postscript" Li Qingzhao wrote about Zhao Tingzhi with respect, referred to him by his title of the prime minister throughout the essay, and had positive things to say about the Zhao family. Those sentiments revealed in the "Postscript" ring true and were not a sham. If she had harsh words about the treatment of her father at the hands of her father-in-law she seemed to have forgiven the latter in her later years. There is no hint of any grudge against Zhao Tingzhi in the "Postscript" whatever her feelings might have been in the heat of the moment. And that would be in line with her character.

The rather lengthy discussion of the conflict between the Reformers and Conservatives, particularly in reference to the Zhao and Li families, and the Su faction, is included because it portrays, first, Li Qingzhao's difficult and delicate predicament in the second year of her marriage. Secondly, one of the major reasons for the decline and end of Northern Song was the unrelenting internecine conflict within officialdom. Among the Reformers and Conservatives there were corrupt officials interested in only safeguarding their positions of power and material benefits, but there were also many sincere and upright scholars in both camps who were infused with the Confucian ethic of serving the country and the public. The party struggle in the end hurt the latter group of officials, Reformers and Conservatives alike, who were unable to carry out any consistent policies of ensuring stability and welfare for the people or strengthening the government financially or militarily. The political vacuum was filled by the corrupt and selfish men of mean character, often joined by unscrupulous eunuchs who had a chance to be close to and, therefore, to influence any emperor. It was then inevitable that crafty politicians like Cai Jing would seize power for their own gain and ultimately so enfeebled the Song Empire that invasion and conquest by Jin was a matter of time. The conquest of Northern Song by Jin would bring widespread destruction of the cities and in the countryside, and cause suffering to millions of people, include Li Qingzhao. This kind of unhappy outcome was what she had lamented as occurring in the Tang dynasty and forewarned as possible happenings in her own time in her two *shi* to rhyme with Zhang Wenqian's poem when she was 17 *sui*.

There is one *ci* that is thought to be written during the political turmoil:

### To the tune of "Walking in Fragrance" (Seventh Night)[6]

Startled by crickets chirping in the grass
Sycamore trees shed their leaves,
In resonance with the intense sorrow enshrouding
    heaven and people.
Clouds form stairs leading to the moon terrace,
But the heavenly palace is still locked behind gate after gate.
Even if I float on a raft hither and thither
We'll not meet.
The magpies span a starry bridge
For the cowherd and the weaving maid to meet once a year.
What endless sorrow their year-long separation must bring!
Perhaps they are still apart.
Why otherwise suddenly sunshine, suddenly rain, suddenly wind?

### 行香子 – 七夕

草際鳴蛩、驚落梧桐、正人間天上愁濃。雲階月地, 關鎖千重, 縱浮槎來, 浮槎去, 不相逢。星橋鵲駕, 經年纔見, 想離情別恨難窮。牽牛

---

[6] The meaning of the title of the tune "Xin Xiang Zi" is not clear. "Walking in Fragrance" is a very literal translation.

織女, 莫是離中。甚霎兒晴, 霎兒雨, 霎兒風。

This *ci* is about the sorrow of partings and the anguish of longing for the beloved from whom the composer was separated. "Seventh Night" of the Seventh Month in the subtitle refers to a well known folklore about the Weaving Maid and the Cowherd. The story varies slightly from version to version. In the main, the Weaving Maid living on one side of the Milky Way was the daughter of the Emperor of Heaven. She wove silk as delicate as clouds into exquisite garments. But she was lonely. Her father allowed her to be married to the Cowherd living on the other side of the Milky Way. Happily married, she had two children but neglected her weaving. In his anger, the Emperor of Heaven recalled the Weaving Maid home. She and her husband could only meet once a year, on the Seventh Night of the Seventh Month, when the magpies would form a bridge over the Milky Way (Hu 1966:71).

The Seventh Night of the Seventh Month was a favourite festival of young women as the Weaving Maid was seen as the model for fine needlework. While there was awareness of the sorrow of parting, there was also the joy of meeting and the festival was usually celebrated by families and friends getting together in the evening. In Li Qingzhao's *ci*, joy is absent, only the sorrows of parting. There is doubt as to whether the once a year meeting between the Weaving Maid and the Cowherd would ever take place. A touch of autumn with the trees shedding leaves conjures up all the gloom. The above *ci* could refer to short separations from Zhao Mingcheng as during this period it was possible that she might have been away from Bianjing to visit her parents. Or it could be about the exile of her parents from the capital and her separation from them. She feels as if she in a fragile raft is being tossed about by strong waves beyond her control as was the banishment of her father and *niangjia* in the political turmoil (Chen 1995:254). Thus her bitter cry in the last line: Why suddenly sunshine, suddenly rain, suddenly wind?

There is another interpretation of Li Qingzhao's *ci* written during the time when her father Li Gefei and other members of the Yuan You Party were exiled. According to this view, a vocal proponent of which is Chen Zumei (1995), Li Qingzhao was banished from the capital and, therefore, separated from Zhao Mingcheng because the ban prohibited marriage between any son or daughter of the Yuan

You Party members with members of the imperial clan. Zhao Mingcheng's family name was the same as that of the imperial clan. Hence, according to this view, Li Qingzhao was also exiled, possibly with her father and she then wrote those *ci* expressing her sorrow in being separated from her husband.

This would have explained the sadness in some of Li Qingzhao's *ci* purportedly written at this time although it should be kept in mind that firm dating of most of her *ci* is quite impossible. However, there is really no historical evidence suggesting that Li Qingzhao was in fact exiled. She and Zhao Mingcheng were already married when the political storm broke out. The ban forbidding marriages involving the Yuan You Party families and the imperial clan did not go so far as to stipulate the dissolution of any existing marriage. Above all, Zhao Mingcheng's family was simply not part of the imperial clan even though they shared the same surname. There is some evidence that Zhao Mingcheng's father Zhao Tingzhi once applied for recognition as part of the imperial clan. This could mean that many generations earlier Zhao Tingzhi's family might have branched off from the Song imperial family. But no official decree of recognition was ever issued. At his death, Zhao Tingshi's various titles did not include one as being part of the imperial clan (Zhuge 2004).

Li Qingzhao could have written about separation from her husband at that time as he might be away collecting his stone tablets or bronze vessels, but it would not be due to her alleged exile from the capital.

## Last Years in the Capital

Two years after their wedding, in 1103, Zhao Mingcheng having completed his studies at the Imperial University gained an official position, most probably due to the influence of his father's exalted status. In the "Postscript," Li Qingzhao does not describe Zhao Mingcheng's official duties but is quite detailed in what he seemed to be doing during what must be called his off-duty time. Li Qingzhao continuing in the vein of approbating the tradition of frugality in the Zhao and Li families, recounts that she and Zhao Mingcheng would economize with more vegetables at meals and plain attire so that Zhao Mingcheng would travel "to the ends of the earth" (Wang 1979:177) in search of ancient inscriptions and records. While Zhao Mingcheng was on his quest, Li Qingzhao most certainly would have been in Bianjing the capital. While there were periods when Zhao Mingcheng was absent from home during his university days, his excursions now would be more extended as he was employed and had a regular salary. And while travelling as a scholar, according to the custom of the day, it would be quite likely that at the end of the day, at an inn or a restaurant, he would be entertained by female singers or dancers. Li Qingzhao would have felt quite lonely during his jaunts abroad.

Nonetheless, both Li Qingzhao and Zhao Mingcheng were enthusiastic about what was done for and in the name of scholarship. According to the "Postscript," his collections increased over months and years. In addition to his personal quest that took him to remote areas, given the high position of Zhao Tingzhi, friends and colleagues including those in charge of the palace library and archive would supply them with missing poetry, lost historical records, and even materials not seen in the collections taken from Kong Fuzi's residence or the mausoleum of King Xiang of Wei (魏襄王).[7] Zhao Mingcheng and Li Qingzhao became more and more interested in copying these ancient texts. They became so engrossed in it that they could not stop. From then on if any famous painting or calligraphy, or relics from the Xia, Shang and Zhou dynasties came to their notice, they would sell their clothes to pay for the treasures.

At around this time someone brought to them a painting of peony by the famous Southern Tang dynasty artist Xu Xi (徐熙) with the asking price of 200,000 copper coins. How could even the wealthy scions of the aristocracy of the day easily come up with such a sum? Li Qingzhao and Zhao Mingcheng kept the scroll of painting for two days but had no choice but to return the scroll to the owner. They commiserated with each other and felt depressed for quite a few days.

It could perhaps be imagined that Li Qingzhao and Zhao Mingcheng sought refuge in the collection of inscriptions, paintings and calligraphy to escape from the pressure of the political turmoil. But when Zhao Mingcheng went away, Li Qingzhao would be very

---

[7] Kong Fuzi's home was endowed with lands and buildings by emperors of successive dynasties. It held many ancient texts. The Kong residence and the tomb of King Xiang of Wei, of Warring States period, were both robbed and valuable texts and books came to public knowledge.

alone indeed.  Li Qingzhao's *ci*, thought to be written at this time, would dwell much on loneliness.  There is a tinge of melancholy.  The following two are such examples:

To the Tune of "Grievance Against the Lord"

Late spring in the imperial capital,
Deep in the courtyard behind locked gates,
Green grass grows in front of the steps.
There is no trace of the wild geese this evening.
Who will deliver my letter to the faraway land
As I remain in my tower in skeins of sorrow?
Sentiments bring these entanglements –
Too difficult to cast away.
It's again the day of Cold Food.[8]
Still is the swing, quiet the street.
The pear blossoms bathe in the radiance of the moon.

怨王孫

帝里春晚, 重門深院。 草綠階前, 暮天雁斷。 樓上遠信誰傳? 恨綿綿。 多情自是多沾惹, 難拼捨, 又是寒食也。 秋千巷陌, 人静皎月初斜, 浸梨花。

The feelings in this *ci* are quite different from those of a carefree

---

[8] One or two days before the Qingming (清明) festival is the Day of Cold Food (寒食).  Qingming is the festival in the spring (always on April 4 or 5 in the Western calendar except in the Leap Year) when people would visit the tombs of the deceased ancestors.  They would sweep away the debris left over the winter and make offerings of food, drink, incense etc. to the deceased.  The origin of the Day of Cold Food is traced to the Spring and Autumn period (春秋時代 770-476 BCE) when a loyal courtier Jie Zitui (介子推) of the Duke Wen of Jin (晉文公) was unwittingly burnt to death in a hill fire which ironically had been set to force him out of retirement.  To commemorate his heroic life and unfortunate death in the fire, people did not cook on that day but ate cold food.  Up to the Song dynasty, the Day of Cold Food was for remembrance of the deceased ancestors and for sweeping the graves.  After the Song dynasty, the Qingming festival began to replace the Day of Cold Food as the day for remembering the deceased.

girl before marriage who enjoys her outing so much that she returns to her boat late and rows into a patch of lotus.  Here the *ci* writer is thinking of a loved one who is away.  Her solitude and desolation are expressed by being alone in the rear courtyard behind heavy doors.  It is springtime.  Grass grows in front of the steps because no visitor treads on it.  In Chinese folklore, the wild geese could carry letters to loved ones far away.  But instead of enjoying the season in his company, she does not even have means of sending him a letter.  She is not at peace.  Her tumultuous feelings are contrasted by the stillness of the swing, which she has enjoyed before, and the quiet, peaceful surroundings.

The following is another *ci* about the red plum blossom.  But gone is the light-heartedness seen earlier.

To the Tune of "Spring in the Jade Tower" (Red Plum Blossoms)

Red blossoms bursting forth will crush the crystalline buds.
I glance at the southern boughs: have all the buds opened?
How much fragrance is contained therein
Like unending sentiments?
Plum branches see me melancholy by the window,
Brushing by the balustrade, in sadness will not on it lean.
Come now and drink to the blossoms if you can;
Who knows if tomorrow will not bring a blustery wind?

玉樓春 (紅梅)

紅酥肯放瓊瑤碎, 探著南枝開遍未。不知醞藉幾多香, 但見包藏無限意。道人憔悴春窗底, 悶損闌干愁不倚。要來小酌便來休, 未必明朝風不起。

This is another *ci* about the plum blossom.  It begins with the beauty of the buds yet to bloom.  But she is beset by melancholic sentiments.  If anyone would like to enjoy the plum blossoms and drink to their beauty, come now as a sudden wind storm may blow the blossoms off the branches and toss them around.  There is an implied lament that the political climate could be just as unpredictable and Li Qingzhao is uncertain about the future (Xu 2002:27-28).

The political climate was indeed unpredictable.  As has been mentioned earlier, on Cai Jing's recommendation, Zhao Tingzhi was made a co-prime minister in 1105. But a few months later, Zhao parted company with Cai and resigned. In the following year Emperor Song Hui Zong had a change of heart. He acknowledged that Zhao Tingzhi's criticisms of Cai Jing were justified, dismissed Cai Jing and recalled Zhao Tingzhi to be the sole prime minister. Furthermore, the emperor began to pardon the Yuan You Party members in 1106 (Xu 2009:26). The stone tablet bearing their names was destroyed and they could become officials again. Li Gefei was among those who regained their freedom and their status. He was restored to an official position (Huang 1974:151) although he did not return from his exile until 1108 (Xu 2009:432).

Zhao Tingzhi's sole premiership did not last long. In the first month of 1107 Cai Jing was reinstated to premiership as well. Cai, a vindictive politician, was not in a mood to forgive Zhao for his earlier dismissal. Less than two months later, Zhao was dismissed from office. He died five days later. The emperor came to the Zhao residence to offer his condolences. The widow and Zhao Mingcheng's mother Madam Guo (郭夫人), in a bold move requested three favours from the emperor. One of them was that the posthumous sobriquet to be bestowed by the emperor would include the character zheng (正 meaning upright). If the emperor would grant this request of hers, she would forego the other two. Despite the widow's tearful entreaty, the emperor's reply was that let the matter wait till later, which really meant that the request was denied. Zhao Tingzhi's posthumous sobriquet was decreed to be Qingxian (清憲). "Qing" means "pure" or "clean," and "xian" means the "basic law" or "constitution." The posthumous title could be loosely interpreted as "upholding the law" (Huang 1974:152; Chen 1995:291).

The matter of the posthumous sobriquet foreshadowed the things to come. Cai Jing most likely had a hand in the actual choice of the characters. Moreover, he would not let things go so easily: he had a score to settle with Zhao Tingzhi for causing his dismissal from the premiership earlier, even though the latter was now deceased. Three days after Zhao Tingzhi's death, Cai fabricated crimes and misdeeds that Zhao Tingzhi allegedly committed. His whole family, possibly meaning only Zhao Tingzhi's three sons, were put in jail. The months dragged on but Cai could not find witnesses or evidence to substantiate the trumped up charges. By the seventh month of the

Chinese calendar, Cai stripped the deceased Zhao Tingzhi of his titles but let the family members go back to their home in the province.

Thus the Zhao family also came to grief. In the "Postscript," conspicuous by its absence is any reference by Li Qingzhao to the misfortune befalling her father or her father-in-law due to political strife. That is to be expected as the "Postscript," undoubtedly the best autobiographical source available to posterity, was written in honour of Zhao Mingcheng's lifelong work. It is about him and his work, not about anyone else, even herself. It would also be out of respect for the memory of her father and father-in-law not to bring up reverses in their lives although her and Zhao Mingcheng's retirement to the countryside was precipitated by the final setback in Zhao Tingzhi's long political career.

Misfortune has a way of bringing its own blessings. Zhao Mingcheng and Li Qingzhao with his mother, brothers and sisters returned to their ancestral province Shandong. It began a period of what Li Qingzhao in the "Postscript" describes as ten years of sheltered life in the countryside (Wang 1979:177). There in banishment and seclusion Li Qingzhao and Zhao Mingcheng spent perhaps the happiest days of their life. They now had all the time to be scholars in the full sense of the word. They had time to write and appreciate all forms of art. Li Qingzhao would produce some of her finest *ci* in the decade spent in the countryside. Above all, they could devote their energy to collecting, systematizing, and preparing the inscriptions for publication.

# 4 Years in the Province

## Retreat to Qingzhou

After Zhao Mingcheng's father, Zhao Tingzhi, died in 1107, the prime minister Cai Jing accused the late senior Zhao of cultivating relationships with the rich and taking bribes, and stripped him of all honorific titles. It was an insult to the memory of the deceased. But it had more dire consequences for his survivors. It meant dismissal from office of the three sons: Zhao Mingcheng and his two elder brothers, Zhao Cuncheng (趙存誠) and Zhao Sicheng (趙思誠). Three days after Zhao Tingzhi's death, they were imprisoned on some trumped up charges of corruption and sedition. After a few months, as no criminal evidence was found, Zhao Mingcheng and his brothers were released (Huang 1974:151-152). Even if allowed to do so, it would be unwise for the Zhao family to remain in the capital. Moreover, the practice was that scholar-officials would retire from public office for three years upon the death of a parent.[1] Zhao Tingzhi's widow, Madam Guo, her three sons and their families retired to the countryside in the province of Shandong where the families of both Zhao Mingcheng and Li Qingzhao had their ancestral hometowns. Li Qingzhao's "Postscript" does not indicate the location of the retreat. There was some uncertainty about the place but today the consensus among scholars is that the Zhao family went to Qingzhou.

It would be a common practice for high officials to expand real estate holdings while in office as land was always considered the ultimate form of economic security in China. Zhao Tingzhi did exactly that. It appears, however, that he acquired an estate not in his ancestral town of Zhucheng (諸城 in Mizhou 密州) but in Qingzhou.

---

[1] Kong Fuzi admonished people to mourn the death of a parent for three years. During the period of mourning a son could not attend festive celebrations, marry, sit for the civil service examination, or be an official. Throughout the dynasties, officials would leave their office and retire to their ancestral town upon the death of a parent. In the Qing dynasty, however, the mourning period was shortened in order not to disrupt civil service unduly.

There were probably several reasons for his choice of retirement site. His nemesis Su Shi was an official in Zhucheng for two years. The elders there might have been on Su Shi's side during the decades of political conflict and repudiated the New Laws espoused by Zhao Tingzhi throughout most of his career. On the other hand, a fellow Reformer was once assigned to Qingzhou and Zhao Tingzhi could have expected a warmer reception there. Another consideration might have been that Zhao Tingzhi's wife, Madam Guo, had her *niangjia* in Qingzhou at the time. Her preference for Qingzhou would have carried considerable weight with Zhao Tingzhi's final decision regarding the location of their estate (Chen 1995:265).

Moreover, Qingzhou was not only a scenic place but an ancient cultural centre since the time of the State of Qi in the Zhou dynasty. By the Northern Song period, many tablets bearing inscriptions and bronze vessels dating back to the Xia, Shang and Zhou dynasties were being unearthed (Deng 2005:70-71). This probably was not the crucial factor in Zhao Tingzhi's decision to settle in Qingzhou after retirement; as it turned out he never lived to enjoy his retirement. However, the location of the estate was a boon for Zhao Mingcheng and Li Qingzhao. With Qingzhou as the home base, Zhao Mingcheng was able to roam around the countryside and add quite a few tablets and bronze vessels to his collection (Deng 2005:71).

Shortly after the Zhao matriarch Madam Guo and her sons settled in Qingzhou, the husbands of two of her daughters, also officials, requested to be transferred there. Thus Madam Guo not only had her sons but also at least two of her four married daughters close by after leaving the capital (Deng 2005:70; Yu 1995).

Li Qingzhao's "Postscript" does not mention the precise year of relocation to Qingzhou. It simply states: "Later (we) retired to the countryside for ten years of sheltered life" (Wang 1979:177). Zhao Mingcheng and his brothers were released from prison in the seventh month of the Chinese calendar in 1107. The retreat would have taken place no later than the autumn of that year (Huang 1984:320; Xu 2009:431).

It was not uncommon for scholar-officials who left their positions voluntarily or for cause to pass their days enjoying nature, writing memoirs or composing poetry, while nurturing their frustration and resentment for leaving office. The retired officials would often pose the quiet and peace of nature as a counterpoint to the officials' lot of tiresome protocols and delicate human relationships that must be maintained assiduously. Yet secretly they might still pine for a return to the power and prestige attached to an official's status.

There was no such secret ambition in the case of Zhao Mingcheng and Li Qingzhao. Quite the opposite, they were simply relieved to be away from the capital and all the political intrigue and conflict that had brought so much grief to the Li and Zhao families. The "Postscript" provides a vivid description of her and Zhao Mingcheng's life in seclusion. They truly emulated the best known reclusive in Chinese history, Tao Yuanming, who in 405 CE, at 41 *sui*, wrote a most celebrated essay on leaving officialdom and retiring to his rustic home. The essay is entitled "Gui Qü Lai Ci" ("歸去來辭") meaning "Return home." Li Qingzhao and Zhao Mingcheng named their study the "Gui Lai Tang" (歸來堂 meaning Return Home Hall) which anyone who had a nodding acquaintance with literature at that time would have immediately associated the home and their occupants with Tao Yuanming's philosophy and example of a simple life in the country.

It was also around this time that Li Qingzhao named her own bower "Yi'an Room" (Deng 2005:68; Zhuge 2004:56-57). The character "*yi*" means "easily" while "*an*" means "contented" or "peace." Thus came her *hao* or sobriquet "Yi'an Jushi" meaning the easily contented inhabitant. The two characters "*yi'an*" also came from two lines in the "Return Home" essay by Tao Yuanming: "Leaning on the south window I surrender my pride to nature, and looking at my little room that barely contains my knees I still feel contented" (Tao 1989:364).[2] If Li Qingzhao was to sign her name in any writings at all, usually at the end of a letter or an essay but not her *ci*, it would be with this *hao*, or simply "(in) Yi'an Room" (易安室). As these pieces of prose appeared later in her life, it is argued by some literary critics that she gave herself this sobriquet after migrating south. But the characters seem to resonate more with her carefree and peaceful mood as she began her time of seclusion than at any other time in her life. No matter when she started using this *hao*, she and her works would be referred to by her *hao* in the *Song Shi* as well as other scholars' writings in the Song and Yuan dynasties.

The choice of characters for their study and her *hao* reflects her

---

[2] The two lines in the original Chinese: 倚南窗以寄傲，審容膝之易安。

deep fondness of Tao Yuanming and his profound impact on her outlook and philosophy of life.   Tao himself was a follower and practitioner of the daoist philosophy expounded by Lao Zi and Zhuang Zi.  Tomes have been written about the book of *Lao Zi* also known as *Dao De Jing*, and the book of *Zhuang Zi*, and still it is quite impossible to encapsulate *dao* or "the way" in a few words.   One important idea in Lao Zi and Zhuang Zi is that human beings are essentially linked to the universe, hence the emphasis on nature in daoist philosophy.   However, this philosophy is not about mysticism as is often the misconception today, especially in the West.   It rather,

> . . . like other Chinese schools of thought, is mainly concerned with politics, governing a society, the inhumanity of war, and survival in the chaotic times of the Warring States period in Chinese history.   It admonishes that in governing people and other human affairs, it is wise to follow the way or principles of nature and not do anything that is contrary to nature (Djao 2003:207).

Coupled with the activist Confucian ethic, the attitude cultivated by scholars throughout the millennia is that one should conduct one's life or work with assiduous efforts.   However, one should be detached from the consequences of success or failure.   If one's efforts are not appreciated but spurned by others, or even when one is successful in one's endeavours, a wise course of action is to detach oneself from the affairs of the world and retreat to a place closer to nature.   It could be a temporary withdrawal or a long-term retreat.

In this Tao Yuanming was a model par excellence.   Due to economic necessity he became an official.   But he found the burden of bureaucracy and the hypocrisy often demanded by officialdom unbearable and decided to return home to be closer to nature and, in particular, to cultivate chrysanthemums for which he had an abiding fondness.

Li Qingzhao has a few *ci,* possibly written at this time, that have explicit references to Tao Yuanming, his "Return Home" essay or to his philosophy.   Li Qingzhao composed one *ci* in praise of the white chrysanthemum to the tune of "Many Beauties" ("多麗" – see the *ci* in Chinese Appendix A).   In it she names four beauties in Chinese history but argues that none of them could compare with the elegance and grace of the flower. Only the character of two poets, Tao Yuanming and Qu Yuan, could match the nobility of the white chrysanthemum. Both of them took leave from public life.

In this fondness and enjoyment of retirement Li Qingzhao was undoubtedly also influenced by Su Shi and his followers. Su Shi wrote 109 poems in rhyme with Tao Yuanming and claimed that he and Tao were essentially the same. One of Su's students, Chao Buzhi also retired to his native Shandong province a few years earlier and gave himself the *hao* of Guilai Zi (歸來子) "One who returned home" (Zhuge 2004:57).

In another *ci*, probably composed soon after Li Qingzhao and Zhao Mingcheng settled in Qingzhou, she incorporates the phrase "return home":

To the tune of "Small Overlapping Hills"

Spring has come to the Long Gate –
Spring grass so green!
By the river some buds of plum blossoms are breaking forth,
Not all open.
Jade green leaves ground to dust[3] –
Spring tea aroma shatters morning dreams.
Flower shadows press on multiple gates;
Loose-woven screen spreads the pale moonlight –
Beautiful twilight, yet
Thrice in two years you have slighted the god of spring.
O Return home!
We must enjoy this spring.

小重山

春到長門春草青，江梅些子破，未開勻。 碧雲龍碾玉成塵。留曉夢，驚破一甌春。花影壓重門，疏簾鋪淡月，好黃昏。二年三度負東君，歸來也，著意過今春。

In the first stanza, she praises spring by pointing to the green

---

[3] A common practice in the Song time was to grind tea leaves to powder.

grass by the gate, the budding plum blossoms and the refreshing new green tea of spring that helps her to wake up. It is a scene in the morning. The second stanza describes the beauty of a spring evening. For three times in the last two years, the person she is writing about has missed spring celebrations in close proximity to nature, the countryside. So, return home and do not fail to enjoy this one!

As this *ci*, like most other *ci* by Li Qingzhao, is not dated, there are different interpretations of the *ci* depending on when and under what circumstances it was supposedly written. The Long Gate in the first line is pregnant with meaning. In the Han dynasty Emperor Han Xiaowu (漢孝武帝) used to favour Empress Chen (陳皇后). But she was a jealous woman and eventually the emperor tired of her. She was sent to the Long Gate Palace, spurned and neglected. Long Gate thus became synonymous with a lonely place where a royal consort who was out of the emperor's favour or any woman cast away by her man would spend her days. Chen Zumei (1995), for example, argues that this *ci* was written, several years later in her stay at Qingzhou, when Zhao Mingcheng might have left Li Qingzhao for another woman or taken to himself a concubine. Li Qingzhao thus feels, according to Chen's interpretation, that she is abandoned and alone as in a Long Gate Palace. She then in this *ci* calls Zhao Mingcheng to come home.

A different view is that this *ci* was written during her time in Qingzhou when Zhao Mingcheng was away, on one of his trips collecting bronze vessels, stone tablets, rubbings of inscriptions, books, antiques or other art works. Li Qingzhao feels lonely as if she were behind the Long Gate. In this interpretation Li Qingzhao is also hoping for her husband's return (Lin and Qing 1986:1-3).

Xu Peijun (2002:94) thinks that this *ci* was written at a much later date, in 1128 when Li Qingzhao first went south to Nanjing. His reason is based on the three consecutive springs during which Li Qingzhao and Zhao Mingcheng were allegedly separated from each other.

Perhaps there is another interpretation. As the Zhao brothers were all dismissed from their offices and banished to the countryside, the family, like Li Qingzhao's father a few years earlier, was experiencing abandonment. The analogy of Empress Chen's story points not to the woman but to the emperor's displeasure. The Long Gate euphemistically was where the dismissed officials went. The political events in the last two years in the capital might have prevented Li Qingzhao as well as other members of the Zhao family from going to the Shandong country estate for three springs. Even though the three brothers had been dismissed from office, now they had returned home, and must celebrate and enjoy spring.

In their retreat to Qingzhou, the Zhao family consisting of Madam Guo and her three sons together with their families would quite possibly have all stayed on the estate. The residence would most likely be built according to the dominant Chinese architectural design with the main gate facing south. Across a courtyard from the gate would be the main hall where important guests were received and the major festivals celebrated, along with offerings to the deceased ancestors. The living quarters would be behind the main hall, consisting of a series of courtyards, all along the north-south axis, with rooms situated at the perimeters of each rectangular courtyard. It was quite likely that each of the Zhao brothers and their respective families would occupy a courtyard or at least a set of rooms within a courtyard. Within each courtyard there would be a small hall as the principal room in addition to bedrooms, a kitchen and storage space. There might even be a second storey above the principal room as Li Qingzhao in her *ci* often mentions a terrace, an upper room or a "tower" (*lou* 樓).

## Collectors and Editors[4]

Li Qingzhao points out in the "Postscript" that in their years of seclusion they lived simply and frugally. With income from various sources they had a bit left over after meeting their needs for food and clothing. She mentions that Zhao Mingcheng was appointed to two official positions. However, Zhao Mingcheng did not re-join the ranks of officials until about ten years later. He might have saved some money from his salaries when he became an official in Bianjing after completing his studies at the Imperial University. But the salary of a junior official would not have lasted very long. Most likely the rents from the land owned by the Zhao family and let to tenant

---

[4] The details about their work and life in this section, unless otherwise stated, are all taken from the "Postscript" (Wang 1979:176-182).

farmers constituted an important source of income not only for Zhao Mingcheng but also for his mother and brothers.

Any money Li Qingzhao and Zhao Mingcheng could scrape together was spent on collecting books, inscriptions, bronze vessels, stone tablets, scrolls of paintings and calligraphy and other art objects. Li Qingzhao admits in the "Postscript" that she was short on patience. In order to indulge in their passion for collecting scholarly works and art objects then and there, instead of waiting for the day when their financial situation would improve, she decided to economize even more. They did away with the second meat dish at dinner and each made do with only one set of decent garments. She owned no jewellery and there were no gold or embroidered decorations in the house.

Whatever book, painting or bronze vessel they acquired, they would examine and fondly admire the piece to their hearts' content. If she and Zhao Mingcheng came across any classics, philosophical treatises, or history books, as long as they were intact and with few errors, they would buy them as spare copies. As the Zhao family had for generations kept various copies and editions of *Zhou Yi* and *Zuo Zhuan*[5], these two books were the most complete and free of errors. The young couple acquired so many books that they were everywhere: on the tables, desk and even beds besides their pillows. All their waking hours and all their energy were given to scholarly work involving books, inscriptions, and art works.

They would compare any book they bought with other editions and copies, then correct errors and proofread their editing. Sometimes they would give it a title. They would repair scrolls of painting and calligraphy, and remount them if necessary so that their collection would be the most excellent among all collections. When a book had been restored to a pristine condition, they would classify and catalogue it, record it in a registry, and then store it in huge book cabinets in the "Return Home Hall." If one of them wanted to take a book out, he/she would unlock the cabinet and enter the title of the

---

[5] *Zhou Yi* (周易) is also known as Yijing (易經) or the *Classic of Changes*. With the use of eight trigrams and 64 hexagrams, this very ancient Chinese text is used to foretell changes. *Zuo Zhuan* (左傳) is Zuo Qiuming's (左丘明) commentary on the *Spring and Autumn Annals*, a history of the state of Lu written by Kong Fuzi. Zuo was a contemporary of Kong.

book in the registry.  If a book was accidentally soiled, the culprit must clean it as a punishment and a reminder not to be so careless in the future.  Although they tried to be carefree and do as they please in their retirement, they ended up being more restricted and worrisome.

Thus Li Qingzhao and Zhao Mingcheng spent their days.  But that was not enough.  They would work into the night, allotting themselves the time of burning one candle.  They would brew tea in the Return Home Hall after dinner.  Li Qingzhao's memory was prodigious.  She would point to a stack of books and ask for the exact location of a certain incident.  The one who could identify correctly the book, volume, page and line would win the chance to drink tea first.  As the winner she would raise the tea cup and laugh loudly.  In her hearty laugh she would spill the whole cup into her lap and ended up drinking nothing.

Humour has never been lacking in thousands of years of Chinese literature.  But descriptions of a hearty belly laugh are not so common to come by.  Li Qingzhao's depiction of herself laughing loudly and splashing tea all over her dress is, therefore, quite unique.  The conduct is unbecoming of a woman of the gentry.  Certainly no gentlewoman has written about herself this way.  This is the unedited Li Qingzhao.

Li Qingzhao writes in the "Postscript" that even though they laboured under difficult circumstances and with limited financial resources, they did not waver in their resolute ambition.  Rather their joy in sorting and comparing ancient texts and in handling and repairing art objects was such that it far surpassed the pleasures sought by the scion of the gentry class:  song and dance in the halls of entertainment, sex, gambling, and keeping dogs and horses.  She even compares their passion for their work as an addiction!  Quite contentedly she announces that they would be happy to grow old as two rustics.


## *Ci*, Anecdotes and Relics

During this period, while Zhao Mingcheng was on his many journeys in quest of books, scrolls of painting or calligraphy, bronze vessels, stone tablets, or simply rubbings of inscriptions on these objects, Li Qingzhao was undoubtedly quite lonely.  She wrote some of the most poignant *ci* on separation from and the absence of a loved one.  The following *ci* are examples; the first one is particularly well known.

To the tune of "Inebriated in the Shadow of Flowers" (*Chongyang*)[6]

> Light mist, thick clouds,
> Sadness persists all day.
> Ambergris incense rises from the burner,
> It's the fair festival *Chongyang* again.
> The midnight chill seeps through
> Jewelled pillow and sheer silk drapery.[7]
> Sipping wine in the evening by the east fence
> Imperceptibly fragrance fills the sleeves.
> How else not be dispirited?
> Curtain furling up the west wind,
> I am more slender than the yellow flower.

醉花陰 - 重陽

薄霧濃雰愁永晝，瑞腦銷金獸。佳節又重陽，寶枕紗厨，半夜凉初透。東籬把酒黃昏後，有暗香盈袖。莫道不銷魂，簾捲西風，人比黃花瘦。

The Yuan dynasty writer Yi Shizhen who recounts the tale that Zhao Mingcheng would be the husband of a female *ci* composer (see Chapter 3) records a rather fetching story about the above *ci* (see Chen 1995:147-148).  Li Qingzhao wrote the *ci* to the tune of "Inebriated in the Shadow of Flowers" on the *Chongyang* festival and sent it to Zhao Mingcheng who was at that time out of town.  Zhao Mingcheng was overwhelmed by the superb quality of the *ci*.  Not only did he admire it, but also felt challenged by it.  He aimed to better it.  For three days and nights he refused to see any visitors.  In fact he neglected to eat or sleep.  Thus he composed fifty *ci*.  He mixed the *ci* sent by his wife

---

[6] The *Chongyang* festival is on the ninth day of the ninth month in the Chinese calendar.  It was often celebrated with outings up some mountains or visits to ancestors' graves.

[7] Beds in China had curtains which also served as a mosquito net.

among his own compositions and showed them to his friend Lu Defu (陸德夫). Lu read the *ci* carefully and concluded that there were only three truly excellent lines. They were the last three lines of the *ci* "Inebriated in the Shadow of Flowers" composed and sent by Li Qingzhao.

Yi Shizhen does not indicate how he came to know these anecdotes about Li Qingzhao and Zhao Mingcheng. Literary critics have always been sceptical about their veracity. While these stories are probably not based on facts, or are much embellished versions of actual events, they do show the genuine fondness with which Li Qingzhao and her *ci* were regarded by posterity.

In the first part of this *ci*, Li Qingzhao expresses how she misses a loved one as the *Chongyang* festival draws near. The gloomy weather accentuates her melancholy indoors: the smoke from the incense burner circles the room while the chill permeates her bed chamber.

The second half of the *ci* is about her loneliness on the festival itself. The eastern fence is a widely recognized reference to Tao Yuanming whose love of chrysanthemum was legendary and who planted it by the eastern fence of his humble dwelling. As Li Qingzhao sips wine and admires the chrysanthemum by her eastern fence, the subtle fragrance of the flower infuses her clothes. She feels despondent and listless. As the west wind stirs up the curtain, she compares herself to the slender-stemmed yellow chrysanthemum. It is an unusual comparison. But the last word in the *ci*, *shou* (瘦), meaning thin and slender, suggests that her being alone is affecting her physical health; she is losing weight during an era when being plump was a hallmark of beauty.

According to Yi Shizhen, shortly after Yi'an (Li Qingzhao) was married, Zhao Mingcheng had to go on a trip to far away places. She could not bear the thought of separation, wrote the following *ci* on a silk handkerchief and gave him at his departure. However, there is no consensus about the date of this *ci*. Many critics do not think that this was written in Bianjing during the early years of their marriage (Chen 1995; Zhuge 2004). It was more likely to have been composed after their departure from the capital.

This *ci* is undoubtedly about separation. It expresses longing for a loved one. The anecdote recounted by Yi Shizhen is probably not based on any actual event as the *ci* describes her feelings after he has left rather than when he is about to depart. The composer is waiting in vain for a letter that the wild geese would bring to her.

### To the Tune of "A Cutting of the Plum Blossoms"

The red lotus scent fades.
Autumn chills the bamboo mat.
Lifting my skirt
Alone I step into the boat.
Who will send a letter through the clouds?
When the wild geese return
Moonlight suffuses the western loft.
Fallen petals float in the unending stream.
The same loneliness
In two places far apart,
How to dispel this feeling?
It slips from the brows,
Only to rise in the heart.

一剪梅

紅藕香殘玉簟秋，輕解羅裳，獨上蘭舟。雲中誰寄錦書來？雁字回時，月滿西樓。花自飄零水自流，一種相思，兩處閑愁。此情無計可消除，纔下眉頭，却上心頭。

Much of the poetic impulse is lost in translation from one language to another. In particular, the translation of the last three lines in this *ci* does not convey the poignant feelings described with the simple words. It does not begin to explain why the three lines are so ardently admired by the Chinese through the centuries. One limp explanation is that set in the watery context of the composer drifting down the stream, feelings of loneliness are given a vivid imagery. One can wipe the sad frown from the eyebrows, but it swells up in the heart.

The following is another *ci* very likely written during the period of seclusion in Qingzhou. On the other hand, it could have been written earlier, perhaps in the first couple years of their marriage when they still resided in the capital. The circumstances would have been similar in that Zhao Mingcheng had gone away in search of scholarly works, inscriptions and art objects.

## To the Tune of "Washing Brook Sand"

Small courtyard,
Idle window,[8]
Deep colours of spring.
Through bamboo screens not yet raised
Shadows falter on each other.
In my bower, wordless,
Plucking at my jade *qin*[9]
Clouds on the distant peaks
Chase away lingering evening glow.
Gentle breeze, light drizzle dim the skies.
I fear the pear blossoms, not resisting, will wilt.

### 浣溪沙

小院閑窗春色深，重簾未捲影沉沉。倚樓無語理瑤琴。遠岫出雲催薄暮，細風吹雨弄輕陰，梨花欲謝恐難禁。

Like the preceding *ci,* this one expresses tender feelings of being alone and thinking of someone who is absent. In the gathering gloom one hears the plaintive music.

In an article in 1992, the famous contemporary *qin* player Gong Yi (龔一) reported that according to oral tradition, the *qin* given to him by his teacher, a famous artist in Nanjing, originally belonged to Li Qingzhao (Xu 2009:394-395). It would have been possible that she brought this instrument with her from Qingzhou to Nanjing. But in the chaotic period of the Jin invasion shortly after Zhao Mingcheng's death, Li Qingzhao left it behind in Nanjing while she tried to catch

---

[8] An "idle window" is one with a balustrade.

[9] *Qin,* sometimes translated into English as the Chinese harp, is a general term for all string instruments. Here it refers to one with a shallow horizontal soundboard that is placed on a stand or low table, similar to the Indian zither. The two characters used here are *yao qin* 瑤琴, *yao* meaning beautiful jade. The words could refer to any beautiful *qin* or to a *qin* inlaid with jade.

up with the fleeing imperial court. If this instrument indeed belonged to Li Qingzhao, it would certainly be one of the few relics or even the only relic of hers to have survived to the present day.

In the late Qing dynasty, there appeared a portrait of Li Qingzhao in one copy of the *Shu Yu Ci*. On the painting is a colophon signed by Zhao Mingcheng with the year (1114 CE) and the place, the "Gui Lai Tang" (Return Home Hall).[10] The late Qing scholar Wang Peng Yun (王鵬運) mentions in his commentary on the portrait, which is included in the said copy of *Shu Yu Ci*, that the portrait "is kept in the ancient city of Zhucheng . . . the ancestral town of (Zhao) Mingcheng" (quoted in Chen 1995:264).

There are several problems with the portrait that raise doubts about its authenticity. One, the style of dress worn by Li Qingzhao is not of the Song period, but more like that of the Ming or Qing dynasties. Two, although Zhucheng was the ancestral town of the Zhao family, Zhao Mingcheng with his mother and brothers did not retire there but to Qingzhou as discussed above. It is obvious in Li Qingzhao's "Postscript" that the "Return Home Hall" was part of her residence in Qingzhou, not Zhucheng. Li Qingzhao and Zhao Mingcheng were living in Qingzhou in the year 1114. Three, Li Qingzhao should be 31 *sui* when the portrait was purportedly painted in 1114, a relatively young woman. The woman portrayed in the painting looks like someone more advanced in years than at the age of about 30 *sui*[11] (Huang 1974:136; Chen 1995).

For these reasons, most Li Qingzhao experts today consider the portrait as fraudulent, fabricated much later in time, although there are still contemporary defenders of the portrait as genuine. Zhuge (2004:67), for example, is of the opinion that the colophon came from the same hand as the extant specimens of Zhao Mingcheng's calligraphy. However, unless there is more evidence unearthed, it is difficult to accept the picture as Li Qingzhao's portrait. It was fabricated possibly by some resident(s) of Zhucheng who thought that Li Qingzhao and Zhao Mingcheng spent their "ten years in the

---

[10] The original Chinese of the caption in the *Shu Yu Ci* and the colophon reads as follows: 四印齋刻<漱玉詞>前附<易安居士三十一歲之照>及明誠題詞：清麗其詞，端莊其品，歸去來兮，真堪偕隱。政和甲午新秋德甫題於歸來堂。

[11] See explanation about the reckoning of age in Chapter 1.

countryside" in that town. Like Yi Shizhen's anecdotes about the famous couple, the person or persons behind the fake portrait might have had a true fondness of Li Qingzhao. But the deception was disingenuous and morally reprehensible.

There were some events in Li Qingzhao's life during the Qingzhou years that could bear much more scrutiny and be found to be factual. Her association with Chao Buzhi was one of them. Chao was one of Su Shi's students. A kindred spirit of Li Qingzhao's father Li Gefei, he once wrote a *shi* about drinking wine on a cold night, singing and composing poems with Li Gefei (Zhuge 2004:60). Undoubtedly Li Qingzhao would have met him in her childhood.

As a member of a faction among the Conservatives known as the Yuan You Party and a close follower of Su Shi, Chao Buzhi was punished more severely and banished earlier than Li Gefei. In 1103 Chao resigned from his position in exile and retired to his ancestral town of Mincheng (緡城 present day Jinxiang 金鄉 in Shandong province). From 1106 on, Emperor Song Hui Zong began to pardon and reinstate some Yuan You Party members among whom were Chao Buzhi and Li Gefei (Xu 2009:424; 428). By 1107, when Li Qingzhao and Zhao Mingcheng were settled in Qingzhou, they would have had the chance to meet Chao Buzhi as Mincheng was not far from Qingzhou. This was all the more probable as in the spring of 1108 Li Gefei was finally able to return from exile to his ancestral province where his daughter and good friend Chao now resided (Xu 2009:432-433).

In the early 1980s, a *ci* by Li Qingzhao, to the tune of "New Lotus Leaves," was discovered in a Ming dynasty edition of a collection of poems. The *ci* is in praise of a birthday celebrant. Most likely Li Qingzhao composed it in 1108 CE in honour of Chao Buzhi's birthday at 56 *sui* (Chen 1995:292; Xu 2002:46-50). In that year he renovated his house in Mincheng and named his study the "Pine and Chrysanthemum Hall" (松菊堂). With his *hao* of Guilai Zi "one who returned home" and the name of his hall, his resonance with the spirit of Tao Yuanming, the famous retiree with a passion for chrysanthemum, was abundantly clear. In turn the impact of Chao on Li Qingzhao was also undeniable. Chao died in 1110 CE (Wang 1984:368).

Chao Buzhi in his last years was very prolific, producing many popular and critically acclaimed *ci*. Li Qingzhao most likely would have sought him as a mentor. They probably spent time together, sipping tea or wine, composing *ci,* showing each other their works, and carrying on discussions about literature, history and current events – all topics that scholar-officials would likely talk about whenever they met. Chao would be quite impressed by Li Qingzhao's breadth and depth of knowledge of history and classics, her creativity, her insights into political development, her organizational abilities in collaborating with her Zhao Mingcheng in his work on *Jin Shi Lu,* and her incomparable scholarship. It was, therefore, with conviction that Chao paid her the highest compliment that could be accorded any man of letters:  calling her a *shidafu,* the scholar-official whose ranks could only be attained after years of study and passing the civil service examinations. Of course, it would be unheard of to have it bestowed on a woman.[12] But both Chao and Li Qingzhao were independent free spirits, not bound by conventions. The generosity on Chao's part in calling Li Qingzhao *shidafu* was only matched by his honesty in acknowledging talent, accomplishment and merit when he saw them.

Many years earlier, Chao Buzhi wrote a critique of seven famous *ci* composers of the early Northern Song period. It is a careful analysis of both the music and the lyrics of the *ci* of those scholars. At the time Chao wrote the critique, Li Qingzhao was only about 10 *sui.* She could have begun composing poetry by then but the essay probably would not be of paramount interest to her. But at the Qingzhou stage in her life, when she was reconnected with Chao, his critical essay on *ci* most probably stimulated her own thinking about *ci* and acted as a catalyst to writing her own essay on *ci* (Chen 1995:63-64; 292).

---

[12] In China's long dynastic history, from time to time women were unofficial scribes and counselors at court although they were not addressed as *shidafu.* The woman who came closest to being a prime minister was Shangguan Wan'er (上官婉兒 664-710 CE) who was an indispensable advisor and strategist to the only female emperor in China, Wu Zetian (武則天) of the Tang dynasty. She also composed many official documents for Wu Zetian who as the concubine and then empress of one emperor, and empress dowager of another emperor began to take control of court affairs in 655 CE, and assumed the title of Emperor Sheng Shen (聖神皇帝) in 690 until her death in 705.

## Essay on *Ci*

Li Qingzhao's essay on *ci* first appeared about 1167 CE in the second volume of an anthology entitled *Tiao Xi Yu Yin Cong Hua* (苕溪漁隱叢話後集卷三十三) collected and edited by Hu Zi (胡仔).[13] The essay is simply inserted after these words: "Li Yi'an says:" (Chen 1995:101) and is followed by Hu's critique.  Li Qingzhao's essay that was included in Hu Zi's anthology could have been part of a longer piece. It did not have any title.  Literary critics later began to refer to it as "*Ci Lun*" meaning "The Theory of *Ci*."

In the "*Ci Lun*," Li Qingzhao comments on the works of sixteen *ci* composers.  As all of these poets lived during the Northern Song period, and none in the Southern Song period, Li Qingzhao most likely wrote the essay before her migration to the south. More specifically, it would be during the years when she lived in Qingzhou and was in contact with Chao Buzhi or shortly after the latter's death (Chen 1995:109; Xu 2002:266-270).

The main thesis of the essay is that *ci* is musical poetry.  Li Qingzhao begins with the story of Li Balang (李八郎) an incomparable singer who lived during the reign of Emperor Tang Xuan Zong. During that period, lyrics were composed to be sung, preferably by star performers in the halls of entertainment.  One day a group of new *jinshi,* who had recently passed the highest civil service examination, wanted to celebrate their graduation and admission into the top rank of scholars.  One of them privately invited Li Balang to the party but asked him not to reveal his identity.  At the party the shabbily clad singer was merely introduced as a cousin and as such was asked to sit at the lowest place.  The new graduates enjoyed themselves with much drinking and singing.  The person who invited Li Balang then told the

---

[13] Hu Zi's anthology has a rich collection of Northern Song writers, especially those labeled as belonging to the Yuan You Party whose works were banned for many years until the ban was lifted by Emperor Song Hui Zong towards the end of the Northern Song period. The first volume of the anthology was completed in 1148, and the second in 1167 in the Southern Song period (Chen 1995:113).  Hu Zi was 11 or 12 years Li Qingzhao's junior and died about 14 or 15 years after her death.  As a contemporary, he would have been familiar with her works.  Li Qingzhao's "*Ci* Lun" is included in Appendix A.

others that he would ask his cousin to sing. The request caused consternation among the graduates, but they reluctantly allowed Li Balang to sing. It was such an excellent rendition that all those present were moved to tears. Only then was the "cousin" introduced to all as the famous Li Balang.

Li Qingzhao's point is that *ci* is as much about music as the lyrics. She has much to say about both as since the beginning of the Northern Song dynasty, with economic development and relative peace in the early years especially, there was a tremendous flowering in literature and all the arts. The cultural development included the elevation of the musical poems, the *ci*, to the status of being worthy pursuits by the scholars among whom were even some of the highest ranking officials. The popularity of *ci* was at an all time high during Li Qingzhao's own life time.

According to Li Qingzhao, *ci* must follow the notes and rules of the ancient Chinese musical scale. The tones of the words must be in accordance with the musical notes. There are also stringent requirements imposed on the lyrics. While the essential function of *ci* at the time was to express personal feelings, Li Qingzhao demands that the sentiments must be genuine and must not degenerate into vulgarity. But there must be something more than mere feelings and emotions: first, the lyrics should describe the setting or the context of the *ci*; second, the *ci* must relate to an actual event; and third, the lyrics must have some allusion to some historical fact or literary quotation.

In the rest of the essay "*Ci Lun*," Li Qingzhao evaluates the works of the famous *ci* composers in the Song dynasty according to her criteria of *ci*. All of the 16 *ci* writers discussed in the essay were men and her elders, of her father's generation or older. Her assessment of each writer is actually succinct and accurate, although her criticisms of Ouyang Xiu (歐陽修), Wang Anshi and Qin Guan are perhaps too harsh (Chen 1995:101-112).

Li Qingzhao's "*Ci Lun*" is highly significant. By emphasizing both the musical and the lyrical components of *ci*, she brings out the specific characteristics of *ci* and thus carves out a special place for *ci*, not just an appendage of *shi*. In her unequivocal words, *ci* "is a genre all its own."

With her tendency towards free and original ways of expression, some of her later *ci* did not always meet the standards of *ci* that she herself established. But in the Southern Song dynasty, the famous *ci* composers all strove to live up to those criteria (Zhuge 2004:71). That was an indication of the influence of Li Qingzhao's essay.

Li Qingzhao's "*Ci Lun*" is the first essay that systematically discusses the special characteristics of *ci*. Significantly it came from the brush of a woman. While Hu Zi did posterity a great service in preserving this essay, he was scathing in his comments about it. Conforming to the suppression of women ideology prominent in Neo-Confucianism that was becoming ever more entrenched in the Southern Song dynasty, Hu Zi was basically sexist. In his anthology, all the works by women were put in an appendix. That Li Qingzhao's writings were an exception was due to her association with Chao Buzhi. Immediately following Li Qingzhao's "*Ci Lun*" in his volume he attacks Li Qingzhao for her critique of the elders by concentrating on all their shortcomings. He heaps scorn on her preposterousness in evaluating and criticizing the well-known *ci* composers, and not minding her own limitations (Chen 1995:114).

Hu Zi's severe reproof of the "*Ci Lun*" essay stems mainly from Li Qingzhao's criticism of the venerated Su Shi who died in 1101. Li Qingzhao sees Su Shi's *ci* as essentially *shi*, with no attention paid to the musical requirements of the former. As Li Qingzhao takes pains to delineate the true character of *ci*, this is an accurate description of Su Shi's *ci*: while his lyrics are elegant and moving they are not musical poems. Insofar as Su Shi was a mentor to Li Qingzhao's father Li Gefei, the lack of deference shown by Li Qingzhao towards all of the *ci* composers and especially Su Shi in her critical essay earned her Hu Zi's disapproval. And Hu Zi's view of her essay became the standard stance taken by most scholars for centuries to come. Even down to the 20th century, Hu Qinping who wrote the first full-length biography of Li Qingzhao in English could categorically say:  "She delivered no message, developed no theory," (Hu 1966:42).

Actually, Li Qingzhao's criticism of Su Shi's *ci* is accurate and unbiased.  However, there might have been other reasons for her critical evaluation. At the time of her writing the essay, around 1108 – 1113 CE, the early years of her stay in Qingzhou, although many Yuan You Party members had been pardoned Cai Jing a Reformer was still the prime minister. Under his watch the writings of the notable Yuan You Party members were still banned. It would be a criminal offence to read or own their books. Any praise or favourable views of their writings, let alone the works of its most respectable leader Su Shi, might be construed as violating the imperial decree. Moreover, insofar as Su Shi was an unrelenting critic and opponent of her father-in-law Zhao Tingzhi, the Zhao family might have expected Li Qingzhao to keep some distance from Su Shi. Consequently some sort of mild criticism of Su Shi's *ci* might have been socially if not politically necessary (Chen 1995:115). However, even without the delicate situation of which she must have been mindful, given her candour and penchant to voice her views, it would not be in character for her to hold anything back. All the same, her criticism is appropriate and not a fabrication. The criticism is mild, merely expressing her dissatisfaction with the works of many *ci* composers. No woman of letters was ever so misunderstood while no man of letters would likely be so easily dismissed.

## Manuscript: *Jin Shi Lu*

All the collecting, editing and compiling were in preparation for the magnum opus *Jin Shi Lu* (*Inscriptions on Bronzes and Stones*). Zhao Mingcheng is the author. But unquestionably Li Qingzhao had quite a hand in the compilation and organization of the material. After Zhao Mingcheng's death and after she was somewhat settled in the south, she further edited and systematized the manuscript, and wrote the "Postscript" in 1134 prior to its publication (Huang 1974:176). Wang Shizhen (王士禎), a scholar of the Qing dynasty, already regarded the book as the joint work of Zhao Mingcheng and Li Qingzhao (Jin 1985:2). Most historians and archaeologists today recognize Li Qingzhao's important and indispensable contribution to the work.

The book *Jin Shi Lu* consists of 30 volumes. The first ten lists the titles and the known authors of the inscriptions in a chronological order. Altogether the book contains over 2,000 inscriptions, covering the entire known history of China, from the ancient Xia, Shang and Zhou dynasties to the period of Five Dynasties and Ten Dynasties. The other 20 volumes provide the actual inscriptions on the bronze vessels and stone tablets. In addition, Zhao Mingcheng wrote commentaries on 502 of the inscriptions, often stating when, where and sometimes the circumstances under which he got the particular inscription (Chen 1995:267).

Prior to the publication of this work, Ouyang Xiu, an essayist and a prime minister earlier in the Northern Song dynasty, compiled a book entitled *Collection of Ancient Inscriptions*. But it contained relatively few inscriptions and they were not in a chronological order. As Zhao Mingcheng states in his own preface to the *Jin Shi Lu*, by correcting the errors in the documents and by presenting what the sages had written since the time of Xia, Shang and Zhou dynasties, he hopes that his book would benefit the scholars in the future. It took him 20 years and many journeys even into foreign places, as he claims, to unearth, collect, compare, edit and compile his *Jin Shi Lu* (Zhao 1985:1-3).

The purpose of Zhao Mingcheng and Li Qingzhao in undertaking this stupendous task of compiling a new collection of inscriptions is stated again in Li Qingzhao's "Postscript": to reconstruct the original texts of the inscriptions as much as possible by comparing the different copies and editions of each inscription. Thus they would follow the way of the sages and correct the errors made by scribes and historians. Their aim was no less than presenting more accurate accounts of history.

The errors in reproducing the inscriptions were unavoidable as before the printing press made possible the mass dissemination of the written word in the Northern Song dynasty, the only means to preserve and distribute any piece of writing were to copy it by hand and since the Tang dynasty also by wood block printing. Even with the printing press, there would still be mistakes. An example of how errors could be inadvertently passed on from generation to generation was given by Zhao Mingcheng's friend Liu Qi (劉 跂) who wrote a postscript for the *Jin Shi Lu* at the time of the near completion of the manuscript by Zhao in 1117. Liu Qi obtained for Zhao Mingcheng the rubbing of an inscription by Li Si (李斯), the prime minister of Qin Shihuang (秦始皇 259 – 210 BCE), the first emperor of China. Li Shi's inscription was carved on stone at the very top of Tai Mountain (泰山 in Shandong province). A comparison of the inscription on the Tai Mountain peak with that in the *Shi Ji*, the 500,000-character book and the first general history of China written by the Han dynasty historian Sima Qian, revealed that of the 146 characters in Li Si's inscription, there were nine errors in the *Shi Ji* (Liu 1985:558-559).

On another occasion, Zhao Mingcheng was able to correct a long held notion in measurement by determining the exact volume of an antique bronze wine vessel. This was the kind of meticulous scholarship that went into the compilation of *Jin Shi Lu* which has had an enormous impact on historical research since the publication of the book in the 12th century (Zhao 1991:310).

Accompanied by his cousins, brothers or friends, he frequented historical and scenic sites near Qingzhou and found inscriptions on stones in many places, such as those from the Qin dynasty on Tai Mountain (Zhao 1991:316-317). He also left his own inscriptions carved on stone tablets at sites that he and his companions visited (Yu 1995:182-186).

In his commentaries on the 502 inscriptions in the book, he would sometimes mention the year and the place of particular vessels or tablets that were added to the collection. Several vessels and tablets were discovered and rubbings of inscriptions taken from the time he and his family left Bianjing in 1107 till 1127 when Zhao Mingcheng went south to the present day city of Nanjing. For example, there was a set of ten bells from the State of Qi (Warring States Period) with an inscription of over 500 words. The bells and many other ancient vessels were found in the fields near Zizhou in 1123 (Zhao 1991:308-309) when he was a magistrate in Laizhou.

Zhao Mingcheng does not record in any of his writings if Li Qingzhao accompanied him on his numerous journeys in quest of authentic inscriptions. On only one occasion does he mention Li Qingzhao and that is in relation to his getting the famous Tang dynasty poet Bai Juyi's calligraphy of the Buddhist sutra *Leng Yan Jing* (楞嚴經). The event took place after Zhao Mingcheng had become an official again. By 1126 he had been transferred to Zizhou (淄州 in Shandong province). In one village where all inhabitants were surnamed Xing (邢), there was a reclusive gentleman and scholar who cultivated a luxuriant garden. He did not dislike Zhao Mingcheng for being an official but received him courteously as befitting a scholar. In time he showed Bai Juyi's calligraphy to Zhao Mingcheng who immediately got on his horse and galloped home to share with Li Qingzhao this precious find. It was already late at night but they warmed up some wine and snacks, and both were beside themselves with ecstasy. They deeply admired and cherished the calligraphy. Even after burning two candles they still did not want to go to bed (Zhao 1991; Huang 1974:161).

By this time, the *Jin Shi Lu* manuscript was nearly complete but they were still adding new discoveries to it. Although Zhao

Mingcheng was already back in public life he still spent time visiting cultural and archaeological sites.    Earlier, during the years of retirement in Qingzhou, he had much more time to roam the countryside.    While Li Qingzhao and Zhao Mingcheng worked together perusing and editing the *Jin Shi Lu* , there were times when Zhao Mingcheng was away.    Both before and after Zhao Mingcheng's reinstatement as an official, Li Qingzhao wrote some moving *ci* about separation and longing for the absent lover as discussed above.

## Reinstatement of Zhao Mingcheng

As has been mentioned at the beginning of this chapter, after Zhao Tingzhi's death in 1107, Cai Jing accused him of corruption and sedition.    Zhao Mingcheng and his brothers were dismissed from office and were imprisoned.    The charges against Zhao Tingzhi could not be substantiated and his sons were eventually released after several months.    But their dismissal from their respective offices was permanent.    As long as Zhao Tingzhi was in disgrace, even if posthumously, his sons could not serve in any official capacity, hence the retirement of the entire family to Qingzhou as discussed above.

The prime minister Cai Jing was dismissed from office in 1111. The indomitable widow of Zhao Tingzhi, Madam Guo, who would rarely take "No" for an answer, lost no time in petitioning the sovereign, Emperor Song Hui Zong, once again.    This time it was to remove all charges against her husband and have him restored to all his achievements and statuses.    The petition was granted.    This meant that her sons could be re-appointed to official positions.    Two of her sons, Zhao Mingcheng's two elder brothers, were indeed back in civil service in the following year.    However, historical records did not reveal any trace of Zhao Mingcheng holding offices until 1121 when he was the magistrate of Laizhou (萊州) in present day Shandong province (Huang 1974:134-135).    On the other hand, as recorded by himself in the *Jin Shi Lu* or by his friends, Zhao Mingcheng travelled quite frequently during the years between 1111 and 1121 in his quest for art objects and inscriptions.    Thus it appears that Zhao Mingcheng and Li Qingzhao stayed in Qingzhou much longer than his brothers, immersed as they were in what they enjoyed doing the most, namely, scholarly work.

In assuming his official duties in Laizhou, Zhao Mingcheng seemed to have gone there by himself, unaccompanied by Li Qingzhao.  She travelled there separately and on the way, while staying in an inn wrote a *ci*.  In one of the rare instances, she mentioned the town, Changle (昌樂), in a short preface and that the *ci* was to be sent to her sisters.

To the tune of "Butterflies Love Flowers"
   – Evening, to my sisters from the inn at Changle

Tears coursing down powdered and rouged faces
Dampened silk gowns.
We sang a thousand times the four stanzas of *Yang Pass*.
They say the mountains go on forever,
And mountains break us apart.
Alone in the inn, there is only the sound of fine drizzle.
Sad partings disquiet the heart, forgetting
If we drank wine in farewell from cups deep or shallow.
Ask the wild geese to carry your letter!
East Lai is not as far as Peng Lai.

蝶戀花 – 晚止昌樂館寄姊妹

淚濕羅衣脂粉滿，四疊陽關，唱到千千遍。人道山長山又斷，瀟瀟
微雨聞孤館。　惜別傷離方寸亂，忘了臨行，酒盞深和淺。好把音書
憑過雁，東萊不似蓬萊遠。

Changle in Shandong province was a town that Li Qingzhao must pass through on her way from Qingzhou to Laizhou, referred to as East Lai in the *ci*, in order to join Zhao Mingcheng who had already been posted in Laizhou.  Peng Lai (蓬萊) is a mythical island in the eastern ocean according to the daoist religion.  Here Li Qingzhao is urging her sisters to send her letters as Laizhou was not so far away.

Wang Wei (王維 701-761 CE) of the Tang dynasty wrote a poem upon a friend's departure for the west.  In it he laments that beyond the Yang Pass there will only be strangers for his friend.  The poem became a popular farewell song, often repeated in its rendition.  In Li Qingzhao's *ci*, she describes her farewell to her sisters as repeating the song many, many times.

That Li Qingzhao composed the above *ci* for her sisters is still immensely fascinating to any readers almost 900 years later. Many poems in Chinese literature were written by men as they bid their male friends farewell. The system of Chinese administration and civil service in sending scholar-officials to various parts of the country, often for a limited period of time, and then assigning them to somewhere else produced numerous meetings and partings among colleagues and family members. In fact voyages by scholars would have been undertaken even earlier than civil service postings as they would have to leave home in order to sit for examinations at the local, provincial and national levels. Thus some of the most touching verses in Chinese literature are about sorrows of partings and of missing family, friends and hometowns. But that was among the male scholars.

Although the women often travelled to the places of their husbands' or fathers' postings, there are not many extant poems about leave-taking and separations from their own friends. There are, however, quite a few excellent poems about missing their husbands. On the whole, fewer women were educated to the extent of being able to compose poetry. Even when they did, their writings were not likely to be included in official dynastic histories or even in anthologies, which were almost exclusively collected and edited by male scholars.

Li Qingzhao's use of the term *jiemei* (姊妹), translated as sisters, in the preface confirms the fact that this literary gem was written by a woman and for other women. It is most significant. First of all, the term *jiemei* consists of two words: *jie* meaning elder sister and *mei* meaning younger sister. So she was writing to a group of sisters, not one individual.

Secondly, the term *jiemei* does not necessarily mean biological sisters. As far as we know Li Qingzhao had only one sibling, a younger brother. But the term *jiemei* as it was used then and still is used today can refer to a variety of women of the same generation or about the same age. In Li Qingzhao's case, they could possibly be Zhao Mingcheng's sisters; as we have seen, two of them also moved to Qingzhou after the death of their father. *Jiemei* could also include sisters-in-law and cousins of either Li Qingzhao or Zhao Mingcheng. It might also include good friends and neighbours. All of these would be addressed as elder sisters or younger sisters depending on the age of any two women in question. In the Chinese naming culture, it would be considered disrespectful to call people by their names. Among the men, the "courtesy names," the $zi$, are used. But even among men and certainly among women, in addressing each other, the person's name would be followed by the relational term of elder sister, younger sister, elder brother or younger brother. That Li Qingzhao intended this $ci$ for her "sisters" means that in Qingzhou at least she had a coterie of close women folks whom she was unhappy to leave.

Lastly, the $ci$ is significant in pointing to the literacy of women of the gentry and how some of them spent their time. This $ci$ of Li Qingzhao takes for granted that her sisters were literate and in fact quite educated. They would not only read this $ci$ that Li Qingzhao is sending them, but Li Qingzhao expects them to write letters to her.

The $ci$ does not describe the women's daily life. Most women in the scholar-officials' households did some needlework, and some might even be quite competent in cooking as at some point in their lives they would be expected to run a household. Nevertheless, there would be servants who did the actual housework. The ladies of the scholar-official class would thus have much leisure time. It is into the leisure time that Li Qingzhao gives the readers a glimpse. Later on she would write a treatise on a gambling game popular among ladies of the gentry. In the preface to that piece of writing she admits that she was very fond of gambling. The $ci$ presented above points to another pastime of the gentlewomen. It appears that they would get together on various occasions and make music and sing, but certainly not always in sorrow. They would have wine and drink to each other's good fortune, health or happiness. When their education was coupled with their social gatherings, it is not too far-fetched to imagine that the women of the gentry would compose poetry as they drank their wine and partook in the repast.

This kind of gathering where food and wine were served and verses were composed was probably quite frequent among the educated women of the gentry. In her earlier $ci$ discussed in Chapter 2 about rowing into a tangle of lotus flowers and the sea gulls getting annoyed at people leaving too early, the excursions were not solitary experiences. They were outings by a group of ladies of the gentry. The gatherings of the *jiemei* could be the celebration of a birthday, a festival, or the New Year. In this case, it was to say farewell with wishes for a safe journey. On these occasions, the *jiemei* would reaffirm their bonds and provide support for each other.

Such groups of literary women could have been quite informal in Li Qingzhao's days.  In the later Ming and Qing dynasties, actual poetry clubs were formed and women's literary productions could be quite prolific.  One such club included three generations of a scholar-official family plus other close friends (see Ko 1994).  Perhaps the best description of the multi-faceted and layered interaction among women in such formal or informal poetry clubs, most likely based on actual literary groups of gentlewomen, is provided by Cao Xueqin (曹雪芹) in his novel *Honglou Meng (紅樓夢 )*, often translated into English as the *Dream of the Red Chamber* or *Dream of the Red Mansions*.  It would not be far-fetched to assert that Li Qingzhao's *ci* here refers to an early example of these poetry clubs.


## Desolation

In the *ci* "Butterflies Love Flowers," Li Qingzhao solicits letters from her *jiemei*.  She wants to be remembered and missed by them.  She in fact was begging for their support and affection because she had reason to be very sad and low in spirits, aside from the separation. We know that she reached Laizhou on the 10th day of the Eighth Month of the Chinese calendar in 1121.  This is stated in the short preface to a *shi* that she wrote upon arrival.

*Ganhuai* (Deeply Moved)

I arrived in Laizhou during the reign entitled Xuanhe (宣和 of Emperor Song Hui Zong) in the year Xinchou (辛丑 1121 CE), Eighth Month, 10th day.  I sit alone in a room that contains nothing that I am used to seeing around me. The *Li Yun* rhyme book[14] is on the table.  I opened it at random and decided to compose a *shi* on the basis of whatever rhyme I happened to come upon.  I obtained the

---

[14] There were various rhyme books in use to facilitate a poet's task.  The *Li Yun* (an abbreviation for *Li Bu Yun Lue* <禮部韻略>) was the official rhyme book in the Song Dynasty.  It alone could be used in the Civil Service Examinations.

word "*zi*" (子).  Using that word I composed the *shi* while my sentiments were aroused.[15]

Cold seeping through the window, broken table,
No books of literature or history.
Pitiful Yuan Shu must have come to an end like this.[16]
Smile all day for delectable wine and lucre,
Which only lead to endless troubles.
Close the door, take leave of guests,
And compose poetry;
There is yet inspiration within the official's residence.
In silence I made fast friends
With Mr. Nothing and Master Void.[17]

### 感懷

宣和辛丑八月十日到萊，獨坐一室，平生所見，皆不在目
前。几上有<禮韻>，因信手開之，約以所開為韻作詩。
偶得"子"字，作感懷詩云。

寒窗敗几無書史，公路可憐合至此。青州從事孔方兄，終日紛紛喜
生事。作詩謝絕聊閉門，燕寢凝香有佳思。靜中吾乃得至交，烏有
先生子虛子。

The poem was originally un-entitled.  But in anthologies of poems since Li Qingzhao's time, it has been given the title "*Ganhuai*" (感懷) as the three characters *ganhuai shi* appear in the last sentence of

---

[15] In this preface, Li Qingzhao actually did not use the first person pronouns at all.

[16] In the dying days of the Eastern Han dynasty, a military leader Yuan Shu (袁術 courtesy name Gonglu 字公路) had no food for his soldiers and followers.  Bereft of any sustenance, he cried out, "So this is the end for Yuan Shu!"  He collapsed, vomited blood and expired.  Li Qingzhao compares herself not to his death but to his bare and empty surroundings.

[17] Mr. Nothing (Wuyou 烏有) and Master Void (Zixu 子虛) are two imaginary characters in a poetic essay "*Zixu fu*" (子虛賦) composed by Sima Xiangru (司馬相如) of the Western Han dynasty.

her preface. The term *ganhuai* is sometimes translated into English as "sentiment" (see Rexroth & Chung 1979: 55). But the Chinese characters for *ganhuai* express arousal of thoughts and feelings. Under the circumstances she was in, it could well be said that she was quite distraught. Zhao Mingcheng had preceded her to Laizhou, the seat of his administration, possibly as early as 1118 and certainly by 1120, so she made her way there on her own. She said goodbye to her coterie of female relatives and friends who no doubt had provided her much solace and support and whose company she had enjoyed for over 10 years. Now she found herself alone in room that contained none of the things which she would usually find around her. Her familiar surroundings would include not only rouge, powder and other articles of toiletry but, more important, the stationery that would be the standard equipment of any scholar. The basic stationery items were and still are today referred to as the four treasures of the study: paper, brush, ink stick and ink stone dish. But Li Qingzhao would have had far more than the four basic treasures. She would have had scrolls of painting and calligraphy, bronze vessels and other antique pieces, musical instruments, and many books. But the room where she wrote her *shi* was bare and desolate, an extension of her inner desolation and unhappiness.

In this *shi*, Li Qingzhao feels deprived as her room has virtually nothing compared to what she has been used to. She also feels neglected as Zhao Mingcheng as an official has a busy schedule. He has to smile all day for the sake of money. But all the feasting and hobnobbing only lead to more troubles. For companionship she turns to the fictive characters, Mr. Nothing and Master Void, who essentially stand for emptiness.

This *"Ganhuai" shi* is quite curious. In her description of her Qingzhou days or even the time when Zhao Mingcheng was still a university student, she was quite willing to economize in order to acquire inscription rubbings or art objects. But now in Laizhou, Zhao Mingcheng would have a salary as an official which would be modest but officials would be given all sorts of gifts, hence the description of him smiling all day. There is no evidence that Zhao Mingcheng was a corrupt official, but it was customary for most officials in all dynasties to become quite rich despite their limited official income. If Zhao Mingcheng was actually becoming better off, why would Li Qingzhao be housed in such shabby surroundings? And why would Li

Qingzhao be chafing under these straitened conditions in Laizhou while she did not do so previously when Zhao Mingcheng was a university student in the capital with little income or when she had to economize on food or forego jewellery as in Qingzhou?

The prevailing interpretation by most Li Qingzhao biographers and experts today is that during this particular period there was a serious rift between Li Qingzhao and Zhao Mingcheng.

According to Owen (1986) Li Qingzhao and Zhao Mingcheng grew apart. Both were totally dedicated to their collection and the scholarly work with the collection. But in Owen's view Zhao Mingcheng's single-minded passion for collecting bronzes and stones led to such an attachment to the objects that they became an end in itself, overriding any affection he might have had for Li Qingzhao or any other concern in his life.

While Owen presented an interesting supposition, the many *ci* from Li Qingzhao's brush do not in any way castigate Zhao Mingcheng for becoming attached to the art objects. Nor does she directly or obliquely voice any complaints about any misbehaviour by Zhao Mingcheng. Her *ci* are simply about the cutting pain and sorrow of the lonely woman who longs for the return of the loved one. Those sentiments are most poignantly expressed in the following ci, which is generally thought by critics to be written around the time of Zhao Mingcheng's resuming an official's posting after years of seclusion in Qingzhou. However, as the vast majority of Li Qingzhao's *ci* bears no indication of the time or place of composition, it is hard to tell.

To the tune of "Reminiscence of Flute Playing on the Phoenix Terrace"

Cold incense in the gold lion burner,
Red waves of the ruffled coverlet[18] –
Arising, I'm too languid to comb my hair.
The cosmetics box is covered with dust,
While the sun climbs up to drapery hooks.
Dreading deeply the bitter sorrows of parting,

---

[18] This line intimates that the poet has had a sleepless night. Her tossing and turning ruffles her red coverlet into red waves.

Wanting to say so many things,
Yet I remain silent.
I have become thin lately —
'Tis not due to over-indulgence in wine,
Nor to the autumnal desolation.
Let it be!  Let it be!
This time go your way;
Singing *Yang Pass* ten thousand times will not hold you back.
I think of the traveller to the faraway Wuling Creek,
My Qin Tower locked in fog.
Only the stream flowing in front of the tower
Will remember my gaze all day long.
Where the gaze is cast
Henceforth gushes a new pool of sorrow.

## 鳳凰臺上憶吹簫

香冷金猊，被翻紅浪，起來慵自梳頭。任寶奩塵滿，日上簾鉤。生怕離懷別苦，多少事欲說還休。新來瘦，非干病酒，不是悲秋。　休休！這回去也，千萬遍陽關也則難留。念武陵人遠。煙鎖秦樓。惟有樓前流水，應念我終日凝眸。凝眸處，從今又添一段新愁。

While the sorrow of separation and the pain of being left alone are seen in many of her other $ci$, in this particular one Li Qingzhao uses literary allusions to examples of men finding new love and abandoning their spouses.  The opening scene in this $ci$ is familiar enough, as seen in other $ci$: she is arising from a much disturbed sleep when the sun is already high in the sky.  But she does not care if her hair is uncombed as she is too weary and listless.  She is losing weight, and here it is quite explicitly stated that it is not due to physical illness or melancholia from the desolate scenes of autumn.  It is due to the departure of a loved one.  Yet as she watches him go, she wants to say many things but feels the futility to speak.  Whatever she says or sings will not deter him from leaving.  Then two allusions in the second stanza pointedly bring up some intriguing scenarios and sentiments.

The line, "I think of the traveller(s) to the faraway Wuling Creek (武陵溪)," in fact consists of only five characters.  The key to understanding Li Qingzhao's misery lies in the reference to the

Wuling Creek.[19] In one of the Southern Dynasties (420 – 589 CE), Liu Yiqing (劉義慶) wrote a story set in the Han dynasty during the reign of Emperor Han Ming Di (漢明帝). Two men, Liu Chen (劉晨) and Ruan Zhao (阮肇), went to Tiantai Mountain (天台山) to gather herbs. They followed the Wuling Creek up and encountered two beautiful fairies. They were so enchanted that they had no wish to return to their wives at home. After living with the beauties for half a year, they returned home only to find that seven generations had passed (Chen 1995:66-67; Zhuge 2004:92).

In the next line, "My Qin Tower locked in fog," Li Qingzhao is alluding to another husband and wife story (Chen 1995:66-67; Zhuge 2004:92). Liu Xiang (劉向) of the Western Han dynasty wrote the story of Nongyu (弄玉) the daughter of Duke Mu of the Qin state (秦穆公 Warring States Period). She loved the flautist Xiao Shi (蕭史 Historian Xiao) and they were married. They lived happily for ten years in the Phoenix Terrace (鳳台), also known as Qin Tower (秦樓). Then they became deities and flew away into the sky. In this myth the couple had a happy ending. However, the famous Tang poet Li Bai wrote a *shi* entitled *Feng Tai Qu* (鳳台曲) about the Phoenix Terrace in which Nongyu was abandoned by the flautist Xiao. The Li Qingzhao expert Chen Zumei (1995:67) is of the opinion that Li Qingzhao had Li Bai's poem in mind when she wrote this line. She like Nongyu had lived happily with her husband in seclusion for 10 years. But as Xiao Shi had left Nongyu, Zhao Mingcheng left Li Qingzhao alone in her Qin Tower enveloped, as if locked up, by fog. Furthermore, Li Qingzhao after Zhao Mingcheng's death wrote a *shi* in which she refers to Zhao Mingcheng as the flautist.

The references to the Wuling travellers and the sad tale of Nongyu and the flautist Xiao go a long way in intimating why she is so despondent, not even bothering to comb her hair; why she is becoming gaunt; why she wants to say many things to her husband but feels how pointless any speech would be; and why no amount of entreaty on her part would keep him from leaving. Her pain is acute.

Many contemporary critics see her other *ci* as expressions of the same sorrow and loneliness as that of Nongyu and wives of the

---

[19] There is no distinction between the singular and plural nouns in Chinese grammar. While she most certainly is thinking about the traveller Zhao Mingcheng in this *ci*, the tale she alludes to is about two travellers.

Wuling travellers. They would see several other *ci* discussed in this book as variations of the same theme, that is, the bitter desolation of a neglected woman. The *ci* to the tunes of "Walking in Fragrance," "Grief Against the Lord" and "Spring in the Jade Tower" discussed in chapter 3 and "Inebriated in the Shadow of Flowers," "A Cutting of the Plum Blossoms" and "Washing Brook Sand" in the present chapter could all be interpreted as songs of loneliness and sadness by a woman whose her husband has other romantic interests.

With our limited knowledge of the details of her life and her relationship with Zhao Mingcheng, and virtual absence of firm dates of most of her *ci*, her poetry is subject to various interpretations, and it is impossible to say if all those cited *ci* express feelings of a neglected wife or simply those relating to separation and longing for reunion. Nevertheless, it was most likely that Li Qingzhao wrote the *ci* to the tune of "Reminiscence of Flute Playing on the Phoenix Terrace" at around the time of Zhao Mingcheng's re-appointment as an official. It is almost certain that the estrangement between the husband and wife involved his bestowing his attention and affection on another woman or other women.

Here then is the puzzle. From Li Qingzhao's autobiographical essay the "Postscript," albeit written several years after Zhao Mingcheng's death, we get the picture of a happy young couple, both utterly dedicated to scholarship and the delights of the fine arts. There was a camaraderie founded on a deep mutual understanding between the two. Even after the decade of seclusion in Qingzhou, through his years of civil service in Laizhou and later Zizhou (~1121 – 1126), based on descriptions in both her "Postscript" and his commentaries in the *Jin Shi Lu* we know that they continued working together on their monumental task of collecting art treasures and compiling the *Jin Shi Lu* .

As she edited and compiled the *Jin Shi Lu* for publication, Li Qingzhao was poignantly reminded of her deceased husband. In her "Postscript" she describes how he worked in their study named the Jingzhi Hall (静治堂) in Laizhou. Every evening after the other officials had left, he would edit two chapters and write commentary on one; each chapter would be the inscription from or description of one antique. Of the two thousand and so chapters, he wrote commentaries in 502 of them. He would also collect every 10 chapters into one pile and fasten them with blue and white ribbons.

Furthermore, as we have seen above, after Zhao Mingcheng's appointment as a magistrate of Zizhou in 1125, when he was shown the rare find of Bai Juyi's calligraphy in the Xing village he rushed home to share it with Li Qingzhao. The two of them were so ecstatic over the find that they did not go to bed until the small hours of next morning. Yet from a certain time on, there emerged all those *ci* by Li Qingzhao with dripping pain, sadness, and unfulfilled longing. To understand the relationship between them, one must have an understanding the life of a scholar-official, the *shidafu*, in the Song dynasty.

A characteristic of the Song dynasty *ci* is that the single most frequent theme is romantic love. Many of the *ci* are about farewells and separations. However, the romantic love is for the most part between scholars and courtesans. Very seldom do we find expressions of affection by scholars for their spouses; Su Shi's *ci* in memory of his wife on the tenth anniversary of her death is a gem of an exception. While some women of the gentry class and several courtesans left behind compositions, most of the *ci* in a woman's voice about romantic love were written in fact by men (Zhuge 2004:95).

Although some literary critics are of the opinion that there were genuine sentiments of love and affection between the scholars and the prostitutes, Zhuge (2004) is of the view that given the social structures and cultural milieu of the Song period, such cases were rare. For the scholars, the prostitutes were mere sex objects or congenial temporary companions in their pursuit of pleasures, especially when the scholars were away from home.

As has been mentioned in Chapter 2, the Song rulers raised the status of civil scholar-officials at the expense of the ministry of defence and military officers. When the founder of the dynasty, Emperor Song Tai Zu, disarmed and demobilized his top generals, he endowed them with lands and wealth, and dismissed them to enjoy a pleasurable retirement. This essentially meant tending to their personal and familial interests, with much wining and dining. At these feastings, there would be music and dancing, performed by the prostitutes and joined in by the scholar-officials. Some girls were trained from childhood in the arts of singing, playing musical instruments, dancing, and rudiments of poetry. These would be high-class courtesans to serve patrons who could lavish money and other gifts on them and their keepers (Zhuge 2004:95-105).

There were three types of courtesans in the Song dynasty. Most of them belonged to the first category: in brothels in the entertainment districts of urban centres. There was over a century of relative peace in Northern Song during which technological breakthrough and flourishing commerce went hand in hand with the development and expansion of many cities. In addition to mercantile traffic, many scholars and officials going to and return from examinations and postings helped to stimulate the hospitality industry. The travellers would gather at tea houses, restaurants and inns where one favourite pastime would invariably involve the composition or singing of *ci* in the company of prostitutes. The second category consisted of prostitutes maintained by the government, central and local, for the purpose of entertaining the officials. The third category was made up of courtesans kept by many wealthy families of the landed gentry and scholar-officials in their estates. They would entertain guests, including such notables as the great scholar Su Shi, when private parties were held (Zhuge 2004).

No matter where the courtesans were kept, their social status was low and they were nothing more than sexual objects. When the famous *ci* poet Jiang Kui (see Chapter 1) created exquisite pieces that greatly pleased a scholar-official Fan Chengda (范成大) who himself was a *ci* composer, the latter rewarded Jiang with a courtesan from the harem kept in his household. Another Southern Song *ci* poet, Xin Qiji (辛棄疾), assigned a household courtesan of his to entertain a physician who was treating his wife (Zhuge 2004:97). Although it would be a very rare case indeed if there were genuine sentiments of love on both parties, and rarer still if such feelings were premised on equality between the genders, the romantic love described in the *ci* composed by scholars often emote deep attachments that promise to withstand the tests of time and space. The few extant pieces written by courtesans expressed very different feelings. Yan Rui (嚴蕊), a military camp prostitute kept by the Southern Song government, sings about intense longings for freedom (Chen & Wang 2001:254). Others bemoan the bitterness of abandonment by feckless lovers despite warnings by their *jiemei*, the other prostitutes (Zhuge 2004:102).

All the same, wining, dining and singing with courtesans made up an integral part of the lives of officials and scholars aspiring to the officialdom. It was quite customary for the scholar-officials when they were posted to the provinces to be accompanied by one or more courtesans. Many would in fact insist on taking them along while leaving their wives and children behind in their ancestral hometowns (Zhuge 2004).

Against this backdrop it would be hard to imagine Zhao Mingcheng not being entertained by courtesans as he wandered all over the country in search of bronze and stone inscriptions, or as an official in the capital or the counties where he was posted later. It would also be quite possible that he might be besotted with one or more of the courtesans at some points in his life.

Aside from the courtesans, there was another situation that would have caused Li Qingzhao pain: concubines. That he had one or more concubines is quite certain with evidence provided in Li Qingzhao's "Postscript." Describing Zhao Mingcheng's illness and death, she writes: "He took up the brush and composed poetry, and expired after writing his last. He left no word regarding making settlements on the concubines or other domestic affairs."

The phrase that Li Qingzhao used regarding concubines in the quote consists of four characters: 分香賣履 (fen xiang mai lü). They allude to the last will and testimony of the famous, or infamous, warlord at the end of the Eastern Han dynasty, Cao Cao (曹操 155 – 220 CE) who held the real power behind the puppet child emperor. Cao Cao left instructions that after his death the many precious gifts presented to him during his long career would be distributed among his concubines.[20] The serving maids would be taught to make shoes which they could then sell to make their living.[21] Cao Cao's words are a testimony to his relatively simple lifestyle and to his abiding concern for his family and household members (Chen 1995:34). Any educated person through the centuries would have recognized the term "fen xiang" as a reference to making arrangements for the surviving concubines.

Zhao Mingcheng's concubines could have been courtesans or young women from some impoverished families. Given the close relationship between Li Qingzhao and Zhao Mingcheng in the early

---

[20] The literal translation of the words fen xiang (分香) is "distributing fragrance."

[21] The literal translation of the characters mai lü (賣履) is "selling shoes."

days of their marriage, Li Qingzhao would feel hurt and neglected as Zhao Mingcheng turned his romantic attention to other women. It was likely that as he was reinstated as an official and assigned to Laizhou, he took one or more concubines with him, leaving Li Qingzhao behind in Qingzhou. Thus she made her way to Laizhou later and upon arrival there was given a cold reception.

All her sadness and sorrows are understandable, especially from the viewpoint of the 21st century. However, in Li Qingzhao's days, concubinage was an expected and accepted practice, especially in the class of the landed scholar-officials. There was nothing extraordinary for a man of means to acquire one or more concubines. Furthermore, there was an apparently sound reason for Zhao Mingcheng to take concubines: Li Qingzhao had borne no son. When she wrote the "Butterflies Love Flowers" *ci* quoted above and the *"Ganhuai" shi*, Li Qingzhao was 38 *sui* and without issue. At that age there would have been no expectation by anyone in the Zhao family including herself that she would produce an heir. She must have been resigned to that state of affairs. But a woman of sharp wit who had a remarkable facility to turn a phrase, she left behind many *ci* expressing her misery and pain.

As it turned out, it was recorded quite clearly by a writer of the Song dynasty that Zhao Mingcheng died without an heir (Chen 1995:64). The phrase *wu si* (無嗣) would usually mean "without a male child." However there is no mention in any records of a child, male or female, of Zhao Mingcheng. It could very well be that he was infertile, despite the acquisition of concubines. But the prevailing medical knowledge of that time was such that the blame mostly likely was imputed on the wife, Li Qingzhao.

Most literary critics today note the fact that in none of her *ci* does Li Qingzhao explicitly give any reason for her unhappiness or name Zhao Mingcheng as the cause of her pain. Most of them assume that it was a sorrow or a shame that she did not wish to reveal or share with others. However, a more likely scenario was that it was not necessary for her to record the cause of her heartache. Her contemporaries, especially her *jiemei* around her, were well aware of the childless family situation, and accepting of or resigned to the practice of concubinage and entertainment by courtesans even if some individuals, like Li Qingzhao, might have felt the injustice of it all to the wives and concubines involved.

Insofar as most of the women's love songs in the Song dynasty were composed by men, and the few extant *ci* by courtesans hardly speak of romantic love, Li Qingzhao's love songs and those of a few other women of the gentry, such as Zhu Shuzhen (朱淑貞) of the Southern Song dynasty, are truly significant specimens of genuine sentiments of women in love. The desperate loneliness and pain she wrote about were indeed wrung from her heart. The readers of the 21st century could only wish, in a silly way really, that Li Qingzhao did not have to experience such anguish and sadness in order to bring forth such exquisite words in her immortal poems.

From Zhao Mingcheng's commentaries in the *Jin Shi Lu*, we know that he and Li Qingzhao were both in Laizhou as late as 1123. In that year, several bronze vessels were found in Zizhou. Among them were ten bronze bells which Zhao Mingcheng described in the *Jin Shi Lu* (Xu 2009:452-454).

By 1125, Zhao Mingcheng was a magistrate in Zizhou. It is unclear when the new posting began. But according to the Song system of administration, officials were assigned to provincial positions for a term of three years. If Zhao Mingcheng began his administration of Laizhou in 1121, then his term there would have ended in 1124. It would be likely that he was transferred to Zizhou early in 1125 (Xu 2009:456-457).

In the eleventh month of 1126, the rising Jin nation from the northeast laid siege to Bianjing, the capital of Song. Thus began a chaotic and tragic chapter in the history of the Song dynasty. In the spring of the following year, 1127, Zhao Mingcheng went south to the present day city of Nanjing to attend his mother's funeral. Li Qingzhao would follow him there later, beginning also a new phase of her life that was drastically different from what she had known so far. She was 44 *sui* then and Zhao Mingcheng 47.

# 5 Moving South

In 1125 Zhao Mingcheng was the magistrate of Zizhou which was an ancient city full of cultural relics. His book manuscript *Jin Shi Lu* was essentially completed by then but he continued to collect bronze vessels and stones with inscriptions, and other art objects. He and Li Qingzhao seemed to have resumed their collaboration in scholarly work and enjoyment of art treasures. Furthermore, in the twelfth month in the Chinese calendar, Zhao Mingcheng was commended in an imperial edict for his impressive performance (Huang 1974:160). However, almost immediately two events also happened which heralded the more drastic changes to come.

First came the tragic news of the death of Zhao Mingcheng's brother-in-law Fu Cha (傅察) who was sent as an ambassador to the Jin kingdom but was killed by the Jin for defending the mandate of his mission (Chen 2001:115-116; Xu 2009:458-459). Second, also in the twelfth month in the Chinese calendar, Emperor Song Hui Zong abdicated in favour of his son who is known in history as Emperor Song Qin Zong. The new year 1126 would see the greatest and final calamity that Northern Song had to face, changing the history and geography of China as well as the course of life of millions of Chinese people, including Li Qingzhao and Zhao Mingcheng.

## Jin Invasion

Emperor Song Hui Zong was on the throne for 25 years, 1100 – 1125 CE. He was one of the worst rulers in dynastic China. He probably did not have any strong preference for either the Conservatives or the Reformers. But by appointing Cai Jing, a Reformer, to be the prime minister, he allowed Cai to unleash the fierce persecution of the Conservatives. Not only were Su Shi and his associates exiled, but the works of Su Shi, Huang Tingjian and other Conservatives were banned and destroyed for most of the time from 1103 until almost the end of Northern Song in 1126 CE. The destructive strife within the literati class created a situation where energy that should have gone into strengthening the civil service and the military defence at a time of external threat was dissipated into petty squabble and personal vendetta.

Emperor Song Hui Zong also personally contributed to the decline and eventual extinction of Northern Song.  He was an accomplished artist, an excellent calligrapher, and a poet.  He created a style of calligraphy known as *shou jin shu* (瘦金書 literally meaning slender gold calligraphy).  His calligraphy style was so exquisite and attractive that even a later emperor of the enemy Jin imitated and adopted it. [1]  While Emperor Song Hui Zong spent his time on enjoying art and beauty and building a fabulous pleasure garden, he left key decisions and the running of the country to Cai Jing, Tong Guan and other corrupt greedy officials and eunuchs.  They collected heavy taxes to support the emperor's hedonist lifestyle and to line their own pockets.  They entertained and flattered the emperor but kept him ignorant of the worsening political, military, economic and financial conditions of the country.  There were several uprisings as the hardships borne by the people were horrendous.  Large numbers of peasants became rebels, bandits or outlaws.

Meanwhile during the reign of Emperor Song Hui Zong, the kingdom of Jin set up in 1115 CE by the Nüzhen ethnic group to the northeast of Song became increasingly powerful and expansionist.  Jin was originally a vassal state of the kingdom of Liao which had for decades encroached upon Song territories in the north and posed a menace to Song.  At first Jin formed an alliance with Song to eliminate Liao.  The poorly organized Song army led by inept officers were quickly defeated by Liao, exposing Song's hopelessly weak position.  Jin took the Liao capital Yanjing (燕京 now Beijing 北京) in 1122.  The Song government was only able to recover Yanjing and other territories previously occupied by Liao by paying vast sums of money to Jin (Bai 2002:249).  It was within this context that Emperor Song Hui Zong abdicated and his son ascended the throne.

The Jin army, having vanquished the Liao Kingdom, marched towards the Song capital Bianjing.  The Jin advance was halted after the Jin leaders were pacified again with gold, silver and territories.  However, in the autumn of 1126, in the eighth month of the Chinese

---

[1] A specimen of Emperor Jin Zhang Zong's (金章宗) calligraphy in the *shou jin shu* style is shown in his colophon on a painting which is kept in the British Museum (Zha 1984:405 vol. 2, figure 4).

calendar, Jin mounted another attack on Song from the west and the east. The Song military leader Li Gang (李綱) was able to beat back the Jin invasion repeatedly. But the indecisive new emperor followed the advice of ministers who had no will to resist and who advocated surrender and a negotiated peace with Jin. The emperor dismissed Li Gang (Bai 2002:250). The Jin army captured Bianjing in the eleventh month of the Chinese calendar and razed it to the ground.

In the "Postscript" Li Qingzhao describes how the news of the fall of the capital to the Jin affected her:

> At the end of the year when His Excellency[2] was the magistrate of Zizhou we heard that the capital had fallen to the Jin invaders. We looked around us – shelves of books and cases of art objects. How we cherished these things though we knew not what to do! But we realized that they would soon cease to belong to us. In the spring of the following year, the third month, His Excellency went south to attend the funeral of his mother. As not all things could be shipped, it was decided not to include duplicate books or those that were very large, then to exclude duplicate paintings, next to exclude ancient vessels that bore no inscriptions, finally to leave behind books, paintings or art objects that were ordinary or too heavy or too big. While the collection was reduced and yet reduced, it still filled fifteen carts. When the cargo reached the East Sea, ships carrying the load were tied together stern to bow. Thus it crossed first the Huai River and then the Long River until it arrived in Jiankang (now Nanjing).[3] In the old house in

---

[2] Throughout the "Postscript" Li Qingzhao uses the title *hou* (侯) meaning a "marquis" or "high official" in referring to Zhao Mingcheng.

[3] The present day Nanjing (meaning southern capital) situated on the bank of the longest river in China, Changjiang (長江 meaning Long River, also known as Yangzi River 揚子江), is an ancient city that was the capital of several kingdoms in the south. It was known by various names. In the

Qingzhou there were still over ten rooms filled with books and sundry articles. The intention was to return the following spring and hire boats to carry them away. But in the twelfth month, the Jin army took Qingzhou. Fire consumed all the things in those storage rooms (words in parentheses added).

From the above excerpt, it is clear that Zhao Mingcheng left for the south in the spring of 1127. But it is uncertain if Li Qingzhao went with him. She did not use any subject, that is, "I" or "we," in the passage after the sentence about Zhao Mingcheng leaving for his mother's funeral. It used to be accepted that she and Zhao Mingcheng went to the funeral together along with their shipment of books, paintings and art treasures, and this view is still held by some (see Zhuge 2004:130). However, Zhao Mingcheng's writings suggest otherwise. As Zizhou was quite close to Qingzhou, it would appear that Li Qingzhao went back to Qingzhou and sorted through the collection there and combined it with whatever valuable articles she had brought from Zizhou. She then, by herself, took those 15 carts of cultural treasures on a long journey and she did not rejoin Zhao Mingcheng in Nanjing until the spring of the following year, that is, 1128 (Chen 2001:118-120).

In the autumn 1127 the Song soldiers staged a rebellion in their city of Qingzhou in which the governor was killed. The Jin army did not take over Qingzhou until the first month in the Chinese calendar of the following year (Huang 1974:163-165; Yu 1995:101). Li Qingzhao left Qingzhou during the rebellion by the Song soldiers, and that their old house in Qingzhou and all the precious articles in it were burnt down at around that time. But on her trip south Li Qingzhao took with her an art work most treasured by Zhao Mingcheng, the calligraphy known as "Zhao Shi Shen Miao Tie" (趙氏神妙帖), which he bought with 200,000 strings of money. She hid it on her body and carried it to safety. Her journey was made even more hazardous by armed outlaws roaming the countryside and sacking cities along their

---

Northern Song period, it was called Jiangning (江寧). Its name was changed to Jiankang (建康) in the Southern Song period. In this book it is called by its present day name Nanjing.

way. No wonder then that Zhao Mingcheng believed the calligraphy had some spiritual power protecting it (Huang 1974:165; Chen 2001:118-119). It thus appears that Li Qingzhao was alone in charge of cartloads of precious cargo on a perilous journey during wartime, unaccompanied by Zhao Mingcheng. The whole journey was quite a feat and demonstrated her indefatigable spirit as well as her exceptional organizational and leadership skills.

Some biographers of Li Qingzhao (for example, Ma 1971; Yu 1995:99; Deng 2005) are of the opinion that Li Qingzhao and Zhao Mingcheng went south separately, but it was the latter who took the 15 carts of cultural treasures to Nanjing. Certainly, the contents of 15 carts could not be selected and put together in a matter of a few days, and Zhao Mingcheng who was in a haste to reach Nanjing for his mother's funeral could not have spent time on getting the cultural treasures ready for transport after receiving word of his mother's death. But their argument that Zhao Mingcheng took the 15 carts south is that the northerners, particularly the officials, saw the writing on the wall that the Jin invasion and war were inevitable and they had made preparations to flee from the enemy, just as careful arrangements were made earlier to get the Zhao matriarch, Madam Guo, to safety in the south. Furthermore, Zhao Mingcheng's record that Li Qingzhao carried only the calligraphy with her in her flight to the south, constantly in danger of being attacked by marauding bandits and rebel soldiers, seems to support the view that she did not travel with the 15 carts.

On the other hand, it could also be argued that Li Qingzhao hid only the calligraphy on her person while overseeing the transport of the 15 carts from Qingzhou to Nanjing. The vivid description in her "Postscript" of how the 15 carts of treasures reached south lends weight to the view that she was with those carts on that perilous journey. It would also be unlikely that while he was hurrying to his mother's funeral, Zhao Mingcheng would have to be encumbered with the care of shipping such a large and important cargo.

Besides the migration of Li Qingzhao and Zhao Mingcheng to the south, there were several other significant events that took place during 1126 and 1127. In the summer of 1126, when the Jin army was advancing towards Bianjing, Zhao Mingcheng received an imperial edict announcing his promotion. The reason for the honour was that as the magistrate of Zizhou he arrested many army deserters and executed them (Xu 2009:461). This would mean that from the summer of 1126 to the spring of 1127, when he received the news of his mother's death, he was essentially relieved of official duties and waiting for a new posting (Chen 2001:116). Most likely he used the time collecting cultural relics from around Zizhou which indeed had many antiques to offer. This is borne out by the commentaries in the *Jin Shi Lu* that describe several significant finds in that year. The visit to the Xing village during which he obtained the calligraphy of Bai Juyi's *Leng Yan Jing* for enjoyment by both Li Qingzhao and himself took place in that year also.

A few years earlier before Zhao Mingcheng was reinstated as an official in 1121 and was then sent to Laizhou and Zizhou, his older brothers were already senior officials serving in the south. As battles among the Liao, Song and Jin armies were ravaging northern China, the Zhao family took the decision that for her safety it was best that the matriarch, Madam Guo, should go south. She probably stayed with her oldest son Cuncheng. She died in Nanjing. Several years later, when both Zhao Mingcheng and Zhao Cuncheng were dead, her second son Sicheng moved her remains to Quanzhou in Fujian province where he was an official and had settled his family.

As Zhao Mingcheng sped southward to Nanjing for his mother's funeral in 1127, a national tragedy was unfolding in the north. After the fall of Bianjing to the Jin, the victors destroyed Emperor Song Hui Zong's pleasure garden and carted away the treasures from the imperial palace. Then in the late spring and early summer of 1127, they took into captivity the old and new emperors together with their empresses, imperial concubines, sons and daughters and their spouses and children, officials, retainers, servants and palace artisans. About three thousand prisoners were forced to leave Bianjing and go on a long journey to the Jin heartland along the Heilongjiang (黑龍江), the river that serves as the present day border between Russia and China in the Northeast of China. There the two emperors and their followers endured years of humiliation, never to return to their homes in Bianjing. Thus the Northern Song dynasty came to an end (Fang 2000:165). Li Qingzhao and Zhao Mingcheng travelled south, in the opposite direction of the journey of the deposed emperors and their entourage, but they were never to return to their home either.

One of Emperor Song Hui Zong's sons was not in the capital when it fell to the Jin. A month after the two emperors were forced to leave the capital, this son ascended the throne to become the first emperor of what the historians refer to as the Southern Song dynasty. His posthumous honorific title is Emperor Song Gao Zong. His first reign period title was Jianyan (建炎).

## Nanjing Sojourn

While Li Qingzhao was still in the north, Zhao Mingcheng was appointed the governor of Nanjing in the eighth month of the Chinese calendar in 1127[4]. Situated on the bank of Changjiang, Nanjing was a large and strategically important city. It had served as a capital for smaller kingdoms and dynasties before. Many of Emperor Song Gao Zong's ministers were advising him at the time to make Nanjing his capital. So for Zhao Mingcheng to be appointed such a high profile position indicated that he received recognition from the fledging court of the new emperor that had migrated south. It was of course also a great honour to the Zhao family. Now Zhao Mingcheng and his elder brothers all held high-ranking positions. This shows that with the northern half of China occupied by the Jin not all capable officials made their way to the south. Those who did were readily assigned to posts as the court was greatly in need of experienced or promising officials.

Li Qingzhao arrived in Nanjing in the spring of 1128, a year after Zhao Mingcheng, together with 15 carts of precious cultural relics and the calligraphy "Zhao Shi Shen Miao Tie." About a month later, on the tenth day of the third month in the Chinese calendar, Zhao Mingcheng wrote a colophon on the calligraphy about the important part Li Qingzhao played in bring it to safety (Huang 1974:164-165).

Although the political situation for the Song government was dismal and far from being settled, Li Qingzhao and Zhao Mingcheng quite reasonably felt that they were personally fortunate to be alive

---

[4] In the "Postscript" Li Qingzhao records the appointment of Zhao Mingcheng as the governor of Nanjing in the ninth month in the Chinese calendar of the second year of Emperor Song Gao Zong's reign. But the local historical record of Nanjing (cited in Huang 1974:163) and Li Xinchuan's (1975a) history of Emperor Song Gao Zong's reign put the time of his appointment one year and one month earlier.

and to be relatively well. They, therefore, hosted a banquet for their close relations. The guests would have included Li Qingzhao's brother Li Hang, Zhao Mingcheng's second brother Sicheng, his sister and brother-in-law Li Zhuo (李擢), his cousin Xie Kejia (謝克家), the cousin's son Xie Ji (謝伋), and their families (Xu 2002:92-93). There could also be Zhao Mingcheng's other sisters and their families. Zhao Mingcheng's eldest brother Cuncheng was not present as he was appointed the governor of Guangdong towards the end of the previous year. On this occasion Li Qingzhao wrote the following *ci* which has the date in the subtitle:

To the tune of "Butterflies Love Flowers"
– A Gathering of Kinfolks on the *Shangsi* Day[5]

The long night, so listless, no joy to speak of –
In a dream of Chang'an[6]
I try to find the road leading to Chang'an.
To announce a beautiful spring this year,
Flowers and the moon
Should reflect each other's brilliance.
Though a simple repast casually prepared,
Fine wine and sour plums[7]
Befit longings of the heart.
Inebriated I stick flowers in the hair,
But flowers, don't laugh yet.
Pity the season of spring
That will grow old like people.

蝶戀花 – 上巳召親族

永夜懨懨歡意少，空夢長安，認取長安道。為報今年春色好，花光

---

[5] *Shangsi* is the name of the date.

[6] Chang'an, present day Xian, was the capital in the Tang dynasty. Li Qingzhao uses this name to denote Bianliang, the capital of Northern Song.

[7] It was customary to drink sour plum juice after consuming wine to lessen the effects of a hangover.

月影宜相照。随意杯盤雖草草，酒美梅酸，恰稱人懷抱。醉裡插花花莫笑，可憐春似人將老。

This is one of Li Qingzhao's rare *ci* that is dated. As one of the earliest written after she and her family migrated south, it contains two new motifs that would be repeated in later *ci*.

First, this *ci* like many others to come laments the lost homeland in the north. There is an intense nostalgia for happier times in the capital. Second, while the *ci* still expresses personal feelings, the sentiments begin to be concerned about the current political situations. She knows the way to the capital in the north but she could only go there in her dream as it is now occupied by the enemy. In her poetry then there now appears a blurring of the distinction between *shi* and *ci*. It was the long held tradition from the first emergence of *ci* to the Northern Song period that *shi* was used as a vehicle to comment on political issues and public affairs while *ci* was meant to express feelings about personal relationships. This view was emphasized in her own essay on *ci*. What is new in her post-migration *ci* is that she is less able to separate her private troubles from the public issues[8]; or she is less concerned with the distinction. While her *ci* written in the south are still deeply personal, some of them are unmistakably tinged with political nuances. The readers are, of course, left wondering if she did it intentionally or inadvertently.

Newly arrived in the region known as Jiangnan (江南), that is south of Changjiang, Li Qingzhao was homesick for her native Shandong province and Bianjing. Based on her sharp perception and assessment of the political situation at the time she probably had an uneasy inkling that she was not going to see the north again. But that did not stop her from complaining poetically how hard it was for the transplanted northerner to adjust to a new place and a different clime, both natural and political, as can be seen in the following *ci*:

To the tune of "The Expanded Plucking the Mulberries" (Banana)

Who planted the banana tree outside the window?

---

[8] The close connections between individuals' private troubles and public issues are well expounded by the American sociologist C. Wright Mills in *The Sociological Imagination* (1961).

It casts
Shade over the centre courtyard,
Shade over the centre courtyard.
Leaves upon leaves, bud over bud,
Enfold boundless tender feelings.
On pillow of woe
Midnight rain
Pitter-patter dripping sadness,
Pitter-patter dripping sadness,
Aggrieves the northerner
Unaccustomed to hearing it upon rising.

## 添字采桑子 – 芭蕉

窗前誰種芭蕉樹? 陰滿中庭, 陰滿中庭, 葉葉心心, 舒卷有餘情。傷心枕上三更雨，點滴淒清, 點滴淒清, 愁損北人; 不慣起來聽。

The tune of this *ci* is also referred to as "the Expanded Ugly Slave" (添字醜奴兒) (see Xu 2002; Wang 1979).

This *ci* is filled with the melancholy felt by a stranger on a rainy night. There is no mention of personal relationship in the *ci*, nor is there an absent lover for whom she is heartsick. There is only the insomniac homesickness. One can perhaps guess what is on her mind. What Li Qingzhao has to adjust to is not only a new place where rainfall is much more abundant than in her native land, but it is also a new political climate. What she is seeing and hearing at that time does not seem to be about resisting the Jin or trying to recover the lost territories but fleeing from the enemy and seeking an uncertain peace in the south.

In this *ci* there is also repetition of phrases and words. Repeating the phrase about the shade over the courtyard emphasizes the luxuriant growth of the banana tree while the repetition of the sound of the mournful rain reinforces the insistence of water dripping (Hu 1966:55). The line about leaves and buds in the original actual reads: "leaf leaf heart heart." Repeating words for emphasis is common in both oral and written Chinese. Li Qingzhao is a consummate wordsmith in the use of double words. Repetition of words in a verse or even in an essay could render the piece too colloquial or even crude. Yet in her *ci*, instead of being dull, the repeated words evoke refreshing imagery and novel sentiments in the reader. There are several examples of repetition of words or phrases in the pieces included in this book. One is to the tune of "Walking in Fragrance" (Seventh Night) in Chapter 3. In the last line, "suddenly" is used three times, although not all next to each other. There are a few other examples of word repetition that will be shown later in the book.

At around the same time, during her sojourn in Nanjing, Li Qingzhao wrote a few *shi* which were more overtly political. In fact they were downright critical of Emperor Song Gao Zong's new government and of the ministers he had gathered around him. There are two extant couplets, fragments of some lost *shi* that are pointedly scornful of the regime. One reads:

> Those coming south yet feel the cold of the Wu River;
> Hunters northward would be grieved by the chilly waters
>   of Yi.

南遊尚覺吳江冷，北獵應悲易水寒。

The Wu River is known as the Suzhou River today (蘇州河, in Jiangsu province). In her journey south to Nanjing in the early spring of 1128, Li Qingzhao had to cross the Huai River (淮河), the Changjiang and the much shorter Wu River. At that time of the year, she describes in her *shi*, she yet feels the cold of the Wu River in the south. She is perhaps more chilled by the political attitudes of the courtiers. The northbound hunters are a euphemism for the two emperors in captivity who have been forced to march north. The Yi River is in the present Hebei province (河北省, north of Huanghe 黃河, the Yellow River). She seems to ask the question if anything is being done about those two captive emperors who would have to endure more severe cold. The real answer was, of course, nothing.

Another couplet expresses similar sentiments but also cites a historical incident:

> Moving south, Wang Dao is missing among the officials.
> From the north, there is no news about Liu Kun.

南渡衣冠欠王導，北來消息少劉琨。

After the fall of the Han dynasty in 220 CE, China was plunged into about four centuries of disunity: first the period of the Three Kingdoms (三國 220 – 280 CE), then the Western and Eastern Jin dynasties (西晉東晉 265 – 420 CE), and then the Southern and Northern Dynasties era (南北朝 420 – 589 CE). In the north, non-Han ethnic groups who had historically harassed and invaded China became even more active and established dynasties in China. The emperor of one Northern dynasty, Liu Cong (劉聰) of the Xiongnu ethnic group (匈奴 a non-ethnic Han group known as the Hun in European history) in 317 CE killed Emperor Jin Min Di (晉愍帝) of Western Jin dynasty, an ethnic Han kingdom. The son of the latter moved south and founded the Eastern Jin dynasty and became known in history as Emperor Jin Yuan Di (晉元帝). What this new emperor did is referred to as "Moving South" (Bai 2002:165; Xu 2002:257). It should be noted, however, that the Western and Eastern Jin dynasties (晉) in the third to fifth centuries was different from the Jin (金) kingdom that invaded Song in the 12$^{th}$ century.

As could be readily seen, there are obvious parallels between the "moving south" of Western Jin to become Eastern Jin, and that of Northern Song to Southern Song. In her couplet, Li Qingzhao cites two loyal officials of Western Jin, one civil and the other military. Among the officials and gentry who fled south with Emperor Jin Yuan Di, there was one by the name of Wang Dao who was not content with the secure and comfortable life of the migrants. He admonished his compatriots to organize and recover the lost homeland instead of merely bemoaning their loss. Liu Kun was a general in the Western Jin army. After the royal house and the court moved south, he remained in the north to resist the enemy until he was defeated and later killed (Xu 2002:257).

By explicitly citing the historical precedents, Li Qingzhao in the poem very boldly mocks the new Emperor Song Gao Zong and his advisors who fear the Jin military might and would be content to lead a comfortable existence in the south. They have no intention or will to recover the territories in the north.

Li Qingzhao was undoubtedly expressing the wishes of many but they were not shared by those in power. The new Song emperor talked about marching north to free his father and elder brother from captivity and to gain back the northern half of the country. But he never put his words into action. He ignored the counsel of officials who advocated resisting and fighting against Jin. Instead he adopted the policy of fleeing from or capitulating to the Jin, and seeking a negotiated peace from a position of weakness. Over time he would recall and dismiss officials with aspirations of resistance from positions of authority and execute others who actually tried to defeat the Jin. Early in his reign, Emperor Song Gao Zong executed a graduate of the Imperial University by the name of Chen Dong (陳東) and a *jinshi* named Ouyang Che (歐陽澈) who spoke out against capitulation. Several years later he would listen to his prime minister Qin Hui (秦檜), who was secretly working for the Jin, and had the famous and well loved military officer Yue Fei (岳飛) killed. At that time Yue Fei was actually defeating the Jin.

Li Qingzhao early in her sojourn in the south sensed the lack of political will of the new regime to fight the Jin and its great inclination towards appeasement in exchange for an existence of ease and comfort. Her ideas and political insights would appear clearly in her *shi* and essays. They would also be in her *ci* where she expounds her sorrow and disappointment more eloquently.

Towards the end of the Southern Song dynasty, a writer by the name of Zhou Hui (周煇) met a relative of Li Qingzhao's and learned about the following:

> When Zhao Mingcheng was in Jiankang, whenever it snowed, Yi'an wearing a bamboo hat and a straw cape would walk around the city looking for scenic snowscape as themes for her poetry. Once she had composed a few lines she would ask her husband to join her in versification. Zhao Mingcheng invariably would be vexed each time (Zhu et al. 1994:11).

The conventional interpretation of Zhao Mingcheng's vexation is that he was the governor of Nanjing and could not be expected to drop everything and join in his wife's poetic whims that entailed tramping around the city in the snow for inspiration. Another reason that is often advanced is that he was not as talented a poet as Li Qingzhao and could with reason expect to be bested by her. A third explanation is that he was an expert epigraphist and not a poet, although Li Qingzhao in the "Postscript" and elsewhere has noted his ability to compose poetry. However, there is perhaps another interpretation of his reluctance in composing poems with Li Qingzhao. Given Li Qingzhao's penchant for candour in expression and ready ridicule of politicians and the state of political affairs, and given his own position as a high-ranking official in the new regime it was in his own interest to be cautious and to refrain from expressing any views that might be construed as critical or as sarcastic as Li Qingzhao's (Chen 1995:80-83).

It could also be imagined that her other relatives in the Nanjing at that time, for example, her own brother and Zhao Mingcheng's relatives, might also shun her public expression of political views. After all they had their careers to protect even if they might feel the way she did. Thus she could have been quite alone among her kinfolks in advocating a more proactive policy of resistance against the Jin. It was a different kind of loneliness as can be seen in the following ci:

> To the tune of "Telling Heartfelt Sentiments"
> – Fragrance of the Wilting Plum Blossoms by the Pillow

> The night approaches –
> Inebriated, I did not remove any adornment,
> Plum blossoms wilting in my hair.
> From such slumber
> Blossom fragrance awakens me,
> Shattering my dream
> Wherein the journey home is broken.
> Voices stilled, silent,
> A lingering, clinging moon,
> Jade green screen hanging:
> Crush some more petals,
> Stir up some more fragrance,
> While away some more time.

訴衷情 – 枕畔聞殘梅噴香

夜來沈醉卸妝遲，梅萼插殘枝。酒醒熏破春睡，夢斷不成歸。人悄悄，月依依，翠簾垂。更挼殘蕊，更撚餘香，更得些時。

This *ci* was probably written in early 1129 during the time of plum blossoms that heralded the end of winter and the arrival of spring (Xu 2002:112). Li Qingzhao is alone with her thoughts. She has been inebriated but the fragrance of the plum blossoms wakes her up. Thus her dream of going home in the north was interrupted. She plays with the flowers to while away the night.

Again she repeats words to describe the silence of the night when others have gone to bed and the moon setting slowly. In the last three lines, the repeated word is *geng* 更, which means "again" or "still more." It is a very simple word but it effectively conjures up the imagery of her doing something again and again without thinking.

In the last line about whiling away time, she actually uses the colloquial Shandong dialect (Xu 2002:113). This is another characteristic of her *ci*. As has been mentioned in Chapter 3, Li Qingzhao is meticulous about her choice of words and the words are always eloquent. Her *ci* are indeed always full of allusions to the classics or poems of the ancients which reflect the depth of her knowledge and scholarship. But every now and then she lapses into the regional dialect which is obviously quite intentional. Far from detracting the excellence of her *ci*, it lends a certain refreshing earthiness to her verses. It is a style all her own, at once showing her simplicity and her originality.

Li Qingzhao's learning and creative use of repeated words are shown once more in the following *ci*, which was composed during her stay in Nanjing in the early spring of 1129 around the Chinese New year (Xu 2002:106; Zhuge 2004:137). This is one of two *ci* that she modelled on a *ci* by Ouyang Xiu, an early Northern Song scholar and statesman, who impressed her with his repetition of words. Although in her essay on the theory of *ci* a decade or so earlier Li Qingzhao had criticized him for composing his *ci* as if it were *shi* with no attention paid to the musical standards required in the former, she obviously was a discerning critic. Wherever she saw excellence, she was forward in her admiration and praise.

To the tune of "Fairies by the River"

Lord Ouyang in his composition "Butterflies Love Flowers" has this line: "How deep is the deep deep?" I am very fond of it. Thus I am also incorporating the phrase "the deep, deep courtyard" in my *ci*. The tune is the same as the old "Fairies by the River."

How deep is the deep, deep courtyard?
Windows and loft locked in clouds and fog.
Willows and plum blossoms gradually budding forth,
Spring returns to the trees of Moling[9]
While guests sojourn in Jiankang.[10]
Once the moon and the wind moved me to sing –
Now I grow old having accomplished naught.
Who pities this creature wasting away, alone?
No interest in admiring the lanterns,[11]
Not in the mood to tread in the snow.

臨江仙

歐陽公作<蝶戀花> 有 "深深深幾許" 之句，余酷愛之，用其
語作 "庭院深深" 數句，其聲即舊<臨江仙>也。

庭院深深深幾許，雲窗霧閣常扃。柳梢梅萼漸分明。春歸秣陵樹，人
客建康城。感月吟風多少事，如今老去無成。誰憐憔悴更凋零。試
燈無意思，踏雪没心情。

The first line in this *ci* repeats exactly that in Ouyang Xiu's original. What is so unusual and yet enchanting about the line is that the word *shen* (深) meaning "deep" is repeated three times without a break. Only master poets like Ouyang Xiu and Li Qingzhao could have carried it off like this with such ease and elegance.

---

[9] Moling in this line was an old name of Nanjing. Jiankang in the text was a new name given to the city in 1129. This *ci*, therefore, could not have been written before that year.

[10] In some texts, the word in this line is "ageing" rather than "sojourning."

[11] The first full moon after the Chinese New Year, which always begins with the new moon, is *Yuanxiao* (元宵) often referred to as the Lantern Festival in English. The phrase in this line reads "testing lanterns" which was used to mean admiring and enjoying the lanterns in preparation for the festival.

As Zhuge (2004:137-139) points out, Ouyang Xiu's $ci$ is about a woman of the gentry who spent her days deep within the confines of the home.    Li Qingzhao, however, uses the same words but transcends Ouyang Xiu's original meaning.    She politicizes the $ci$ by first of all referring to the city of Nanjing by two different names.    She certainly would not have been ignorant of the suggestions at that time by many patriotic officials that Emperor Song Gao Zong should make Nanjing the capital.    With its strategic location on the southern bank of the river Changjiang, it would be an ideal place to launch any military campaign to recover the northern territories.    But the reality is different as the emperor and his close advisors have no such intentions.    Li Qingzhao thus writes that although another spring is around the corner, she feels withered inside.    She feels lethargic and uninterested in her surroundings just as the new regime is lethargic and has no ambitions for the future.    Whereas she has always been an active lover of nature, now she simply wants to hide deep, deep in the house, beyond the courtyard.    Like her many other $ci$, this one expresses sorrow, but it is not private pain but it is sadness fraught with social and political meanings.

Zhuge (2002:139) points out that this $ci$ gives us a better idea of Li Qingzhao's mood at that time.    As mentioned by Zhou Hui above, Li Qingzhao liked to wander around Nanjing in the snow in search of poetic inspirations.    It could be that her tramping around Nanjing was her way of relieving her grief of losing her homeland and her repugnance at the defeatist attitude of the government.    But she had no inclination to do so when she wrote this ci.

## Leaving Nanjing

Zhao Mingcheng's tenure as the governor of Nanjing was short-lived. He was dismissed from office in the spring of 1129.    Li Xinchuan (李心傳 1166 – 1243 CE) who lived in the Southern Song dynasty wrote the history of the early Southern Song dynasty, concentrating on Emperor Song Gao Zong's 35-year reign, entitled *Jianyan Yi Lai Xi Nian Yao Lu* ( 建 炎 以 來 繫 年 要 錄) meaning *Chronological Record of Important Events Since the Jianyan Years* (henceforth referred to as *Chronological Record*).    In it he describes an incident on the fifth day of the second month in the third year of *Jianyan* of Emperor Song Gao

Zong (that is, 1129).[12] There was a plot by the imperial guards led by Wang Yi (王亦) to rebel in Nanjing. But another official Li Mo (李謨) got wind of it and reported the impending mutiny to chief administrator Zhao Mingcheng who, however, disregarded the intelligence. Li Mo then took drastic action on his own and directed the militia to set up a blockade. A fire broke out in a daoist temple at midnight, probably as a signal for the rebellion. The guards moved around the place noisily. But because of the barricades the mutiny leader Wang Yi could not reach the rebels to lead them. He eventually hacked open the south gate of the city with an axe and escaped. At first dawn, Li Mo went to see Zhao Mingcheng but Zhao Mingcheng and two other subordinate officials had let themselves down the city wall with a rope and left the city. Later the two subordinate officials were demoted in punishment (Li 1975a:91-92).

In his *Chronological Record*, Li Xinchuan (1975a:91-92), citing sources of his information, mentions that at that time Zhao Mingcheng was already given notice to transfer to Huzhou (湖州). Li adds that the demotion of Zhao Mingcheng's two subordinate officials was meted out in the second month (of the Chinese calendar) but there was no date given for Zhao Mingcheng's transfer (Li 1975a:92). He does not appear to regard Zhao Mingcheng's transfer from Nanjing as punishment.

In the "Postscript" Li Qingzhao puts the time of his leaving his position in Nanjing in the third month of the Chinese calendar. And later in the "Postscript" Li Qingzhao records that Zhao Mingcheng was given order to move to Huzhou in the fifth month of the Chinese calendar. Thus Li Qingzhao in the "Postscript" is clear about the fact that at the time of Zhao Mingcheng's departure from Nanjing he was

---

[12] Li Xinchuan's history of Southern Song dynasty, *Jianyan Yi Lai Xi Nian Yao Lu (Chronological Record of Important Events Since the Jianyan Years)* written in the tradition of recording historical incidents for the purpose of learning from the past and thus dealing with the present according to moral principles, is a highly regarded scholarly work. Jianyan was the first reign title of Emperor Song Gao Zong who became emperor in 1127 and changed his reign title later during his 35 years on the throne. Li Xinchuan's magnum opus has 200 chapters. It is a year by year and month by month, and sometimes even day by day record of events in the early Southern Song period. Modern historians still use Li's *Chronological Record* as an authoritative and reliable source.

not yet appointed to any position in Huzhou.

It appears that Zhao Mingcheng was dismissed from the position of the governor of Nanjing in the second month of the Chinese calendar for deserting the strategically important city entrusted to his care and, therefore, for dereliction of duty. As it was a delicate matter Li Qingzhao in the "Postscript," which is a tribute to Zhao Mingcheng, does not go into the details of the reason for his dismissal. Possibly for the same reason, Li Xinchuan's sources refer to Zhao Mingcheng's dismissal from Nanjing and his much later appointment to Huzhou as simply "transfer."

On the other hand, Zhao Mingcheng's non-action when he received the intelligence about an impending military coup and his escape from Nanjing under the circumstances should be seen in context. It was a chaotic time. In the preceding month (that is, the first month in the Chinese calendar) the Jin army moved south. It took cities north of the Changjiang in quick succession. By the beginning of the second month, the new emperor himself was on the run. Many civil and military officials simply had no confidence that the Song could really resist the Jin. It would not have been the first time if some commanding officer decided to withdraw their allegiance to the Song emperor and to set up a base of their own, as a group of bandits more or less, or to capitulate to the Jin. This was what happened in their hometown Qingzhou after Zhao Mingcheng and Li Qingzhao left for the south. There was a military coup and the magistrate of Qingzhou was killed. If it could have happened in a small provincial city, it would very likely occur in an important city like Nanjing. Communication links and the chain of command in the Song government at that time were broken or in flux. Zhao Mingcheng, quite rightly perhaps, felt that he had no authority or means to deal with the rebellion. After all he was a scholar, an expert in cultural artefacts, who had no experience in military manoeuvres at a time when expertise in such matters was needed more than ever. His flight is cowardly but understandable.

Of course we the readers almost 900 years later must wonder about Li Qingzhao's whereabouts when Zhao Mingcheng managed his escape. Did he see her before he took leave? Or did she perhaps advise him to leave by whatever means? After all, the civil officials with no military training would certainly be killed by rebel soldiers as had happened elsewhere in those turbulent years. Unfortunately we would never know if or how Li Qingzhao was involved in this escapade.

What we do know is that some of the dates and incidents mentioned in Li Qingzhao's "Postscript" are at variance with historical records. For example, she has the wrong year and the wrong month for the appointment of Zhao Mingcheng to the position of the governorship in Nanjing. She also blames the Jin soldiers for the fire that destroyed her collection of cultural treasures contained in the ten rooms in Qingzhou whereas the fire was set by the rebel Song soldiers. When such discrepancies occur in a writer's memoir, it does not necessarily mean that the other historical records are correct. But with regards to the "Postscript" there are multiple historical records that corroborate each other which, therefore, raise questions about the accuracy of some details in this document.

There are several reasons for the factual errors in Li Qingzhao's "Postscript" according to Ma Bin (馬彬 pen name Nan Gongbo 南宮博 1971:2). First, the "Postscript" was written in 1134 CE when she was 51 *sui*, seven or eight years after moving south. While she would not be considered old by today's standards and certainly far from being senile, as could be seen in her fine writings in the years that followed, she would be thought of as aging in her days. A more likely contributing factor to her lapse in memory would be that she was living in very unsettled conditions when she wrote the "Postscript." She was constantly on the move, essentially fleeing from the Jin army and trying to catch up with Emperor Song Gao Zong. The reasons and details of her following the emperor will be made clear later in this chapter. To add to her anxiety, she had to safeguard and move the priceless art treasures and cultural relics. Moreover, she was still grievously mourning Zhao Mingcheng's death and had been seriously ill herself. It would be understandable if her ability to recall details was compromised at that time.

A second reason for the inaccurate dates and minor details is that later collectors and editors of her writings made errors in copying. This was definitely plausible. Even though the printing press was much used by that time, someone still had to set the type.

Lastly, there were perhaps reasons for her not being too clear or explicit about certain events. She had to be careful in recounting incidents that might involve the emperor. This point will be addressed in the final section of this chapter.

## Moving Inland

According to the "Postscript," after leaving Nanjing, she and Zhao Mingcheng boarded a ship and sailed into Lake Wu (蕪湖) and then entered the province of Anhui (安徽).　Their aim was to go further inland and settle somewhere along the Gan River (贛水), in the province of Jiangxi (江西省).

After leaving Nanjing, Li Qingzhao and Zhao Mingcheng sailed to Wujiang (烏江) in Anhui province north of Changjiang.　There she recalled a historical event that took place over thirteen centuries earlier and wrote the most quoted of her *shi*.

After the death of China's first emperor Qin Shihuang, his son who succeeded him was a mere puppet in the hands of the prime minister.　Rebellions broke out in many places and warlords battled each for control of the empire.　The conflict came down to two strongmen:　Liu Bang (劉邦) and Xiang Yu (項羽).　The latter descended from the royal house of the southern kingdom of Chu before the First Emperor united all of China.　Xiang Yu led a well equipped army to win his empire but was eventually defeated by Liu Bang.　He alone escaped to the banks of Wujiang.　There a boatman offered to take him across to the eastern shore with the assurance that since he operated the only boat thereabouts, Liu Bang's soldiers in pursuit would have no means of crossing the river.　Xiang Yu, however, declined with a smile saying that tens of thousands of the sons of Chu had followed him across the river to win the empire.　None of them returned.　Even if the fathers on the eastern shore would have pity on him, he had no face to see them.　He then cut his throat with his own sword (Xu 2002:239).[13]

When Li Qingzhao and Zhao Mingcheng arrived at the shore of Wujiang, she certainly thought of this historical incident.　Thus Xiang Yu is the hero in this *shi*, with the unspoken accusation against Emperor Song Gao Zong and his men who not only had crossed Wujiang but were shamelessly carving out a cowardly existence in the south.

---

[13] The tale of Xiang Yu is also immortalized in the Beijing opera entitled *Farewell My Concubine* (霸王別姬).

Wujiang

Living, be of noble character,
Dead, be a heroic ghost.
Today I commemorate Xiang Yu
Who refused to cross the river eastward.

烏江

生當作人傑，死亦為鬼雄。至今思項羽，不肯過江東。

Today admirers of Li Qingzhao often apply her own words in this *shi* to herself. She was of noble character and heroic in expressing these lofty ideals with implicit scathing criticisms of the regime while the officials were too cowardly to say anything.

In the fifth month in the Chinese calendar, when it was already summer, while they were at Chiyang (池陽), still within Anhui province, Zhao Mingcheng received the imperial edict that assigned him to the position of the magistrate of Huzhou and commanded him to see the emperor. So he let his family stay put in Chiyang and went to assume his new posting alone. He left on the thirteenth day of the sixth month in the Chinese calendar.

Li Qingzhao describes that he began his journey by "leaving the ship and going ashore." This is curious as most people would embark on a trip by boarding a ship. What this indicates is that as they had left Nanjing by ship they were still living on board the ship at this time. That was quite a long time to be living in a floating home, from the third month to the sixth month. However, it should also be mentioned that ships in Song times could be quite substantial. There was a variety of ships, some for inland waterways while others for sea voyages. "A Song Dynasty ship used in both inland and sea-going navigation combined the bottom of a lake-boat, the deck of a warship and the bow and stern of a sea-going vessel" (Zhou 1986:483). Some of these ships had a loading capacity of 800 tons. The largest Song paddle-wheel boats were 110.5 meters long and 12.6 meters wide (Zhou 1986:479-493). While there is no record of the type of ships used by Li Qingzhao and Zhao Mingcheng, it would be reasonable to think that they had the cultural treasures, previously carried in 15 carts from Qingzhou, now on board one or more ships.

In the "Postscript" Li Qingzhao further describes Zhao Mingcheng's appearance as he went ashore. He was wearing summer clothes and his head scarf exposed his forehead. He was energetic and spirited as a tiger, and his eyes shone brightly as he waved goodbye to Li Qingzhao on board the ship. But Li Qingzhao was feeling not at all well. She shouted to him asking what she should do if there was any emergency in the city, that is, in case of a Jin attack and occupation, or an army rebellion.

In some detail, Li Qingzhao recounts Zhao Mingcheng's reply. He raised his hand to her and said,

"Follow the crowd. If it could not be helped, discard first the heavy cases, next the clothes, then books and scrolls, and lastly the ancient bronze vessels. Only copies of the inscriptions on the bronze vessels of the ancient rulers you must carry with you. They survive or perish with you. Don't forget!" Then he galloped away.

There it is: from first to last, Zhao Mingcheng was concerned about the collection! But one could say with certainty that even without Zhao Mingcheng's instructions, Li Qingzhao would have set the same priority, putting the security of the collection ahead of personal safety.

That Zhao Mingcheng was re-assigned a senior position so soon after his dismissal was most likely due to some good word put in by his brothers, relatives or loyal friends who held high offices. He was well liked. On the other hand, as mentioned earlier, the Southern Song government was in need of officials.

Zhao Mingcheng was very much in a hurry to reach the court so that he would begin his term of office. He probably wanted to prove to his superiors anew after the debacle of his flight from Nanjing. Besides, although he held other honorary positions, none of those constituted a substantial source of income. The Zhao family no doubt owned land in their ancestral province Shandong but the Jin occupation of the north would have cut off any rents from land tenancy. Moreover, the position of the magistrate would ensure enhanced military protection against Jin invaders as well as bandits and rebel soldiers. Although as a former governor he might have retained a few soldiers and he would most certainly have hired mercenaries to safeguard their personal safety and the invaluable collection which they were carrying, a real magistrate would have much more resources for protection at his disposal.    Thus for financial and security reasons as well as to gain back his reputation, becoming a senior official again was of paramount importance to Zhao Mingcheng (Ma 1971:14).

The "Postscript" continues that in his haste to assume his posting, Zhao Mingcheng pushed himself tirelessly in the scorching heat.    He was ill by the time he reached the imperial court pro tem in Nanjing. Li Qingzhao received word that he was bedridden at the end of the seventh month.    She was extremely alarmed and fearful because she knew that Zhao Mingcheng was impatient, and that if he had a fever, he would have taken all kinds of medicine, appropriate or not, to get rid of it.    Thus Li Qingzhao also left the ship and tried to reach him by land transport.    She travelled non-stop and covered over 300 *li* everyday.    When she reached his bedside, she found him suffering from malaria and dysentery, and that he had indeed taken the wrong medicine.    By then he was beyond saving.    Li Qingzhao was overcome with grief and did not have the heart to ask how he would like to have things settled after his death.

On the eighteenth day of the eighth month, as he lay dying, he took his brush and composed poetry.    Then he breathed his last, without leaving instructions about future arrangements for the family. It was at this point in the "Postscript" that Li Qingzhao used the phrase for "settlements on the concubines" that made it quite clear that Zhao Mingcheng had concubines (see Chapter 4).    However, the same phrase also denotes that the departing husband had tender feelings for his wife and concubines, and was sad to be about separated from them.

Zhao Mingcheng was buried in Nanjing.    There is no record of the funeral.    Li Qingzhao wrote an essay in lamentation but only twenty words were preserved in the writings of Xie Ji, the son of Zhao Mingcheng's cousin Xie Kejia (Wang 1979:192.   See Appendix A).    The essay was titled "In Memory of Zhao Huzhou."    Thus he is immortalized with the name of the place where he would have served as a top official.

There are several *ci* and *shi* written by Li Qingzhao in memory of her husband, the following pieces clearly showing the depth of her grief.    The flautist in the first *ci* is quite obviously a reference to the

deceased Zhao Mingcheng.   According to Xu (2002:123-125) this *ci*
was most likely written in the winter, the season of plum blossoms,
after his death.

### To the tune of "The Lone Wild Goose"

It has been said that any *ci* about the plum blossoms would always
sound common from the start.  I tried my hand at it and discovered
how true the saying was.

> Rattan bed, paper screen,
> Awaking into early dawn,
> No joyous thought, only that which is unutterable.
> Incense burnt out, the jade brazier cold,
> Feelings in my breast are still as water.
> "Plum Blossoms in Three Melodies" from the flute
> Urging them to hasten budding forth
> Is so fraught with spring love!
> Gentle breeze, fine rain interminably
> Bring on a thousand tears again.
> The flautist departed, the jade bower empty,
> With whom can I share gut-wrenching pain?[14]
> A branch of blossoms in hand,
> Heaven and earth,
> To none can I send it.

### 孤雁兒

世人作梅詞，下筆便俗。予試作一篇，乃知前言不妄耳。

藤床紙帳朝眠起。説不盡，無佳思。沉香烟斷玉墟寒，伴我情懷如
水。笛聲三弄，梅心驚破，多少春情意。小風疏雨瀟瀟地，又催下
千行淚。吹簫人去玉樓空，腸斷與誰同倚？一枝折得，人間天上，
沒個人堪寄。

---

[14] In the English lexicon, the metaphor for visceral sorrow is the broken
heart.  In Chinese, especially poetry, it is the broken bowels.  I decided to
retain the metaphor used by Li Qingzhao in the original.

In the above *ci,* there is a short preface about composing with the plum blossom as the theme. While many *ci* about the plum blossoms by others are often quite common and mediocre, this piece by Li Qingzhao and the one immediately following are anything but. Here again are the hallmarks that render her compositions so appealing: sincerity, simple and effective language, and startlingly fresh imagery.

### To the tune of "Clear Peaceful Joy"

Year after year when it snowed,
Plum blossoms in my hair,
I was intoxicated with happiness.
Now rubbing the petals brings me no joy,
Only tear stains on my dress.
This year at the ends of sea and sky,
Frosted is hair on my temples.
As I look on gusty wind tonight –
It will be difficult to see plum blossoms again.

### 清平樂

年年雪裏，常插梅花醉。挼盡梅花無好意，贏得滿衣清淚。今年海角天涯，蕭蕭兩鬢生華。看取晚來風勢，故應難看梅花。

Like the previous *ci,* this piece was also composed in the winter after Zhao Mingcheng's death (Xu 2002:126-127).

At that time, Li Qingzhao was travelling all over the Jiangnan region in order to reach the Emperor Song Gao Zong who was fleeing from the Jin invaders. This could explain the rather crude furnishings in her room – the rattan bed and screen of paper – in the first *ci* as she would be staying in an inn. As the emperor went on a sea voyage, so did Li Qingzhao. This could explain her hair turning grey as she journeyed to the ends of the sea and sky.

The following is a *shi* expressing nostalgia for happier days with Zhao Mingcheng.

### By Chance

Fifteen years ago under the blossoms and the moon,

Together we admired flowers and composed poetry.
The moon and blossoms appear the same,
How could the sentiments be like the past?

偶成

十五年前花月底, 相從曾賦賞花詩。今看花月渾相似, 安得情懷似昔
時?

While it is not certain when this *shi* was written, it was most likely
in the spring of 1132 when Li Qingzhao, following the emperor, came
to stay in Lin'an, the present day Hangzhou.  Fifteen years earlier
would be 1117 when Li Qingzhao and Zhao Mingcheng were happily
retired in Qingzhou.  This would fit in with several *ci* she composed in
praise of the chrysanthemums, osmanthus, and begonia during her
time in Qingzhou (Xu 2002:220).

The above poems and others were written in mourning for Zhao
Mingcheng.  Nevertheless, during the same period, beset by illness
and grief, Li Qingzhao continued to criticize the political events taking
place, like the *shi* "On History" discussed below.  A year after Zhao
Mingcheng's death, in the late autumn of 1130, Liu Yu (劉豫), a Song
general, capitulated to the Jin invaders.  As a traitor he was rewarded
by the enemy with the throne and became the puppet Emperor of
Great Qi (大齊).  Li Qingzhao was outraged and wrote the *shi*.  In it
she refers to the two Han dynasties, the Western Han and the Eastern
Han.  The Han imperial family was by the surname of Liu, all
descended from Liu Bang, mentioned earlier in this chapter in
connection with Xiang Yu.  Between the Western and Eastern Han
dynasties, there was an interlude when an empress's nephew by the
name of Wang Mang (王莽 54 BCE – 23 CE) usurped the throne and
founded the short-lived Xin (新室 meaning new) dynasty (8 – 24 CE).

In the second part of the *shi*, Li Qingzhao alludes to another
historical figure Ji Kang (稽康 223 – 262 CE) who was an official and a
son-in-law in the royal family of the Wei kingdom during the time of
the Three Kingdoms.  A friend of his decided to join the clique of the
Sima clan that used to serve the king of Wei but was waxing strong
and about to replace the Wei kingdom with their own dynasty.  Ji
Kang severed their friendship with a letter in which he denounced the
founders of the ancient Shang and Zhou dynasties because they

usurped their overlords, the rulers of their respective previous dynasties.

## On History

Two Han dynasties were of one house,
The New house a mere tumour.
Thus Ji Kang to his last breath
Denounced Shang and Zhou dynasties.

咏史

兩漢本繼紹，新室如贅疣。所以稽中散，至死薄殷周。

What Li Qingzhao is saying is that Northern and Southern Song dynasties are the legitimate rulers. The puppet emperor of Great Qi was an ugly tumour like Wang Mang and a usurper like the founders of the Shang and Zhou dynasties.

This *shi* stirred up some interesting criticism of Li Qingzhao. The poem itself was recorded in the writings of the famous Southern Song neo-Confucian philosopher Zhu Xi whose low opinion of women comes through in his commentary. First of all, he categorically states that in the Song dynasty there were only two notable women of letters, Li Qingzhao and Madam Wei. This was certainly not true. At a time when the writings of women were typically left out in most anthologies and official records, there remain to this day many *shi, ci* and other writings by women of the Song period that were fondly read and kept by literary critics generation after generation. Most of them were of very high calibre.

Secondly, Zhu Xi castigates Li Qingzhao for lumping Wang Mang with the founders of the Shang and Zhou dynasties. Wang Mang in the eyes of virtually all Chinese historians up to his day was always a villain whereas the founders of the Shang and Zhou dynasties were held in high esteem. Zhu Xi concludes that a discussion of such issues as those about usurpers and dynasty founders would be beyond the capability of women. This criticism from Zhu Xi was unsurprising as he espoused and promoted the neo-Confucian ideology of the suppression of women that includes sayings such as: "Women without ability are virtuous," and "It is a small matter if women starve to death, but a grave matter if they lose their chastity." In the view of Zhu Xi and other neo-Confucian ideologues, women should be virtuous, particularly in chastity, which meant virginity before marriage, obedience and fidelity to husbands, and no re-marriage in widowhood. But women should not be capable, and most emphatically were not to interfere in public affairs. This ideological burden was placed on Chinese women for centuries to come although in real life women's conduct did not always conform to this ideology.

As Zhuge (2004:136) points out, the meaning and the underlying political outrage of Li Qingzhao's verse entirely escaped Zhu Xi; instead this neo-Confucianist was so muddle-headed that he could only pass a sexist judgement on Li Qingzhao, missing her political acumen and patriotic feelings. Through the centuries after Zhu Xi many writers followed his lead and continued to cast aspersions on Li Qingzhao for overstepping her limits in writing this *shi*. But every now and then, there would also be scholars who would praise her for superior views and works (see Xu 2002:219).

## Li Qingzhao and the Collection

With Zhao Mingcheng's death, Li Qingzhao became the sole custodian of the still considerable collection of cultural relics and art treasures. The collection would bring her much added grief in the next few years.

In less than a month after Zhao Mingcheng's death, in volume 27 of Li Xinchuan's *Chronological Record* is recorded a very curious incident. In the intercalary eighth month,[15] a former imperial doctor and now an instructor by the name of Wang Jixian (王繼先) offered to buy her ancient vessels with 300 ounces of gold. The preposterous offer prompted Xie Kejia, a high official in the Ministry of Defence, to

---

[15] As has been pointed out in Chapter 1, the Chinese calendar follows both the solar and the lunar cycles. It has 30 days for a long month and 29 days in a short month. Once every few years, an additional month, the intercalary month, is added to make up the difference between a year of twelve lunar months and a solar year (Bai 2002:58). The intercalary month in 1129 was added after the eighth month. Thus there was a "second" eighth month in the year of Zhao Mingcheng's death.

write a memorial to Emperor Song Gao Zong thus:  If word of the offer to purchase was spread afar, it might injure the glorious virtue (of the emperor); please put a stop to it.  This was approved by the emperor and Wang Jixian was investigated about this (Li 1975b:37).

Xie Kejia was a cousin of Zhao Mingcheng; their mothers were sisters.  It was apparent that he did not hesitate to safeguard the collection of precious objects amassed by Zhao Mingcheng and Li Qingzhao, thus rendering some service to Li Qingzhao.

It was wise and necessary for Li Qingzhao not to mention this incident in her "Postscript" as it involved the new emperor.  Xie Kejia most certainly interpreted Wang Jixian's offer to purchase the collection as not having originated from him.  As a doctor and an instructor, Wang Jixian could not have been the real buyer.  It was most unlikely that he would have 300 ounces of gold ready at hand to purchase the priceless art treasures.  As the proposed purchase was most egregious coming so soon after Zhao Mingcheng's death, it could have come only from someone far more powerful and with ready cash at his disposal, Emperor Song Gao Zong.  The new emperor, like his father Emperor Song Hui Zong, was already known as an art collector.  Most biographers of Li Qingzhao would agree with the interpretation that the offer to buy the art treasures would most likely have come from him (Ma 1971:18; Yu 1986:388-391).  This was the first serious incident concerning the collection after Zhao Mingcheng's death.

In the "Postscript" Li Qingzhao only wrote that after Zhao Mingcheng's funeral she did not know where to go.  She was seriously ill.  While she was incapacitated, the political situation worsened. The young emperor and his court were fleeing from the Jin army again. The emperor despatched the imperial womenfolk inland under the guardianship of Empress Dowager Meng (孟皇太后), the former consort of Emperor Song Zhe Zong.  Li Qingzhao also heard rumour that no ship could sail upstream in the Changjiang.  But she still had over 20,000 books, 2,000 inscriptions from stones and bronze vessels, utensils and beddings that could accommodate a hundred guests, and many other treasures.  At that time, Zhao Mingcheng's brother-in-law Li Zhuo was a high official in the Ministry of Defence.  He was part of the imperial guard protecting the Empress Dowager and the women of the imperial family in the city of Hongzhou (洪州, present day Nanchang 南昌 in Jiangxi province).  Li Qingzhao decided to send the bulk of her collection and possessions there with two trusted retainers. But by the winter, in the twelfth month of the Chinese calendar, the Jin soldiers occupied Hongzhou. All the things sent there were lost, including the books that had been carried in ships that were joined together in crossing the Huai River and the Changjiang. All that remained were the fairly light objects such as copies of poems by Li Bai and Du Fu, essays by Han Yu (韓愈) and Liu Zongyuan (柳宗元), some classics, rubbings of inscriptions on stones from Han and Tang dynasties, and inscriptions on bronzes vessels from Xia, Shang and Zhou dynasties, together with some hand-copied books from the Southern Tang dynasty. These were in her possession because she kept them in her bedroom to console herself in her illness and convalescence.

As the upstream of the Changjiang was now inaccessible, the "Postscript" continues, and the movement of the Jin army could not be predicted, Li Qingzhao thought of joining her brother Li Hang who was an official in the imperial court and would be in the province of Zhejiang.[16]  The route of Li Qingzhao's travels after Zhao Mingcheng's death described in the "Postscript" is very circuitous. She seemed to have gone from Nanjing south to Taizhou (台州 in southern Zhejiang province) first, then backtracked north to Shengxian (嵊縣), and turned southward again to Huangyan (黄岩) where she embarked on the maritime journey. The entire trip described in the "Postscript" would entail over two thousand *li*. The brevity of the essay makes the route she took very puzzling. There could have been errors in the names of places made by copy editors and printers in the centuries after the *Jin Shi Lu* and the "Postscript" were first published.

Huang (1984: 331-334) reconstructs the most probable route taken by Li Qingzhao that would be in lock-step with Emperor Song Gao Zong's journey as follows. In 1129, Zhao Mingcheng died on the 18th day of the eighth month of the Chinese calendar and was most likely buried in the following month, the intercalary "second" eighth month that year. By that time the threat of the Jin invasion had reached a critical stage. Emperor Song Gao Zong left Nanjing on the 26th day of the intercalary month and fled in the southeast direction

---

[16] Li Hang was in charge of compiling all the imperial edicts into book volumes (Wen & Qian 1987: 239).

with the Jin army hot on his heels.  He travelled through the present day Suzhou, Hangzhou, Shaoxing (紹興, called Yuezhou 越州 at that time) in a matter of a few months and reached the present day Ningbo (寧波) on the coast in the eleventh month of the Chinese calendar. From Ningbo the emperor took to the high seas on the 15th day of the twelfth month, eventually reaching Wenzhou (溫州).

As is mentioned in the "Postscript," Li Qingzhao intended to follow the Empress Dowager Meng to the present day Nanchang in her flight from the Jin invaders.  But she changed her plan and decided to follow the trail of the imperial entourage.  There was an imperative reason for her to reach the emperor.  In the "Postscript" she records that during Zhao Mingcheng's illness a scholar by the name of Zhang Feiqing (張飛卿) brought a jade teapot to see him.  As Zhao Mingcheng had achieved the solid reputation of an expert in assessing and authenticating art treasures and antiques, Zhang Feiqing's visit was for the purpose of seeking Zhao Mingcheng's expert opinion on the value of the teapot.  Li Qingzhao states that Zhang left with the article, which was made of stone, not jade.  She did not know who spread the rumour but it soon came to be known that they, Zhao Mingcheng and Li Qingzhao, intended to give the jade teapot to the enemy, the Jin invaders, in a conspiracy against the Song. This was a treasonable crime and extremely serious.  Moreover, there was rumour that a secret memorial had been sent to the emperor about the alleged treachery of Zhao Mingcheng and his wife.  Li Qingzhao was, of course, very alarmed.  She dared not speak out against the calumnious accusation but neither did she dare to drop the matter.  So she decided to present all the antique bronze vessels and other treasures to the imperial court.  Aside from the loss of antiques and art treasures through war, plunder and theft, this was the second grievous incident involving the collection.

Thus Li Qingzhao also left Nanjing and, according to Huang (1984), proceeded southward in order to catch up with the imperial court.  She went to Hangzhou and Shaoxing.  By then she found out that the emperor had gone on to Siming (四明), the present day Ningbo.  When she reached Ningbo in early 1130 the emperor had already sailed off to the southern coastal city of Wenzhou.  As the imperial party very likely had commandeered most if not all of the seaworthy ships in Ningbo, Li Qingzhao had to take the land route through Fenghua (奉化) where she lost some scrolls of painting and calligraphy (Xu 2009:479); Shengxian where she abandoned most of the clothes, linen and blankets; and Taizhou to reach Huangyan on the coast. There she was able to hire a ship to follow the route taken by the emperor's entourage that had at one time stayed in nearby Zhang'an (章安), but had by then sailed to Wenzhou.

In the third month of the Chinese calendar in 1130, Li Qingzhao, again following the imperial party, left Wenzhou and sailed northward to Ningbo. She returned to Shaoxing in the following month. Later in the same year, the imperial court released all officials, permitting them to flee from the Jin invaders on their own, each taking whatever expedient routes available. The emperor himself went to Quzhou (衢州) and so did Li Qingzhou. Then in the spring of 1131 CE she followed the emperor back to Shaoxing. It was at this time that Emperor Song Gao Zong changed his reign title from Jianyan to Shaoxing, and the city of Yuezhou also changed its name to that of the emperor's new reign title (Huang 1984:334; Xu 2009:479-482).

In 1130 while Li Qingzhao was sailing along the coast of Zhejiang province and trying to catch up with Emperor Song Gao Zong, the open sea must have impressed her immensely. The following *ci* was likely written at that time as it opens with a description of vast seascape.

To the tune of "The Fisherman's Pride"

Sky joining the sea in the mist of dawn,
The Milky Way is about to leap over
The thousand ships with full sails
Dancing in the wind.
The spirit in a dream seems to ascend to the heavenly court;
Heaven caringly enquires where I would go.
I respond that the journey is long
And the sun about to set;
I have learned to compose *shi*
What good is it to me when no one uses my astounding lines?
The roc wings through ninety thousand *li*,
O Wind, do not stop,
Blow this tiny boat to the Three Heavenly Mountains.

漁家傲

天接雲濤連曉霧，星河欲渡千帆舞。彷彿夢魂歸帝所，聞天語，殷勤聞我歸河處. 我報路長嗟日暮，學詩漫有驚人句。九萬里風鵬正舉。風休住，蓬舟吹取三山去。

This *ci* is outstanding in several ways. Li Qingzhao actually uses the first person singular pronoun "I" twice in two lines as translated above.

In this *ci*, Li Qingzhao incorporates ideas from both the daoist religion and the daoist philosophy. [17]    The *ci* is replete with descriptions of nature which is very important in daoist philosophy. It opens with an expansive vista of the sea and many ships bobbing on it.    She dreams that she ascends to heaven.    In the dialogue described in the *ci*, she uses only the word *tian* (天), meaning the sky or heaven, and not the term *tiandi* (天帝), meaning heavenly emperor. But as she has a conversation with *tian*, most interpreters take it to mean the heavenly emperor, a deity in the daoist religion.    However, it should be pointed out that the concept of sky or heaven in Chinese culture or daoist religious mythology does not have the same meaning or significance of Heaven in the Judaeo-Christian tradition; similarly the heavenly emperor in daoist religion is very different from the Hebrew or Christian God (see Djao 2003:105).    The Three Heavenly Mountains at the end of the *ci* refer to three imaginary islands in the eastern ocean, again very important places in the mythology of daoist religion.    Given the popularity of the daoist religion during the Song period, images of the daoist religion can be found in a few of Li Qingzhao's writings.

Quite possibly the reference to the heavenly court and her dialogue with heaven have only superficial religious meaning.    As Chen (2001:148) explains, Li Qingzhao was eager to reach the earth-bound Emperor Song Gao Zong and his undeniably very mobile court.

The roc, the giant bird, is taken from the book *Zhuang Zi* in which the philosopher Zhuang Zi of the Warring States period describes a mythical giant bird like the roc whose back is as long as

---

[17] See Note 4 in Chapter 2, and also my discussion of Chinese philosophy (Djao 2003: 205-211).

the Tai Mountain range and wings as wide as the clouds.  He, like Lao Zi before him, promotes the notion of non-action as this is nature's way and an aspect of *dao*.  People are part of nature, the vast universe, just like the roc or the tiny butterfly.  They come from the universe when they are born.  They will return to it when they die as their bodies decompose into elements of the universe.  Zhuang Zi's ideas are not religious although some of them have been incorporated into the daoist religion.

As pointed out in Chapter 2, Li Qingzhao was very fond of nature and always remained close to it.  The experience of travelling by sea exposed her to another experience of nature and its vastness.  While she is a tiny speck on the surface of the sea, her spirit like the gigantic roc soars over the expansive waters into the sky and engages heaven in a conversation about writing poetry.  In this imaginary escapade she emulates the attitude often displayed by scholars.  When disorder prevails over the country and the rulers are neglectful of their duty to restore order, turning a deaf ear to the advice of upstanding officials as like the times in which she lives, the scholars would pine to withdraw from the world and return to a simple rustic life to be close to nature.  As she tries to reach the emperor and with her grief for Zhao Mingcheng's death still raw, it is understandable that she longs to be up, up away like the roc.

This *ci* also raises the question of the rather artificial classification of *ci*.  Some critics would divide *ci* into two styles:  the *haofang* (豪放) and the *wanyue* (婉約).  *Haofang* means "forthright" and "unrestrained."  *Ci* in this style are said to be bold and uninhibited, the expression of the undaunted heroic spirit.  Su Shi of the Northern Song period and Xin Qiji of the Southern Song have always been held up as the quintessential models of this style of *ci*.  Many *ci* in this style are means by which the poets unburden their feelings about their country and the land.  *Wanyue*, on the other hand, means "gentle" and "gracious."  *Ci* belonging to this style are elegant and graceful.  They are simple and brief.

If we follow Li Qingzhao's theory of *ci*, a cardinal quality of *ci* is genuine personal emotions.  Women since the Tang times and particularly during the Song period, insofar as they were removed from affairs outside the home, would express their feelings in personal relationships in *ci*.  Their *ci* would then be categorised as *wanyue*.  Li Qingzhao certainly wrote many *wanyue ci*, and is often labelled as the prototype of this style. But the above *ci* and others are not solely about personal feelings; instead they describe nature and deal with affairs of the state. In the final analysis, the classification of *ci* into these two styles does not add to the value of the *ci* or the reader's enjoyment of them, except that the *haofang* style appears to be entirely populated by men and all women *ci* composers seem to fall into the *wanyue* style. Li Qingzhao certainly crosses over these artificial boundaries.

As has been described above, Li Qingzhao after Zhao Mingcheng's death was anxious to prove her loyalty to the emperor. In her attempt to reach the emperor she dared not keep the antique bronze vessels in her own possession. She stored the antiques and some handwritten books in Shengxian. Later, Li Qingzhao found out that after the government army had put down the rebel soldiers, a certain General Li seized all her art treasures stored there.

Only about half of the original collection remained by then. She had in her possession about seven cases of books, paintings and ink stones. Wanting to make sure that these remaining treasures would be within her reach all the time, she kept them under her bed and she alone could open or close the cases. In 1131 when she was back in Shaoxing, Li Qingzhao was boarding at the house of a resident surnamed Zhong in Guiji (會稽) which was close to Shaoxing. One night a burglar dug a hole in the wall and made off with five of the seven cases. She was inconsolable and posted a reward for the recovery of the articles. Two days later, a neighbour by the name of Zhong Fuhao (鍾復皓) came with eighteen scrolls of calligraphy and painting and asked for the reward. She knew then that the thief had not gone far. But she never recovered the rest of the stolen art despite her tireless efforts. But at the time she wrote the "Postscript" in 1134 CE she knew that all the purloined articles were bought at a very low price by a transportation agent by the name of Wu Yue (吳說).

Thus in a few years she had lost about eight-tenths of the collection. Some were lost in the ravages of war, others abandoned, looted or stolen. Although it was not explicitly stated in the "Postscript," part of the antiques and art treasures no doubt was presented to the imperial court as she recorded her travels in Zhejiang province in the footsteps of the emperor for that purpose. The calumnious rumour that she and her husband intended to give art treasures to the Jin invaders likely was started after the physician and instructor Wang Jixian was refused the preposterous offer to buy her collection. It could have been instigated by Wang or his powerful backers, first among whom would be the emperor, as a means to pressure Li Qingzhao to relinquish her cultural treasures (Yu 1995:389; Wang 1979:244-245).

The evidence that some art works got into the imperial collection was provided by Zhao Mingcheng's cousin Xie Kejia. A few years later, in 1133, in the ninth month of the Chinese calendar, Xie Kejia came across in the Buddhist temple Fa Hui Si (法慧寺) in Hangzhou a scroll of calligraphy entitled "Jin Xie Yu Ci Shi Juan" (進謝御賜詩卷) by Cai Xiang (蔡襄). In the colophon that Xie Kejia inscribed on the calligraphy scroll he recalls with much sorrow that while the scroll was in Zhao Mingcheng's possession, his cousin showed it to him several times. But so soon after Zhao Mingcheng's death it had fallen into other hands. Citing sources in *Chronological Record* by Li Xinchuan, Yu (1986:390-391; 1995:120) shows that Fa Hui Si was designated as a government archive earlier in 1133, so the calligraphy scroll was already part of the imperial collection.[18] Cai Xiang's calligraphy scroll remained part of the imperial collection till the last dynasty, the Qing.

Some antiques and art works so cherished by Li Qingzhao ironically might have been saved for the posterity by her presenting them to Emperor Song Gao Zong. Emperor Song Hui Zong was an avid collector and art connoisseur and greatly enriched the Northern Song palace collection of antiques and art treasures he inherited from his predecessors. Most of the items in that collection were taken by the Jin invaders. But Emperor Song Gao Zhong, the first emperor of the Southern Song, was also an art and antique collector. The imperial collection of the later Yuan, Ming and Qing dynasties originated in that of the Southern Song dynasty (National Palace Museum 2000). The items collected by Zhao Mingcheng and Li Qingzhao that eventually ended up in Emperor Song Gao Zong's possession would be part of the Qing collection, and possibly housed today in the Palace Museum in Beijing or in the National Palace Museum in Taibei.

---

[18] According to Wang (1979:255) this scroll was among the art treasures that were stolen from Li Qingzhao while she was staying in the house rented from the Zhong family in Shaoxing.

Whatever remained in Li Qingzhao's possession, according to the "Postscript," consisted of one or two incomplete volumes of books and about three scrolls of calligraphy not of top quality. Yet she cherished and protected them as if they were, in her own words, "her head and her eyes." She laughed at herself for being so foolish!

As we shall see in Chapter 7, Li Qingzhao understated in the "Postscript" the quantity and value of books, paintings and calligraphy left in her care. But it was expedient that she should describe as incomplete and inferior what she still had in her possession at the time of writing the "Postscript." Given the watchful and greedy eyes trained on her treasures, she could not say more; she had had enough experiences of plunder and theft by people from high places and low.

The last part of the "Postscript" contains her final view of the collection. She praises Zhao Mingcheng's manuscript *Jin Shi Lu* based on the collection and the meticulous care he took in commenting on many of the pieces in their collection. Most of the contemporary biographers of Li Qingzhao agree that the "Postscript" was written in 1134 CE, which would be five years after Zhao Mingcheng's death. In the "Postscript" she mentions that his handwritten manuscript was still fresh yet the tree at his grave had already grown to maturity requiring both arms to embrace it. Then she goes on to describe what she really thought of the collection by citing two rather unsavoury characters in history. This is very intriguing given the blood and sweat not to mention money that had gone into collecting the articles piece by piece, and the lengths to which she had risked her life in protecting the collection. She laments the loss of the major portion of the collection, but she also puts the collection and the hard work that had gone into it as well as the manuscript into historical perspective. She cites the cases of Xiao Yi (蕭繹) and Yang Guang (楊廣). The former was Emperor Yuan of the short-lived southern Liang dynasty (502 – 557 CE) during the period of disunity known in history as the Southern and Northern Dynasties. He collected books and paintings with a passion. When his capital Jiangling (江陵 another name for Jingzhou in Hubei province 湖北省荊州) fell to the invading Northern Zhou army, he did not regret the loss of his kingdom but he burnt over 140,000 volumes of books and scrolls of paintings as he did not want his collection to go to other hands.

Yang Guang was the second emperor of also a short-lived Sui dynasty, which is nonetheless referred to as the second empire because Yang Guang's father united China after the Southern and Northern Dynasties.   Yang Guang also had a passion for his collection of books and art.   When he travelled, he would have much of the collection with him.   He was assassinated by his general Yuwen Huaji (宇文化及) at Jiangdu (江都).   Yuwen tried to ship his collection back to the capital but the ship was caught in a storm and capsized. Thus the collection of tens of thousands of books and art scrolls was lost.   It was as if Yang Guang did not mind losing his life but wanted to make sure that in death he repossessed his books and paintings.

In the "Postscript" Li Qingzhao wonders if things – be they books, or art, or antiques, or pepper, or money, or anything – to which people have attached their life's interest could never be let go, in life or in death; if it is the will of heaven that she is not blessed to enjoy these rare and precious yet enticing things; or if perhaps the dead are still fond of those things and would begrudge their being left behind for the living.

Li Qingzhao ends the "Postscript" with a lamentation that for 34 years, since the age of 18 when she was married to Zhao Mingcheng, she has gone through so much sorrow and tribulation, collecting things and then losing them!   Finally she writes philosophically:

> As there is "having," then there will surely be "not having."   As there is getting together, there is also dispersal.   This is to be expected.   Someone loses something, someone gains it.   What else can you say? Thus here is a detailed record of the beginning and the end of the collection.   It also serves caution to collectors and connoisseurs of art and antiques in posterity.

The final words of "Postscript" have been interpreted as sour grapes, as a way of consoling herself after losing most of the collection (see Zhuge 2004).   But a careful reading shows an attitude that is steeped in Lao Zi's dialectics.   The actual words for "having" and "not having" in the essay are *you* (有) and *wu* (無).   The literal meaning of *you* is "having" as in possessing things.   On the other hand, *wu* means "nothing."   This pair of contradictory words appears in the first chapter of the book *Lao Zi* popularly known in the West as the *Dao De Jing*: ". . . *Wu* is the beginning of heaven and earth; *you* is the mother of everything. . . . These two have the same origin but have different names" (*Lao Zi*).

This is not the place to delve into the philosophy of *dao* in *Lao Zi*. For our purposes here, it suffices to say that the rather short treatise *Lao Zi* in about 5000 words and 81 chapters presents many pairs of words that are contradictory: *you* having things vs. *wu* nothing, high vs. low, hard vs. soft, strong vs. weak, elaborate and attractive vs. simple, active vs. quiet, etc. In *Lao Zi*, as Lau (1967: xix; xxix) points out, the preference is always for the "less," the "lower" or the negative part of each pair. For example, in Chapter 78, it says:

> Nothing under heaven is softer or weaker than water. Yet nothing is like water in overcoming the hard and the strong, because nothing can replace water. Weakness can overcome power. Softness can conquer strength. People all understand this (principle), yet none can act accordingly. (Translation by author)

This line of thinking is indeed difficult to put into practice. But it appears that Li Qingzhao at the time of writing the "Postscript" was adopting this attitude of detachment from the much loved collection and becoming at ease with its loss and all it entailed, that is, the loss also of prestige and security associated with the high monetary value placed on each of the items. The collection had given her and Zhao Mingcheng immense joy and pride, but it had also brought on grief and worry. It was time to let go. But obviously she was not totally detached from the collection as she still possessed several pieces that she would admire fondly from time to time. That in itself was also a contradiction which both she and Lao Zi would no doubt recognize and consider as an aspect of practising *dao*.

Li Qingzhao shows that she recognized and accepted the elusiveness of things and the distasteful and indeed harmful side of the priceless collection in her choice of the two examples of collectors' passion and single-mindedness. Both Xiao Yi and Yang Guang were selfish rulers, uncaring of the welfare of people but always indulging in their own pursuit of pleasure. In both cases their selfish pursuit included the collection of art and books. They would be the very antithesis of the benevolent and caring ruler held up as the ideal in the Confucian tradition. As Owen (1986) points out, Li

Qingzhao most certainly was also referring to another imperial art collector, Emperor Song Hui Zong. However, I would argue that one could even go further: she was also implicitly referring to the emperor then sitting on the throne, Emperor Song Gao Zong, who coveted her collection.

Whatever ruler she had in mind when she composed the "Postscript" the essay was written first and foremost for the manuscript of *Jin Shi Lu* that was being prepared for publication, and that was the masterpiece by her husband and herself. Owen (1986) is of the opinion that Li Qingzhao in the end resented Zhao Mingcheng for his attachment to the collection. There was, therefore, a rift between her and Zhao Mingcheng. Zhao Mingcheng was totally engrossed in the collection, according to Owen, while she remained devoted to the scholarship of editing and compiling the inscriptions. This would be too simplistic an interpretation of Li Qingzhao's view towards the collection or Zhao Mingcheng. Nor was there evidence of Zhao Mingcheng's deviation from his original and consistent goal of acquiring inscriptions and other art works and cultural relics for the purpose of scholarship as well as for personal enjoyment.

If the "Postscript" is read through the lens of *Lao Zi* there is another interpretation of Li Qingzhao's choice of the examples of Xiao Yi and Yang Guang. In the very beginning of the "Postscript," after stating the purpose of the book *Jin Shi Lu*, in an unusual and unexpected turn of thought she refers to Zhao Mingcheng's and her own passion for collecting inscriptions and art works as well as for the collection itself as an addiction. She cites four historical figures as examples. Two prime ministers in the Tang dynasty both came to a violent death. One hoarded books, calligraphy and paintings, while the other tons of pepper among other things. A third historical figure was obsessed with money and the fourth with the book *Zuo Zhuan*. Li Qingzhao points out that they were addicts. The only difference was the object of their compulsive need, be it art, books, pepper, money or a particular book.

Although she states at the beginning of the "Postscript" that the 30 volumes of *Jin Shi Lu* were written by Zhao Mingcheng, and he remains to this day as the official author, in the rest of the essay it is quite clear that she was very much Zhao Mingcheng's collaborator and a co-author. More significantly, it was mostly after his death that the collection was lost through ravages of war, plunder, theft, or offering to the emperor.  It was she who felt the anguish as bit by bit the collection was diminished.  She thus admits that she no less than her husband was addicted to the collection.  As Zhao Mingcheng was already deceased by the time she wrote the "Postscript" she alone can "recover" from such profound fascination and obsession with the collection by acknowledging that "having things" and "having nothing," and "gathering" and "dispersal" are routine happenings.  Her final words are a warning to all collectors of antiques and art works.

Li Qingzhao wrote the "Postscript" in 1134.  But before that year another event took place in her life which would have spurred her even more to adopt Lao Zi's attitude towards having things.  This will be discussed in the next chapter.

# 6 Remarriage and Divorce

Several things happened in the life of Li Qingzhao in 1132. Her writings that can be traced to this year reflect a range of feelings and moods about various events and personal experiences. The *shi* "By Chance" mentioned in the last chapter was most likely written in this year. In it she recalls her life with Zhao Mingcheng in Qingzhou fifteen years earlier when they were able to enjoy poetry and blossoms in the moonlight.

While she still missed the company of Zhao Mingcheng, she was also becoming more aware of what was going on around her, and her sharp wit would give rise to some incisive words. In the third month of the Chinese calendar, the top graduate in the *jinshi* examination that year was by the name of Zhang Jiucheng (張九成) who wrote some obsequious lines in honour of Emperor Song Gao Zong. Using a few of Zhang's own words as well as his name in a pun, Li Qingzhao composed a couplet to mock his fawning disposition.[1]

It was also in or around 1132, after her arrival in Hangzhou, that she wrote another exquisite *ci* that expresses her nostalgia for her northern homeland (Xu 2009:485).

### To the tune of "Bodhisattvas' Headdress"

A gentle breeze,
Pale daybreak,
It's not quite spring.
Changing to a lined garment
I'm in a happy mood.
Awaking I feel a slight chill;
Plum blossom has withered on my temple.
Where is homeland?
Unless inebriated I forget it not.
Incense lighted before bedtime has burnt out.
Its fragrance has dissipated but not the taste of wine.

---

[1] Li Qingzhao's couplet mocking Zhang is included in Appendix A.

菩薩蠻

風柔日薄春猶早，夾衫乍著心情好。睡起覺微寒，梅花鬢上殘。故
鄉何處是？忘了除非醉。沉水臥時燒，香消酒未消。

In this *ci*, spring has not quite arrived yet.  In China warm
clothing for the winter usually means jackets padded with silk or
cotton fibres.  The poet has already made her seasonal change in attire,
from the heavy padded winter clothing to garments that are simply
lined, but not padded, suitable for the spring weather.  She is in a
happy frame of mind to welcome the change of season.  But she
cannot forget her hometown and all it means except when she is
intoxicated.  When she wakes up from the drunken slumber the plum
blossom has withered and the incense has burnt itself out.  The
unspoken sentiment is that the political climate has not changed and is
not likely to change, and she can only pine for her homeland but not
return to it.  While the *ci* begins with the anticipation of happiness, it
ends with the lasting sadness of nostalgia and displacement.


## Mystery of Second Marriage

One event that took place in Li Qingzhao's life in 1132 still
intrigues us today.

There are many gaps in our knowledge of Li Qingzhao's life, such
as who her mother was, where she was born, when most of her *ci*
were written, and so forth.  There is debate over each of these issues.
However, the greatest controversy has been about whether or not Li
Qingzhao remarried.[2]

---

[2] A 20th century example of the heated debate over Li Qingzhao's second
marriage broke out in the 1960s over the serialized historical novel of Li
Qingzhao's life written by Ma Bin (1971:i).  Readers' reaction to Ma's
account of her life was so vociferous that he himself collected over 270
articles that appeared in the newspapers in Taiwan and Hong Kong.  One
leftist newspaper in Hong Kong even published on the front page a full-
page criticism of his work.  The bone of contention was Ma's plot regarding
the later years of Li Qingzhao's life.  Specifically it was Ma's portrayal of her
as remaining faithful to the memory of Zhao Mingcheng in her widowhood.

Historical records reveal little about her second marriage. There is more information about her divorce. She herself wrote a letter to a high official by the name of Qi Chongli (綦崇禮), which provides the most details about her re-marriage and divorce. But it still leaves many important questions unanswered, such as: Who was the man she married? Where did she meet him? And, the most intriguing question: Why did she get married again?

The following facts are drawn or deduced from Li Qingzhao's letter and other historical records. She was married for the second time sometime in the fourth or the fifth month of the Chinese calendar in 1132. She was divorced about one hundred days later, in the ninth or the tenth month of the Chinese calendar in the same year, after bringing a criminal charge of corruption against her husband by the name of Zhang Ruzhou (張汝舟).

As has been mentioned in the last chapter, after Zhao Mingcheng's death in 1129, Li Qingzhao spent the next two years trying to catch up with Emperor Song Gao Zong in order to offer her antiques and art treasures to the court, and to prove her loyalty to the Song regime and innocence of any treasonous acts. The emperor on the other hand was fleeing from the Jin invaders who had swept through many cities south of Changjiang. By 1131 both the emperor and Li Qingzhao were in Yuezhou where the emperor changed his reign title to Shaoxing; Yuezhou changed its name, too, to that of the reign title. It was there while staying in the Zhong residence that she had many art treasures stolen from her. Shortly after the Chinese New Year in 1132, Emperor Song Gao Zong went to Hangzhou and Li Qingzhao, as noted in her "Postscript," followed. It would appear that both the imperial court and Li Qingzhao took a respite from fleeing and intended to stay there for good. Although Emperor Song Gao Zong would leave Hangzhou two years later in the wake of another invasion, he would return there and Hangzhou would be the capital of the Southern Song court until the Mongols under Kublai

---

In other words, in Ma's historical novel, Li Qingzhao did not marry a second time. Even before the serialized novel was finished, Ma felt that he had made a mistake about this event in Li Qingzhao's life. He never published the novel as a stand alone book. Ten years later, in 1971, Ma wrote a scholarly book on the life of Li Qingzhao after moving south. His later work about Li Qingzhao is cited extensively in this book.

Khan conquered all of China about 140 years later.

Li Qingzhao seemed to have followed the movement of the emperor quite closely during those years. Aside from the reason of presenting items of her collection to the court, she might have become part of her brother Li Hang's household by the time she reached Shaoxing and Hangzhou. Li Hang was in charge of compiling the imperial edicts. While his was not a very high position, he would be part of the imperial entourage.

It is not known where or for how long Li Qingzhao had known Zhang Ruzhou before she married him in the summer of 1132. Most biographers of Li Qingzhao have tried to fathom her reasons for her remarriage, especially in view of the generally accepted depiction of her character that she was self-confident, independent and a prudent decision-maker. Perhaps it was precisely in accordance with her independent spirit that a few years after Zhao Mingcheng's death that alone and lonely she would wish for the love and companionship of a husband and the warmth of a loving family again (Zhuge 2004: 163-164).

There was perhaps a more pragmatic consideration. Insofar as she had lost sizeable portions of the collection through false accusation, theft and plunder, and she had seen how people from the emperor to the village neighbour had coveted her treasures, she might have felt the need of a protector, not so much to guard her personal safety as to ensure the security of the collection.

Another speculation is that her brother Li Hang might have instigated and encouraged the match. It was not unknown before or after Li Qingzhao's time that a brother or former parents-in-law would marry off a widow in order to lessen the financial burden on themselves.

## Divorce

Whatever the reasons, her second marriage was not a happy one and did not last long. In the *Chronological Record* (Li 1975b: 2) is an account of events related to her divorce. In the ninth month of the second year of reign title Shaoxing (1132), Zhang Ruzhou who was an auditor of army expenditures was accused by his wife nee Li for getting his official position fraudulently. Li Xinchuan, the author of *Chronological*

*Record,* explicitly states that this Madam Li was the daughter of (Li) Gefei, and that she composed songs and gave herself the *hao* of Yi'an Jushi.

Zhang Ruzhou's crime that Li Qingzhao reported to the authorities was cheating and falsifying records in order to be appointed an official. In the Song dynasty, with its emphasis on promoting civil servants, a scholar who had failed the provincial examination a certain number of times, on condition that he had also reached a certain age, could still be able to attain an official appointment (Chen 2001:169). Apparently Zhang Ruzhou reported untruthfully the number of times he had sat for the provincial examination and, therefore, gained his official position unlawfully. As it was war time, the Southern Song court regarded military expenses and provision of military equipment and materials to be of utmost importance. Zhang's crime would have been punishable by death.

According to the Li Xinchuan's *Chronological Record,* however, Zhang Ruzhou was stripped of his official title and exiled to Liuzhou (柳州) by imperial edict. This meant that he had been convicted of a less serious offence, "a private crime" (Li 1975c:21), rather than a crime against national security. Thus he escaped capital punishment.

The description in the *Chronological Record* is about Li Qingzhao's charge against Zhang Ruzhou and his conviction, not about her marriage or divorce. A more detailed account of these important personal events was given by herself in a letter to Lord Qi Chongli to thank him for his assistance in the criminal proceedings against Zhang Ruzhou.

After Li Qingzhao brought charges of falsifying records and corruption against her husband Zhang Ruzhou, she herself was put in jail. This happened because according to the Song criminal code, when a husband committed a serious crime, his wife and children would also be incarcerated (Ma 1971:38). In her letter Li Qingzhao mentions that she was also imprisoned but only for nine days. It appears that Lord Qi Chongli rendered her timely assistance so that her stay in prison was short. Her early release might have helped to commute the husband's crime to a lesser offence. If Zhang Ruzhou was convicted of a capital crime, it could mean that Li Qingzhao would have to serve the full two-year term.

This Lord Qi Chongli's mother was the sister of Zhao Mingcheng's father Zhao Tingzhi; thus Qi Chongli and Zhao

Mingcheng were cousins. Qi was also connected by marriage to Zhao Mingcheng's cousin Xie Kejia. Xie Kejia's son Xie Ji had a son who was married to Lord Qi Chongli's daughter. In other words, Lord Qi Chongli was the father-in-law of Xie Ji's son and Xie Kejia's grandson. As has been mentioned earlier, the mothers of Zhao Mingcheng and Xie Kejia were sisters, surnamed Guo. Xie Kejia had helped Li Qingzhao shortly after Zhao Mingcheng's death in rebuffing the offer by a former imperial doctor Wang Jixian to purchase her collection of antiques and art treasures for 300 ounces of gold. It would seem that when Li Qingzhao was imprisoned, the relative of the Zhao family, Xie Kejia, again stepped in and asked his grandson's father-in-law to exert his political influence in gaining her speedy release.

Lord Qi Chongli was indeed most able to offer succour as he was situated in the right place at the right time. Back in 1129 when Emperor Song Gao Zong was forced to take to the sea in order to avoid the Jin invaders, many high ranking officials were reluctant to follow suit. They claimed poor health or other excuses. Some tendered their resignation. Qi Chongli was among the few who bravely followed the emperor to the high seas for an uncertain future. While at sea, Qi Chongli was in charge of the emperor's edicts and other official documents. Having weathered a very difficult time together, Emperor Song Gao Zong was appreciative of Qi Chongli's loyalty. After the court was established in Hangzhou, Qi Chongli was one of the emperor's trusted officials (Huang 1984: 343).

Lord Qi Chongli's intervention on Li Qingzhao's behalf had a prompt and favourable result (Ma 1971:40). It would be quite plausible that the emperor himself gave his special dispensation so that Li Qingzhao was released after only nine days, although the emperor's part was not recorded in any official documents. There is no record that Emperor Song Gao Zong had heard of Li Qingzhao's second marriage. But, as indicated in her letter to Lord Qi Chongli, it was quite certain that Qi would have informed the emperor of Li Qingzhao's separation from Zhang Ruzhou and her role in Zhang's criminal conviction.

Furthermore, Lord Qi Chongli appeared to have secured for Li Qingzhao the retention of all her properties whereas a criminal's wife would have all her possessions confiscated. She still had several choice pieces of art in the years to come. His intervention possibly also helped to retain her status as *mingfu* (命婦), which was an honorific title for a married woman, depending on the rank of her husband's official position. *Lingren* was one of the ranks of *mingfu*[3]. Xie Ji in his writings referred to Li Qingzhao as Zhao Lingren Li (趙令人李), meaning Lingren Li of Zhao, and this was after Zhao Mingcheng's death and Li Qingzhao's divorce (Ma 1971:40).

Based on the time of Zhang Ruzhou's crime mentioned in the *Chronological Record*, the letter of thanks to Lord Qi Chongli would have been written in the ninth or tenth month of the Chinese calendar, that is, the autumn or early winter of 1132. In the letter, Li Qingzhao states that she was with Zhang Ruzhou for only 100 days, hence the time of marriage would be in the fourth or fifth month in the same year. Her divorce from Zhang Ruzhou was only obtained after the bitter law suit.

In the letter, Li Qingzhao does not mention when or where she had first met her second husband, but she describes how she became married to him. The letter has four parts (see Yu & Shu 1999:261). What follows is a summary of her letter, without any of the allusions to historical events which are numerous in the letter.[4]

The first part is about the circumstances surrounding her marriage. Li Qingzhao was very ill at the time of the proposal for marriage. She was in fact delirious and near death, so much so that preparations were being made for her funeral. Her younger brother was administering medication to her and taking care of her, but he was inexperienced and was easily bullied. There was only an old servant in attendance. The situation was pitiful. Into this state of affairs came the suitor who was never identified by name in her letter. He was silver-tongued. With eloquent words and persuasive pretexts he pulled wool over her and her brother's eyes. Her life was hanging on a thread but the suitor advanced his proposal aggressively and forcefully. Before she could consider the matter carefully and make her decision, she was married.

The second part of the letter is about the ill treatment she

---

[3] The *mingfu* in the Song dynasty had these ranks: *shuren* 淑人, *shiren* 碩人, *lingren* 令人, *gongren* 恭人, *yiren* 宜人, *anren* 安人, and *ruren* 孺人 (Ma 1971: 40; Zhao & Li 2003: 240-242).

[4] See Appendix A for the complete text of Li Qingzhao's letter to Qi Chongli in Chinese.

received after marriage and reveals Zhang Ruzhou's ulterior motive for marrying her. She writes that once she was recovered from her illness and could see and think clearly, she found that she could not live with the kind of person he was. She asked herself how someone in the last years of her life could be paired with a despicable, dishonest man like him. To stay with him would be contaminated with the foul odour that he exuded. Her only wish was to get away from him. But he had from the start planned that as soon as he had Li Qingzhao's possessions in his hands he would put her to death. Thus he was violent towards, punching and kicking her. She was a delicate woman, a scholar. How was she to withstand such physical abuse?

In the third part she describes the law suit and her divorce. She was determined not to suffer abuse any more. She called on heaven and earth for justice but there was no one to help her, so she took matters into her own hands. Although it was a small personal matter, the emperor heard about it. Thus she had to go to court. With handcuffs and leg shackles she was to bear witness against this violent and detestable scoundrel. As she was utterly different from him, she was most desirous to sever all association with this person and be freed from his threat of death. By then she did not care if she was compensated for her financial loss. In her own words:

> . . . I was a companion to this violent knave for one hundred days; it was my fate. I was jailed for nine days; I could not blame anyone else. I was cheated and suffered substantial loss; what benefits could there be in return? Since I smashed my head against the wall, the consequences were as expected. I was foolhardy, knowing full well that I could be imprisoned once I brought charges against him. . . .

In the final part of the letter, Li Qingzhao thanked Lord Qi Chongli and expressed her contrition. Throughout the legal proceedings Qi Chongli in his illustrious position had given her assistance and delivered her from prison. Li Qingzhao praised him for his incorruptible and upright character; there was no other under heaven that could be compared to him. He was a virtuous and meritorious official, contributing to the welfare of the country. She had no one to turn to but in his magnanimity Qi Chongli prevented a white-haired old woman from the tribulations of a prison term. How could she examine her own heart and not be ashamed of herself? Li Qingzhao accused herself of misconduct. Having lost virtue and reputation she understood that she would be laughed at by posterity. How could she ever face anyone in public? How could she ever stop people from gossiping about her? Li Qingzhao made it clear in her letter that only someone with Qi Chongli's eminent prestige and impeccable reputation could put a stop to the baseless slander. People in high and low places were different, just as fire and water could not co-exist. She asked Lord Qi Chongli to make an assessment of her situation and thus cleanse her of the dirt that had been smeared over her. She promised that she had learned her lesson and would begin anew. She would like to retire to the countryside and live a simple life. She would have to wash the filth from her many times and apply fragrance to herself many times. Finally, although she and Lord Qi Chongli were distant relatives, she apologized for disturbing him with this mundane affair.

Li Qingzhao's letter to Lord Qi Chongli makes clear a few points about her marriage and divorce. She was ill and not thinking clearly when marriage was proposed. The suitor was dishonest and proposed under false pretexts. His motive for proposing the marriage was material gain: he coveted her money and possessions. Needless to say, the collection of treasures was the real reason. According to Li Qingzhao, he would kill her as soon as he possessed the treasures. Li Qingzhao was physically abused by her husband. Once she saw things clearly she wanted to dissolve the union.

It would appear from the letter that her way of getting away from Zhang Ruzhou was to accuse him of a crime. She must have done some digging into his background to discover that he had attained his official position fraudulently. She knew that if she brought the charge against her husband, she herself would have to go to jail, but she did it anyway. An emperor would not ordinarily hear about divorces among the gentry class. But very likely he was made aware of the law suit that Li Qingzhao brought against Zhang Ruzhou. Zhang's responsibility of auditing military expenses was an important one and if he had obtained his appointment fraudulently, his whole character and discharge of duty came under suspicion.

Lord Qi Chongli helped Li Qingzhao to get her release after nine days, and this was the reason for her gratitude. Although Li Qingzhao does not mention the divorce as such in her letter, it is obvious that she considered herself and Zhang Ruzhou to be worlds apart in character and she did not want to be connected with Zhang Ruzhou in any way.  She got her divorce only after the unpleasant experience of criminal proceedings and imprisonment.

The fact that Qi Chongli was related to Zhao Mingcheng and by marriage to the family of Zhao Mingcheng's cousin indicates that through her second marriage and divorce, she did not sever her ties with the Zhao family completely.  For the rest of her life, she would refer to herself as a widow or as a *mingfu*, a titled lady of the Zhao family.  She leaves no other writings about her re-marriage or divorce besides the letter to Qi Chongli, although these events in her personal life were mentioned by other Song writers in her own life time or shortly after her death.

## Controversy about Remarriage

It was in the Ming dynasty (1271 – 1644 CE), during the reign of Wanli Emperor[5] (萬曆皇帝 1573 – 1620 CE), that a certain Xu Bo (徐渤) of Fujian province first raised the argument that Li Qingzhao's re-marriage could not be true (Huang 1984:335; Ma 1971:28).  He basically had two reasons.  First, he asserts that by 1132 Li Qingzhao was 52 *sui* and, therefore, old.  No woman would re-marry at that age.  Second, as the daughter-in-law of a prime minister and the wife of a senior official she was a *mingfu*.  Given her social status, she could not have remarried.

Since that time many other scholars have taken up this revisionist view of Li Qingzhao's life.  In the Qing dynasty there were several who denied that Li Qingzhao ever remarried.  They felt that those who wrote about her remarriage had slandered her out of malice for her vocal opposition to the government policy of appeasing the Jin

---

[5] It is a convention, still practised today, to refer to the emperors of the Ming (1368-1644 CE) and Qing (1644-1911 CE) dynasties by their reign titles instead of by their posthumous titles as used with emperors of earlier dynasties in this book.  Most of the emperors of the Ming and Qing dynasties only had one reign title each.  Wanli Emperor was the emperor whose reign title was Wanli.

invaders.    The revisionists felt that they needed to defend Li Qingzhao's reputation and virtue by setting the record straight.    The most vociferous and influential revisionist biographer of Li Qingzhao was Yu Zhengxie (俞正燮) who wrote a long essay about the life of Li Qingzhao.    This biographical essay was endorsed by other scholars, reprinted and distributed widely.

Much of the information about Li Qingzhao in Yu Zhengxie's essay was taken from her own essay, the "Postscript."    But his denial of Li Qingzhao's remarriage was based on the premise that mean and despicable *xiaoren* (小人)[6] falsified records.    His motive for the passionate defence of Li Qingzhao's virtue in not marrying again in widowhood was best expressed in his own words:    "I have always detested the claim that Li Qingzhao married Zhang Ruzhou" (quoted in Huang 1984:335).    He simply did not like the idea of Li Qingzhao's second marriage, so he set out to deny it!

Yu Zhengxie was disingenuous in attacking Li Qingzhao's letter to Qi Chongli.    He claimed that its composition was of poor quality and low standard; therefore, it could not have come from Li Qingzhao's hand.    But as Ma (1971:35) points out, Li Qingzhao's letter is a piece of flawless prose and an excellent specimen of *pianti* (駢體) style, much used in the official documents of the Tang dynasty. The special characteristic of this style is that many sentences are of four and six characters long, and they are presented in couplets. According to Ma, if an essay of *pianti* style is constructed well, with appropriate allusions to historical events, and if arguments are expressed cogently and convincingly, then it is outstanding.    Yu Zhengxie would be acting contrary to his better judgement if he indeed thought that the composition of the letter was inferior.

Regarding the content of Li Qingzhao's letter, Yu Zhengxie

---

[6] *Xiaoren* (小人) as a term used to describe a person has been in use since at least the time of Kong Fuzi two thousand and five hundred years ago. Literally it means a small human being.    But the "smallness" refers to the person's character rather than the physical stature.    In Kong Fuzi's teaching, a *xiaoren* is mean-spirited, dishonest, void of human feelings, and untrustworthy, the very antithesis of the ideal "human-hearted person" called the *junzi* (君子 literally meaning the "gentleman").    The latter are the virtuous people who are magnanimous.    The Master said:    *Junzi* is broadminded (treating all others with kindness) but not conspiring.    *Xiaoren* is conspiring (as in being partisan) but not broadminded (Lunyu 2:14).

contended that it was preposterous to say that the matter of her remarriage and divorce would have come to the attention of the emperor. But as has been explained about the letter above, given the circumstances of the case and Qi Chongli's personal relationship with the emperor, it was not surprising that the emperor would have known about the criminal case Li Qingzhao brought against Zhang Ruzhou and, therefore, about her marriage and divorce. According to Ma (1971:39-40) there were in fact cases of marriage involving the families of high ranking officials that had come to the attention of earlier emperors of Northern Song.

Yu Zhengxie and others also questioned how Li Qingzhao could retain her *mingfu* title of Zhao *lingren* or her status as the widow of Zhao Mingcheng in later years if she had remarried. As has been mentioned above, it could be that when her marriage to Zhang Ruzhou was dissolved, she was able to retain her properties and her social status. More historical research would be needed to clarify which law of the Song dynasty would have been invoked in her divorce or if it involved the special permission of the emperor. But what is known is that in later years, there would be at least three occasions on which exchange of documents took place between Li Qingzhao and the imperial court. First, the court ordered the Zhao family and eventually Li Qingzhao to surrender *Zhe Zong Shi Lu* (哲宗 實錄 translated into English as the *Historical Record of Emperor Zhe Zong)*. Second, Li Qingzhao in her status as a *mingfu* composed celebratory poems that were presented to the court. Third, Li Qingzhao presented Zhao Mingcheng's *Jin Shi Lu* to the court (Ma 1971:40-41).

All three occasions will be discussed later. The point is that the emperor and the court continued to recognize Li Qingzhao as a *mingfu* and the widow of Zhao Mingcheng even though all had known about her remarriage and divorce.

Yu Zhengxie and other revisionists argued that the poorly written letter by Li Qingzhao to Qi Chongli – with outrageous claim that even the emperor had heard about Li Qingzhao's law suit and imprisonment – was fabricated by enemies of Li Qingzhao, such as Zhang Feiqing who visited Zhao Mingcheng with the stone teapot. But this argument does not hold water because, as Ma (1971:30-40) points out, there were eight writers in the Southern Song dynasty who directly referred to her second marriage or alluded to it. At least two but perhaps three of these wrote about Li Qingzhao's remarriage while she was still alive. This is what they wrote:

1. Yu Zhengji (俞正己) mentioned Li Qingzhao in his book on poetry: "Regarding women who could write poetry in the current dynasty, there was formerly Madam Zeng. Then there is Li Yi'an. When she was married in the Zhao family, in the early *Jianyan* years when he was the governor of Jiankang, she wrote the verses: "Those coming south yet feel the cold of the Wu River . . . (quoted in Ma 1971:30).

Yu Zhengji's book was published before 1148 when Li Qingzhao was still living. The implication of "when she was married in the Zhao family" is that she was married to someone else later.

2. One of the eight writers, Hu Zi, a contemporary of Li Qingzhao wrote in his memoir: "Yi'an was married once more to Zhang Ruzhou. But not long after she was estranged (from him). She had a letter to Qi Chongli with lines like, 'How could someone in the last years of her life be paired with a despicable, dishonest man like him?' All who heard this laughed at her" (quoted in Ma 1971:31).

3. Wang Zhuo, another contemporary of Li Qingzhao wrote: "Yi'an Jushi, the daughter of Li Gefei of the Ministry of Justice, Eastern Region, was the wife of Zhao Mingcheng the governor of Jiankang. After Zhao's death, she remarried. Then she brought a law suit against him and divorced him. She drifts in her old age with no one to rely upon" (quoted in Ma 1971:31). According to its preface, Wang Zhuo's book was written in 1149 when Li Qingzhao was still alive. Hence there was no mention about her death. This Wang Zho was the same writer who praised Li Qingzhao's *shi* and ability but criticized her *ci* (See Chapters 2 and 3).

4. As we have seen in Chapter 3, Chao Buzhi, a friend of Li Qingzhao's father Li Gefei, called her a *shidafu*. His nephew Zhao Gongwu recorded in his book that Li Qingzhao had published her works in 12 volumes, and that she was first married to Zhao Mingcheng. She passed away after drifting around the country (cited in Ma 1971:31-32). The implication of Zhao Gongwu's description of Li Qingzhao was that there was not only the first marriage but that there was another.

5. Hong Gua (洪适 1117-1184 CE) was also a contemporary of Li Qingzhao but younger than she. He was a renowned scholar. His father was sent to Jin as an envoy and then was kept by the Jin as a hostage for 15 years. Hong Gua himself shared in Zhao Mingcheng's

passion for inscriptions and his book about inscriptions on stone tablets and calligraphy was similar to Zhao Mingcheng's *Jin Shi Lu* . He mentioned Li Qingzhao in his book in a commentary on Zhao Mingcheng's book *Jin Shi Lu* : ". . . In the mid-Shaoxing[7] years, (his) wife Yi'an Jushi presented his book to the emperor. Mr. Zhao had no son. Li married again. His book has been widely distributed but his tablet no longer exists. . . ." (quoted in Ma 1971:32).

6. Another writer, Zhao Yanwei, deserves the credit for recording the entire letter of Li Qingzhao to Qi Chongli . His memoir was published in 1206 CE, about half century after Li Qingzhao's death. However, he was a member of the imperial Zhao clan and would have had access to documents kept in the palace archives. He would not have included Li Qingzhao's letter in his book if it or the reference in the letter to the emperor was untrue.

7. Li Xinchuan's (1975c) *Chronological Record of Important Events Since the Jianyan Years* contains the account of Li Qingzhao's law suit against Zhang Ruzhou which has already been discussed above.

8. Lastly, an author by the name of Chen Zhensun (陳振孫) recorded that the "*Shu Yu Ji*, one volume, by Yi'an Jushi, Li surname Qingzhao, daughter of renowned scholar Li Gefei (style name) Wenshu, married to Zhao Defu[8] of Dongwu. She lost her chastity in her later years" (quoted in Ma: 1971:33).

Five of the eight authors mentioned above were contemporaries of Li Qingzhao. Four of the eight references (that is, Yu Zhengji, Hu Zi, Wang Zhuo and Zhao Yanwei) to Li Qingzhao's remarriage appear in memoirs. It could be said that their writings would be more subjective as memoirs typically are. However, of the other four, Li Xinchuan's *Chronological Record* is a history book while the other three were works in specialized fields as two were catalogues of published works and the third was about calligraphy and inscriptions on stone tablets. It would be most unlikely that these authors, living in different times and places, would agree on fabricating Li Qingzhao's remarriage (Ma 1971:34).

The questions then arises as to why some scholars of the Ming

---

[7] Shaoxing was the second reign title of Emperor Song Gao Zong. It covered the years 1131 – 1162 CE.

[8] Zhao Defu was the style name of Zhao Mingcheng.

and Qing dynasties were so vociferous about defending Li Qingzhao's honour and virtue, and bent on rewriting her biography. To understand their taking that stance requires an explanation of the mores and ideology of their times which conditioned their views about women. But Li Qingzhao lived in a different cultural milieu. The views held by the later Ming and Qing writers were quite different from those prevailing in Li Qingzhao's time.

Patriarchy had existed in China since the late neolithic period as shown by the archaeological evidence at the sites of Longshan, Qijia (齊家文化), Qujialing (屈家嶺文化), Dawenkou (大汶口文化) and other cultures (Bai 2002:40). However, oppression of women varied in different periods of time and by region. Generally speaking it intensified in the later dynasties and centuries. Up to the Northern Song dynasty, women were free to divorce their husbands and widows to remarry, although from time to time some scholars wrote tracts that promoted the ideology that women should do neither.

It may be worthwhile to keep in mind what is meant by an ideology. An ideology is not a true or veritable explanation of people's behaviour or any social phenomenon. As a system of ideas that partially and apparently explains human behaviour or social phenomenon, it more specifically defines how people ought to behave or conduct their affairs.[9] An ideology usually benefits its proponents in some material way. The ruling class of a society always has its ideology or ideologies about the social order and proper behaviour for the people (see *The German Ideology* by Marx and Engels 1970). An ideology is part of the ideal culture. But how people actually live, which is the real culture, may or may not be in accordance with the ideal culture.

How Chinese women, including Li Qingzhao, lived is an empirical question. Historical records contain a social class bias insofar as more has been written about the women of the gentry than of the peasant or working class. Those records show that in China's long history, the upper class widows and divorced women often

---

[9] The way "ideology" is used in this book is based on the definition of ideology given by Gould and Kolb (1964:315, parentheses in the original): "a pattern of beliefs and concepts (both factual and normative) which purport to explain complex social phenomena with a view to directing and simplifying socio-political choices facing individuals and groups."

remarried. From the Western Han dynasty to the period of the Five Dynasties and Ten Kingdoms period, it was not uncommon for widowed princesses or widows of the gentry to remarry. Some widows remarried multiple times. One of the generals who helped to found the Western Han dynasty, Chen Ping (陳平), married a woman who had been widowed five times previously (Zhuge 2004:171). During the period of the Three Kingdoms (220 – 280 CE) Empress Zhen (甄皇后) of Emperor Wei Wen Di (魏文帝) was a widow when he married her (Zhuge 2004:171).

Early in the Tang dynasty, the Emperor Tang Tai Zong, in order to increase population and stimulate the economy, proclaimed in an edict in 627 CE that specifically encouraged early marriage (men at 20 *sui* and women at 15 *sui* and above) and the remarriage of widows. Upper class women of the Tang dynasty were still quite able to exert their will. That dynasty saw the only female emperor Wu Zetian ruling China. Altogether 23 princesses of the Tang dynasty remarried, and four others married three times (Zhuge 2004:172). Some of them remarried in widowhood while others did so after divorce.

During the period of Five Dynasties and Ten Kingdoms, Emperor Zhou Tai Zu (周太祖) of the Later Zhou dynasty married four times and each time the bride was a widow (Zhuge 2004:172).

In the Northern Song dynasty, following the tradition established in the Tang and Five Dynasties, widows and divorced women continued to remarry. The sister of the founder of the Song dynasty, Emperor Song Tai Zu, remarried after the death of her husband. At the age of two *sui*, the famous Northern Song scholar and statesman Fan Zhongyan (范仲淹) lost his father. His widowed mother remarried. In fact Fan Zhongyan used his stepfather's surname Zhu until he passed the *jinshi* examination and became an official. Later in life, in his instructions to the Fan clan about financial arrangements and management for the clan, he stipulated that women on their remarriage would receive 20 strings of money (Zhuge 2004:172).

Wang Anshi, the Reformer and prime minister to Emperor Song Shen Zong (see Chapter 2) had a son who was mentally ill. In his deranged state, the son accused his wife of infidelity and constantly harangued her. Wang Anshi knew that his daughter-in-law was blameless. He was also cognizant of the fact that given his son's condition, her chance of remarriage on her own after divorce would be slim. He wisely arranged a match for his daughter-in-law (Ma

1971:39; Zhuge 2004:172-173).

Even in the Southern Song dynasty, when the ideology of the chaste woman was becoming more prevalent, women continued to remarry. Lu You (陸游 1125 – 1210 CE), born shortly before the extinction of Northern Song dynasty, is known as the patriotic poet. He expressed in his poetry a deep love for the lost territories in the north and a longing for their recovery. He and his first wife Tang Wan (唐婉) loved each other very much. But his mother disliked her and forced the couple to divorce. They both remarried, she to a Zhao Shicheng (趙士程) who was a member of the imperial clan. Years after their divorce, Lu You and Tang Wan met in a private garden. They both wrote *ci*, to the same tune, expressing their regrets and unwavering deep affection for each other.

About a century after Li Qingzhao's death in the Southern Song dynasty, a Madam Huang was married twice before she became a lady-in-waiting in the household of a prince who was the son of Emperor Song Li Zong (宋理宗). She bore this prince a son who later became Emperor Song Du Zong (宋度宗) who reigned from 1264 to 1274 CE (Zhuge 2004:172).

In addition to the freedom of women to remarry, the Northern Song women had the right to speak out about politics. We have seen Li Qingzhao's mother-in-law Madam Guo addressing and writing to Emperor Song Hui Zong. As Ma (1971:45) points out it was not uncommon for women to attend banquets and other social gatherings at which they readily expressed their views. Li Qingzhao provides a record in the form of a *ci* of a banquet she hosted (see Chapter 5). She no doubt was not reticent about airing her views publicly on those occasions.

Unfortunately for Li Qingzhao and all Chinese women after her, from the Northern Song to the Southern Song periods, there was a marked and steady decline in the social status and freedom of women as the ideology of suppressing women was increasingly embraced by the literati class. Early in the Northern Song dynasty, the second emperor, Emperor Song Tai Zong (宋太宗) and brother of the founding emperor Song Tai Zu, decreed in an edict the prohibition of women of the imperial clan to remarry (Zhuge 2004:173). This could explain why of all the Song princesses of the blood royal, only the sister of these two emperors remarried. However, other women of the imperial clan continued to remarry. During the reign of Emperors

Song Ying Zong (宋英宗 r. 1063 – 1067 CE), Song Shen Zong, and Song Zhe Zong (r. 1085 – 1100 CE), there were edicts granting permission to specific women of the imperial clan to remarry (Huang 1984:347).

It was in the Southern Song dynasty that the ideas of the Cheng brothers of the Northern Song period gained widespread acceptance among the ruling elite, that is, the landed scholar-official gentry. Cheng Yi had this to say about women: "It is a small matter if they starve to death, but a very serious matter if they lose their chastity" (quoted in Zhao and Li 2003:130). At the same time the saying that women without ability were virtuous became more popular. Li Qingzhao was born in a world, the Northern Song period, that was drastically different from the one in which she died, the Southern Song period.

The Southern Song dynasty was followed by the Yuan dynasty (1271 – 1368 CE) founded by Kublai Khan. As Ma (1971:45) explains, the loss of rights and freedoms by Chinese women coincided with the founding of the Yuan dynasty when for the first time in history the whole of China was conquered and occupied by a foreign power, the Mongols. The Yuan dynasty was replaced by the Ming dynasty which was founded by a Han Chinese. However, during the Ming dynasty the fear of the resurgence of the Mongols in the north persisted for quite a long time. There was no going back to the relative freedom enjoyed by the women in the Northern Song and earlier dynasties; instead suppression and restriction of women continued. By the Qing dynasty, when the revisionists of Li Qingzhao's biography were most prominent and active, the suppression of women intensified to such a degree that the women of the gentry were most often hidden inside the household. By then women's virtue was defined almost exclusively in terms of chastity which was interpreted to mean virginity before marriage and no other sexual partner besides the husband after marriage. In other words, widows should not remarry as it would mean being unfaithful to the deceased husbands. As Huang (1984:347) puts it, while women's remarriage was often looked upon with disfavour in patriarchal China, it was only in the Ming and Qing dynasties that it was considered as immoral.

There was a deeper current of ethos underlying the ideology of women's chastity. The Chinese word used for virginity and chastity is *jie* (節). Ma (1971:45) explains the intensification of safeguarding women's *jie* during the Qing dynasty in terms of the changing definition of this word. The original meaning of the word was broader, beyond chastity, to encompass integrity-cum-loyalty. This would entail loyalty to one's country in the face of adversity. Those who did not surrender to the enemy or become traitors even when threatened with death were said to have kept *jie*.

The Qing imperial family and rulers, like the Mongols of the Yuan dynasty, were also foreigners, the Manchu from the northeast. The Manchu rulers of the Qing dynasty, nonetheless, retained the administrative structures, including the civil service system, established by the Ming dynasty. The broader notion of *jie* essentially would subvert the rule by foreigners (Huang 1984:347). However, the Han Chinese male scholar-officials served the foreign rulers. In terms of the moral code for the Chinese people as a whole, these officials having lost *jie* were disloyal to their own people by serving the Manchu foreigners. Thus the educated Chinese, Han and Manchu alike, put the entire burden of *jie*, that is integrity and loyalty, on the shoulders of women while at the same time reducing the meaning of *jie* to chastity alone. Widows who refused to remarry were praised as having kept their *jie*. In this way, women's *jie* became "a cover-up for the loss of *jie* by men as they served foreign masters" (Ma 1971:45). Women thus came under insufferable bondage imposed by patriarchy.

An example of bondage was foot binding. While the origin of foot binding is not entirely clear, according to one view, it was introduced into China by the dancers from the Western Regions during the late Tang dynasty or the period of Five Dynasties and Ten Kingdoms. What is certain is that during the Song dynasty, both the Northern and Southern Song periods, foot binding was a practice only found among prostitutes or dancing girls in entertainment establishments. Other women, especially among the gentry, did not bind their feet (Ma 1971:45). Li Qingzhao most definitely did not have bound feet. But by the Ming and Qing dynasties, foot binding became the custom among even the women of the gentry. The three-inch feet were a sign of beauty and gentility.

Foot binding seen within the historical perspective was only one manifestation of the declining position of women and their loss of control of their own lives during the Ming and Qing dynasties. However, for this downward spiral of women's status to evolve, it was supported and justified by the ideology of the womanly virtue of *jie* that came into prominence in the late Southern Song dynasty.

Within the cultural milieu of the Qing dynasty, Yu Zhengxie and other revisionists felt the compulsion to defend Li Qingzhao's *jie*. This they could only do by denying her second marriage. But Li Qingzhao was born into a different cultural environment of the Northern Song period where women's remarriage was not a shameful deed; it was, in today's lingual, "no big deal." But by the time she died in the Southern Song dynasty, however, the loss of women's *jie* was already ideologically important. The drastic change in cultural mores can be seen in the last known event of Li Qingzhao's life which was recorded in the tombstone inscription of one Madam Sun (孫夫人).

Madam Sun's tombstone inscription was composed by the patriotic poet Lu You mentioned above. It reads in part thus: "Madam (Sun) was virtuous from a tender age. The wife of the late Zhao Mingcheng of Jiankang, Madam Li, well known for her literary works, wanted to pass on her learning to Madam (Sun) who, at the time past the age of 10 *sui*,[10] declined with thanks saying, 'Literary ability is not the concern of girls.'" (Lu You as quoted in Huang 1974:181). Madam Sun, the wife of an official in the capital, died in 1193. It can be seen that by that time the ideology of keeping women ignorant and without ability was already widely accepted among the gentry class and, of course, only that class had the means of educating its daughter if it so chose.

It is somewhat surprising that Lu You would have written such an inscription. Even though he was about 30 years younger than Li Qingzhao, one would have thought that he might have been a kindred spirit of hers in that both earnestly grieved the loss of half a country to the Jin and fervently expressed the longing to recover the lost territories. Moreover, Lu You's first wife Tang Wan whom he apparently loved all his life was also an accomplished *ci* poet and had a second marriage. In the tombstone inscription he obviously was praising Madam Sun for her perspicacity in describing the proper upbringing of a young lady: virtuous but without education or ability. This was expected in any tombstone inscriptions as it was meant to be a eulogy. But one also wonders if this was in fact a back-handed

---

[10] The term used in describing Madam Sun's age could be anywhere between 11 and 19 *sui*, all of which would be past the age of 10 *sui*.

compliment. Madam Sun might have been clever and "virtuous" enough to have learned the mores of the culture of her time as to refuse Li Qingzhao's kind offer, but against the backdrop of the latter's integrity, nobility of character, and the intellectual and literary stature, Madam Sun was truly ignorant and foolish.

The true intention of Lu You could never be known. What this tombstone inscription indicates is the immense cultural change that accompanied the transition of the Northern Song into the Southern Song, spanning the years in which Li Qingzhao lived. Perhaps Lu You and Madam Sun both in fact harboured antipathy towards Li Qingzhao for her remarriage. Whatever the case might have been, Madam Sun's words resonated with the characterization of Li Qingzhao's remarriage as a matter of loss of virtue in the writings of her contemporaries which have been presented earlier in this chapter. Words like those of Madam Sun's also formed the basis for the denial of her remarriage by the Qing writers. Women without learning or ability were virtuous. But Li Qingzhao had tremendous abilities and used them to the full. How could the Qing writers reconcile her abilities with her virtue? For them, Li Qingzhao could only be virtuous if she kept her *jie* and did not remarry.

In the opinions of those who deny that Li Qingzhao married a second time, the Southern Song writers wrote about or intimated her second marriage in order to malign her character. The motive behind such calumny was that Li Qingzhao was steadfastly opposed to the Southern Song government's peace-at-any-cost policy and was a vocal advocate of military campaigns to resist the Jin and to recover lost territories. Quite often officials who espoused the resistance policy were dismissed, demoted, banished or even killed. Insofar as Li Qingzhao was a woman and, therefore, was never an official, the best way of punishing her would be to decry her loss of virtue.

The debate about Li Qingzhao's second marriage continues to the present. There were writers in the twentieth century who did not think that Li Qingzhao remarried (see Xia 1974; Huang Mugu 1984; and Tang and Pan 1984). In their view the Southern Song scholars mentioned above wrote unfavourably about the aging Li Qingzhao and showed no sympathy for her as she drifted around the country in her old age. Instead, in order to vilify her for her political stance, these writers sneered and laughed at her for having lost her virtue by marrying again in her widowhood. This revisionist view of her life persists in a recently published biography of Li Qingzhao written by Xie Xueqin (謝學欽 2009).

It is indeed reasonable to think that Li Qingzhao's detractors would have preferred to attack her political stance openly and that she was maligned for political reasons.   Indeed, insofar as she was a woman, her critics could really only attack her about her personal life and loss of virtue.   But it does not necessarily mean that the Southern Song scholars conspired to spread falsehoods about her life.   The fact that she a widow remarried gave them grounds for castigating her without having to reveal the political motives for their aspersions. The contemporary writers who deny Li Qingzhao's second marriage might have carried the "maligning hypothesis" a bit too far.

In Ma's 1971 evaluation of Li Qingzhao's life, she was the last of the outstanding women in Chinese history before Chinese women began to lose their rights and human dignity.   While there were published women writers in the later dynasties, none of them measured up to Li Qingzhao's talents or achievements.   Li Qingzhao in her lifetime published her works – *ci, shi*, essays, rules of a gambling, and others – in 12 or 13 volumes.   She expounded on the theory of *ci*. She expressed her ideas on historical events and current political affairs.   She dared to satirize the rulers and officials in powerful positions.   She collaborated with her husband on the most complete treatise on the inscriptions on bronze vessels and stone tablets since antiquity.   She was in every sense a *shidafu* except for the actual appointment to an official position.   She did not allow herself to lag behind men.   In fact she aimed right at surpassing them, as another Qing writer Li Tiaoyuan (李調元) enthusiastically claimed (quoted in Wang 1978:323)).   Most critics today would acknowledge her as a literary giant of the Song dynasty, ranking her right after Su Shi and Wang Anshi (Ma 1971: 46).   In the opinion of this writer, her *ci* are second to none, before or after her, male or female.

For all of this, she did not and does not need any scholar to defend her virtue. She kept her *jie*, to herself and to her country, right through her remarriage and divorce.

# 7 Later Years

Li Qingzhao's divorce and release from prison closed a short but most vexing episode in her life. It could be imagined that she would be in low spirits towards the end of 1132. She was likely to be in poor health too as she had been ill after Zhao Mingcheng's death and at the time of her marriage to Zhang Ruzhou. It must have been a desperately unhappy time for Li Qingzhao. She stayed on in Hangzhou, possibly with her brother Li Hang. Given the war time conditions that still prevailed at that time, it would be safer for her and what remained of her collection of art and antiques to be part of a larger and more secure household.

Demoralized and unwell after her release from prison, Li Qingzhao took time to recover. She probably spent her time reading and writing in seclusion. With an indomitable spirit and a proactive attitude towards life, Li Qingzhao did not wallow in her misery for long. Beginning in the summer of 1133, she seemed to be very productive for the next two years as shown by her extant writings that can be dated.

## Poems in Honour of the Envoys

In 1133, in the fifth month of the Chinese calendar, Emperor Song Gao Zong announced that he would send a delegation to the Jin kingdom to visit his father Emperor Song Hui Zong and his brother Emperor Qin Zong in captivity. In the following month, Li Qingzhao composed two *shi* in honour of the envoy Han Xiaozhou (韓肖冑) and the vice-envoy Hu Songnian (胡松年)[1] as they began their journey. In the preface to the poems, Li Qingzhao mentions that her father and grandfather were students of Envoy Han Xiaozhou's ancestors. She claims that her family were by then too few in number and too lowly in status to approach the eminent envoys; in fact she indicates in the second poem that she sent the poems not directly to the two envoys but to Envoy Hu's secretary. Moreover she had been ill and poorly in spirit. But as this was an important event, it must not be forgotten, so

---

[1] See Appendix A for the two *shi* in Chinese.

she was composing two *shi* in commemoration.

Missions to the Jin kingdom were taken very seriously. Envoys were often humiliated or taken as prisoners. They could even be killed as was Zhao Mingcheng's brother-in-law Fu Cha. Envoy Han Xiaozhou's family had been much honoured with high positions. His great grandfather and grandfather were prime ministers to altogether five emperors in the Northern Song period. He himself was now ready to serve his country with his life if necessary. As he took up the mission, he told the court that it would be good if he could achieve genuine peace between Song and Jin. However, Song should continue to prepare for Jin's invasion and go to war if necessary, without worrying about his safety (Ma 1971:51). It was recorded in his biography in the official *Song Shi* that when Lord Han Xiaozhou went to bid his mother Madam Wen (文夫人) farewell before going on this mission, she told him: "The Han family of ministers have been serving the country for generations. You have now received your orders. Go right away. Don't worry about your old mother" (quoted in Wen and Qian 1987:197). When Emperor Song Gao Zong heard about this, he granted her the title of *Rong Guo Tai Furen* (榮國太夫人 meaning the Duchess Dowager who glorifies country) in praise of her spirit of *jie*[2] (Wen and Qian 1987:197).

In the two poems, Li Qingzhao reveals her views on the current affairs of her time. She was not at all pleased with the cowering attitude and the resultant policies of retreat and appeasement adopted by the Song court as it complied with all demands by Jin for land, gold, silks and other goods. There was no political will to retake the north. By this time it was also quite obvious to all who cared to observe that Emperor Song Gao Zong was reluctant to secure the release of the captured emperors as the return of his elder brother Emperor Song Qin Zong would spell the end of his own reign. Thus in her *shi* Li Qingzhao expresses sadness and anger at the perils suffered by her country while she also satirizes the emperor and his policies.

The first poem was addressed to Envoy Han Xiaozhou. Li Qingzhao begins with words of praise for Emperor Song Gao Zong for thinking of his father and brother in captivity and sending the envoys northward to visit them. This is actually more sarcastic rather than complimentary as six years had elapsed since the two emperors

---

[2] See Chapter 6 for a discussion of *jie*.

were marched unceremoniously north. Li Qingzhao also praises Envoy Han for his courage in taking on the ambassadorial role. She makes a reference to the words of farewell that he had said as mentioned above. She also comforts him and tells him not to worry about his wife and family. Then she throws some darts at the court. In his instructions to the envoys, Emperor Song Gao Zong had told them not to quibble too much about the language of protocol in their negotiation with the Jin but to be humble in words and generous in gifts. Neither should they be miserly in agreeing to the demands by the Jin for tributes in money or in kind. Ostensibly in her *shi* Li Qingzhao is repeating the words of the emperor. But any educated persons reading between the lines of the *shi* would have recognized that she was in fact mocking the emperor. They would have understood as no doubt the envoys did too that she was in fact giving them a contrary message that they should cherish the land and the riches of the country, and should not squander them. Pursuing the policies of the emperor and the court would only betray their country to the enemy.

In the second *shi* in honour of Lord Hu Songnian, Li Qingzhao praises his virtue and high moral standards. Later during the mission Hu Songnian would live up to the high standard of honourable behaviour that Li Qingzhao and the people had expected of him. When Liu Yu, the puppet emperor of Great Qi set up by the Jin, wanted the envoys to address him as an emperor, Envoy Han Xiaozhou did not quite know what to do. But the Vice-Envoy Hu Songnian without hesitation replied that they were all subjects of the Song emperor as Liu Yu himself was a former Song official (Zhuge 2004:179-180).

Further in the second *shi* Li Qingzhao acknowledges the difficult task Hu Songnian had ahead of him. She emphasizes the danger inherent in their mission. She brings up the story of the task given to the emissary sent by the Prince of the State of Yan (燕國) during the period of the Warring States to assassinate the King of the State of Qin. That plot failed and the King of Qin eventually became the first emperor of China, Qin Shi Huang. However, the present mission would be different, Li Qingzhao opines optimistically.

Li Qingzhao then openly denounces the Jin as untrustworthy who had repeatedly broken earlier peace treaties. She proceeds to caution Vice-Envoy Hu Songnian against the enemy's treachery.

Rather it would be well for him to listen to ordinary folks who were not in official positions.

In the poem dedicated to Hu Songnian, she again brings up the fact that her father and grandfather were from Shandong province. They were well known and honourable, often engaging scholars in lively discussion about politics and current affairs (see Chapter 2). But their descendants were now mixed with migrant refugees drifting hither and yon. She ends the *shi* with the wish if she could only send her blood and tears to the hills and rivers of Shandong in homage to the graves of the ancestors.

In these two *shi* in honour of Envoys Han and Hu, Li Qingzhao not only expresses her patriotic sentiments and the plight of the migrant refugees like herself, but also points out the strategic location of her ancestral province of Shandong. In the occupied north, the Jin like other conquerors of China, including the Japanese army in the 20th century, controlled the cities, but the vast numbers of people in the rural areas were ready to join in any uprising. Of all the officials who moved south, Hu Songnian alone saw the importance of Shandong where the Jin did not have total control and where the people deeply resented the puppet Liu Yu in their midst. If Southern Song would only take back Shandong province then recovery of the entire north would be possible. Unfortunately the Southern Song court did not and would not follow this line of action (Ma 1971:50).

Although Li Qingzhao calls herself a widow in the two *shi*, she was writing very much as a member of her family of origin, that is the Li clan. Her references to her father and grandfather, and to her roots in Shandong, show that she was deeply concerned with the events there. Most likely she was still in her brother's household and involved with the welfare of the Li clan (Ma 1971:51).

## Hangzhou 1133 – 1134

In the late summer of the same year, 1133, still residing in Hangzhou, she composed the *ci* known as "Blossoms on the Hill" (山花子) also recorded as composed to the tune of the "New Version of Silk Washing Brook Sand" (攤破浣溪沙 Zhuge 2004:181).

## To the tune of "Blossoms on the Hill"

Recovering from an illness –
Temples turning grey,
Reclining, I watch the waning moon
Climb to the laced window.
Stemmed nutmeg simmers,
But there is no tea ceremony.
Poems spread on the pillow -
They are good for idle moments.
The scenery in front of the gate
Is more exquisite in the rain.
The osmanthus fragrance warmly greets me
All day long.

山花子 (四印齋本調作攤破浣溪沙)

病起蕭蕭兩鬢華，臥看殘月上窗紗。豆蔻連梢煮熟水，莫分茶。枕
上詩詞閑處好，門前風景雨來佳。終日向人多蘊藉，木樨花。

Composed in convalescence, this *ci* speaks not of pain or despondence so often associated with illness. Amidst the little things that a recovering patient does or observes, Li Qingzhao seems to be listless and weary of idleness. The mood is calm. There is a hint of impatience for greater activity as she busies herself with books and poetry even if she is in bed.

The twenty-first century literary critic Xu (2002:119) dates this *ci* to 1129, the year of Zhao Mingcheng's death as Li Qingzhao mentions in the "Postscript" that she was gravely ill after his passing. However, if this was indeed written earlier than 1133, one would expect more of the raw pain and sorrow that Li Qingzhao was so capable of conveying in a *ci*. Insofar as she is somewhat idle and paying attention to *shi*, *ci*, the scenery and the fragrance of osmanthus, the invalid did not appear to be steeped in acute bereavement. As Li Qingzhao was also ill before and after her second marriage, it would be reasonable to put this *ci* as composed during her recovery after her divorce. The osmanthus, also known as cassia flowers, bloom in late summer and early autumn. As her divorce took place in mid- to late autumn of 1132, this *ci* could not have been written in the year of her brief imprisonment and divorce.  Zhuge (2004:181-182), a biographer of Li Qingzhao and Zhao Mingcheng, dates the *ci* to 1133.

There is another *ci* that was most likely composed around this time.  It is entitled *Chang Shou Le* (長壽樂), meaning "Happy Long Life."  It has a subtitle of Nanchang's birthday.  It is a celebration of the birthday of a high ranking lady who had the title of Nanchang.  It describes her as a bright pearl born into an illustrious family, married to an honourable husband, and raising sons who attained high positions.  All those who came to congratulate her were high officials.  The *ci* ends with wishes that the lady would live a long time like the ancient pine tree.  According to Xu (2002:136), this *ci* was composed in honour of Madam Wen, the mother of Envoy Han Xiaozhou, already mentioned earlier in this Chapter.  The *ci* has a lively mood and paints a vivid picture of wealth and glory.  Otherwise it does not have much artistic merit.  But it does indicate that Li Qingzhao was well connected with the social elites in Hangzhou.

In the following year, 1134, Li Qingzhao possibly began to compile and edit all her writings with a view to publication.  As has been indicated in Chapter 1, in the years after her death, her works were mentioned as collected in six volumes of *ci* and seven volumes of essays and other writings.  This would mean that someone, most likely herself, would have selected the writings, compiled them and prepared them for publication.  She would write more in the years to come.  But in her convalescence, spreading the poems in front of her, she might well be sorting and arranging them in order for publication later.

During this time, she most certainly also re-read and edited the *Jin Shi Lu* manuscript.  She always knew that Zhao Mingcheng had meant to publish his magnum opus of which she was a collaborator.  In connection with it, in the eighth month of the Chinese calendar in this year, she wrote the "Postscript" to the *Jin Shi Lu* .

Other dates for the "Postscript" have been suggested by biographers: two years earlier or one year later than 1134.  The most widely circulated version of the "Postscript" is taken from the edition of *Jin Shi Lu* that was printed in the Qing dynasty (Xu 2009:313).  It bears the date of composition as the second year of Shaoxing (i.e., 1132 CE), 8th month, 2nd day, in Yi'an Room.  Shaoxing was the second reign title of Emperor Song Gao Zong, the first being *Jianyan*. Scholars in dynastic China often used the emperors' reign titles to date their writings.  However, based on careful research, Huang (1974:176) and the majority of Li Qingzhao experts today are quite certain that Li Qingzhao completed the "Postscript" in the fourth year of Shaoxing (i.e., 1134 CE) and that the earlier year was an error in copying.

Shortly after the completion of the "Postscript," in the ninth month of the Chinese calendar, the Southern Song Court in Hangzhou was threatened again. This time it was the army of the puppet emperor Liu Yu of Great Qi together with the Jin forces. They launched this invasion because Liu Yu had been greatly alarmed by the success of the much admired and fearless Song General Yue Fei in recovering parts of Hubei and Henan provinces. Liu persuaded the Jin lords to mobilize their troops. With his son and nephew acting as guides for the Jin army, Liu Yu led the combined forces and marched south. They were poised to attack several counties south of the Huai River.

Having experienced Jin invasions several times in the preceding years, Li Qingzhao like many others in Hangzhou was extremely fearful and prepared to flee again. She most likely left Hangzhou with her brother's family as he was a court official and fled to Jinhua (金華) in southern Zhejiang province. She described the chaotic conditions of the refugees on the move as follows:

> When word of impending invasion reached the people of Jiangsu and Zhejiang provinces, those in the east went west and those in the south went north. Those who lived in the forested mountains rushed to the cities while the urban dwellers went into the mountains. There was a constant movement of people all day long. All were quite lost (Li Qingzhao as cited in Huang 1974:157-158).

Li Qingzhao herself went by boat going upstream on the Fuchun River (富春江), risked the danger of the Yan Sandbar, and arrived in Jinhua. She stayed in a house belonging to the Chen family (Huang 1974:157-158).

As she passed the Yan Sandbar she wrote a *shi* in honour of Yan Guang (嚴光) of the Eastern Han dynasty after whom the sandbar was named. Yan Guang was a schoolmate and close friend of Liu Xiu (劉秀) who restored the house of Liu to the throne and established the Eastern Han dynasty after the usurpation of the interloper Wang

Mang for several years.  After Liu Xiu became an emperor, Yan Guang changed his name and became a hermit.  Even when the emperor's emissaries found him he refused all official positions offered to him.  Yan Guang found his retreat by the banks of the Fuchun River and became a fisherman (Wen and Qian 1987:211).

Li Qingzhao admired Yan Guang's virtue of not seeking fame or fortune in high places.  As she sailed by the sandbar that bore his name, she was touched and wrote:

### Crossing the Yan Sandbar at Night

Big ships pass by in search of riches,
Small boats also come for fame.
Coming and going, all should be shamed by your virtue,
Hence I sneak by the fisherman's terrace under cover of night.

夜發嚴灘

巨艦只緣因利往，扁舟亦是為名來。往來有愧先生德，特地通宵過釣臺。

In Li Qingzhao's view most of the high officials close to Emperor Song Gao Zong connived to enrich themselves instead of working for the good of the country.  Even the emperor was no better as he had no political will to fight the Jin.  Deprecating herself as too ashamed to sail past the place where Yan Guang used to fish in broad daylight, she would only steal by in the dark.

## The Year in Jinhua

Li Qingzhao arrived in Jinhua in the tenth month of the Chinese calendar (in 1134).  Her stay there seemed to be conducive to prolific creativity.  Rested and recovered, with a change of scenery even in those troubled times, she continued to write which began about half a year after her divorce.  Meanwhile the panic that had gripped the refugees subsided somewhat as the crisis of the combined invasion by the Jin and Liu Yu eased.  Early in the tenth month, Emperor Song Gao Zong had decided to lead the military campaign of resistance personally.  Although he did not really go to the front, his decision boosted the morale of the Song soldiers.  Led by capable generals they were able to defeat the invaders in several important battles.  While the war was not actually won, local Song officials stopped deserting cities or counties in their charge (Ma 1971).

Sensing that the war conditions were not entirely hopeless, Emperor Song Gao Zong after over twenty days of procrastination left Hangzhou and marched north, purportedly to the front.  As the Song forces recovered some cities and territories, the invading armies retreated to the north side of the Huai River due to a considerable extent to the fact that the Jin emperor was gravely ill.  By early eleventh month, Emperor Song Gao Zong even appeared to be eager to cross the Huai River in pursuit of the enemy.  Of course he never acted on his heroic sentiments but the Song people could collectively heave a sigh of relief and relax a little (Ma 1971:63-64).

Under these changing circumstances, Li Qingzhao and the rest of her family felt more at ease which she mentioned in her writings at this time.  It would appear that as a refugee in temporary quarters, Li Qingzhao was with her family of origin.  The younger generation would consist of the children, particularly the daughters of her brother and possibly other members of the Li clan.  She and her clanswomen spent their evenings gambling.

About a month after her arrival in Jinhua she produced one of the most curious and fascinating documents of all time, not only among her own writings but in all Chinese literary works.  She wrote a trilogy on the gambling game *dama* (打馬) which literally means whipping the horses.  The trilogy consists of *Dama Tujing Mingci (打馬 圖經命詞)*, a treatise on the illustrated rules and principles of the game with her commentaries;  a preface for it, dated the 24th day of the 11th month in the Chinese calendar;  and a poetic essay, an established Chinese literary genre known as the *fu* (賦), about it.[3]

Gambling has always occupied a prominent place in Chinese folk culture.  Betting on the odds of winning, often with the challenge of employing stratagems, is highly alluring to many Chinese from those

---

[3] *Dama Tujing Mingci*, its Preface and the *"Dama Fu"* are included in Appendix A.

in the most exalted positions to those occupying the lowest.  In the Song dynasty, a game of chance popular among the women of the gentry class was the *dama*. It was played on a board like the game of chess but the pieces were called horses.  This game was still played in the Ming and early Qing dynasties.  It disappeared from popular culture sometime during the Qing dynasty.  However, some writers, for example Xie (2009), believe that the *dama* game evolved into the popular game of *majiang* (麻將) also known as *mahjong* of today.

While other writers have described the rules and procedures of gambling games, Li Qingzhao's trilogy alone is valued as literary gems. This is because the three pieces of prose are excellent specimens of elegance infused with deep and genuine feelings.  Imagery is vivid, conveying her meanings incisively and clearly.

In her preface, Li Qingzhao mentions three variations of the game: *guanxima* (關西馬), *yijingma* (依經馬) and *xuanhema* (宣和馬).  Of the three she claims that she prefers *yijingma* because winning in this game depends not only on luck or chance but requires forethought and daring (see her "*Dama Fu*" and "Preface to *Dama Tujing Mingci*"). As Li Qingzhao points out in the "Preface," the chess game could only be played by two people.  The *dama* games, on the other hand, are more flexible, for any group of two to five players.  But it would be too unwieldy to follow the rules and too noisy if there are more than four or five players (Xu 2002:373).

In the "Preface" and a short Forward to her *fu* on the game, Li Qingzhao gives her reason for writing about the *dama* game.  She describes, as has been mentioned earlier, the chaotic situation earlier when the people of Jiangsu and Zhejiang provinces upon hearing the invasion by the combined forces of the Jin and the puppet king Liu Yu went hither and yon.  However, by the time she was settled in the residence of the Chen family in Jinhua city, the threat of enemy occupation diminished and she felt at ease to engage in some games of fortune with the female members of her family.[4]

In the "Preface" Li Qingzhao lists over 20 different such games. But she finds fault with those games.  Some are too common and vulgar.  Others are too fast-paced in producing winners and losers, or too restrictive on the number of players.  Yet others are unsophisticated such that no intelligence is involved.  As she loves the

---

[4] See Ma (1971:63-64) for a description of the development of war.

game of *yijingma* above all others, she decides to write a few words on each of the moves and ask someone to draw illustrations of the game so that the younger generation would learn it. Thus we also see her didactic intentions in writing about the *dama* game.

The fact that she could easily rattle off 20 some games of fortune shows her familiarity with gambling. That she was fond of gambling she readily acknowledges in the "Preface." With intelligence, she reasons, one could understand everything, and with concentration one reaches a level of expertise in comprehending all its nuances and subtleties. This was how she felt about gambling. In fact in the short Forward to her *fu* on the game, she unabashedly owns up that she excelled in gaming, to the point that she would play day and night foregoing food and sleep.

After coming to the south, she no longer had the game boards or pieces but she had not forgotten the *dama* game. Thus she prepared the book of illustrated rules. She ends the preface by saying that she wants all posterity, up to tens of thousands of generations, to know that the *dama* game was first committed to writing by her, the Yi'an Jushi. It is interesting to note that this comment about a gambling game is the only known instance in which she expresses a wish for immortality through her writings.

In the *Dama Tujing Mingci*, she records the rules and basic principles of the game. In addition, after each rule or principle, there is a commentary in the *pianti* style[5] (Jiang and Jiang 2008:228), alluding to historical events and suggesting winning strategies. Elegantly composed, her comments are ostensibly about the game, but they reveal her thoughts about public affairs of her time. As Ma (1971:68) points out, although at the time of writing the immediate crisis of yet another Jin invasion was contained, the Southern Song government was fraught with problems. Emperor Song Gao Zong and his highest ranking ministers were easily scared by news or rumours of invasion. The emperor was reluctant to act and whenever threatened by the invaders could only think of capitulation and negotiation for peace. To compound the problems, two leading military officers, Han Shizhong (韓世忠) and Liu Guangshi (劉光世) had such bad blood between them that they would not come to each other's aid in critical times of need. Li Qingzhao's comments on the *dama* game offer

---

[5] See Chapter 6 about the *pianti* style.

counsel in dire military situations but are also satirical about the turn of events that she was witnessing (Ma 1971:68).

The poetic essay, *fu*, is a time-honoured literary genre in which the writer focuses on an event or object, and then expresses her views, aspirations and feelings about it. In the "*Dama Fu*," Li Qingzhao also uses the *pianti* style. She first briefly states that hundreds of thousands of cash could be wagered in gambling. At social gatherings, the inebriated host and guests readily enter into it. Then Li Qingzhao refers to the words of Kong Fuzi (*Lun Yu* 17:22) that an idle person is good for nothing and that playing a game of chance or chess would be better than idling one's time away. In Li Qingzhao's view, *dama* is a delightful game, a cut above the run of the mill forms of gambling, and could be enjoyed by gentlewomen in their inner quarters.

In the greater part of the *fu*, Li Qingzhao launches into vivid descriptions of many famous horses in history and personages associated with horses. It is obvious that horses on the *dama* game board could be compared to numerous situations in real life. Thus by discussing the *dama* game Li Qingzhao is expressing her views about past events with which she then analyzes or criticizes the current affairs. She describes dire setbacks faced by players of the game, which are of course not unlike the experiences of the Southern Song government. This would be followed by elucidation on ways of overcoming the crises. By then, Li Qingzhao is no longer writing about a gambling game but stratagems employed in military campaigns. In this she utilizes the admonition from Lao Zi and Kong Fuzi. In line with the teaching of Lao Zi, she notes that Liu Xiu, the founder of Eastern Han dynasty, personifies the principles of weakness overcoming strength ( see *Lao Zi* Chapter 35 and other chapters) and of knowing when it would be time to stop (see *Lao Zi* Chapter 44). Liu Xiu leading a few thousand daredevils defeated the usurper Wang Mang whose army numbered millions of soldiers.

On the other hand, Li Qingzhao expostulates that there are occasions that call for righteous military expeditions led by legitimate rulers. An example would the legendary Huang Di the Yellow Emperor, revered as the progenitor of all Chinese, who defeated the enemy Chi You (蚩尤) in a decisive battle. Huang Di's victory would be in accordance with Kong Fuzi's teaching that the name and the title must befit a person honestly and legitimately. If not, the person's words would not be in accord with the truth of things (*Lun Yu* 13:3).

In all of this, Li Qingzhao is devising military campaigns for the Southern Song court to undertake in order to defeat the enemy and reunite the country.

It is evident in the "Preface" that she was fond of all forms of gambling with the boast that she would win most of the time. No doubt that was an exaggeration. However, in both the *Dama Tujing Mingci* and the "*Dama Fu*" it is also apparent that she was familiar with military stratagems. She no doubt felt keenly that as a woman she was unable to take up arms and contribute her efforts on the battlefield in defence of her country. This is revealed towards the end of the *fu* when she praises and expresses admiration for one of the most cherished heroines in Chinese history, Hua Mulan (花木蘭), of the Southern and Northern Dynasties period, who took up the challenge of defending her country. Hua Mulan disguised herself as a man, took the place of her father in military campaigns against northern invaders, and proved herself as a brave soldier and a capable officer.[6]

The *Dama* trilogy is a manifesto of Li Qingzhao's feelings about national salvation and her ambitions of recovering the lost territories from the Jin invaders. In it she shows herself to be a most gifted and versatile thinker and writer. It was unusual for any writer, let alone a female, to elevate the manual of a gambling game to the status of a literary masterpiece. It is certainly fascinating to see the same woman expound on military manoeuvres through the movements of the chess pieces on a game board. She did it all with such clarity and literary finesse. It is little wonder that readers and critics through the centuries have been unable to contain their admiration for such a writer.

It is customary every spring in China for people to spend a day outdoors to enjoy nature as it resumes its mantle of greenery. This would usually take place on or around the *Qingming* festival which comes 105 days after the Winter Solstice. This was also the custom in

---

[6] Hua Mulan lived in a period of disunity in China, referred to as the Southern and Northern Dynasties, when China was invaded by non-Han ethnic groups from the north, northeast and northwest. Short-lived dynasties were set up and some of these in the north were by non-Han peoples. Hua Mulan fought and eventually led an army during the reign of Emperor Taiwu (魏太武帝 424 – 452 CE) of the Northern Wei dynasty (Xu 2002:371), established by the Tuoba (拓跋) clan of the non-Han Xianbei tribe (鲜卑族). To this day she is revered by the Chinese for her bravery and military acumen as well as her filial piety.

Li Qingzhao's time.  By the beginning of 1135, as the threat of an actual invasion by the combined forces of the Jin and Liu Yu lessened, the refugees who had fled to Jinhua felt more relaxed.  Many of them thought of visiting the scenic spots around Jinhua on a fine spring day. Li Qingzhao's relatives and friends very likely took the opportunity to visit the area around Shuang Xi (雙溪 meaning Double Brook).  The place is listed in the *Zhejiang Tongzhi* (浙江通志, the *Historical Records of Zhejiang Province*) as one of its famous scenic sites.  It is situated south of Jinhua city (Xu 2002:142).  Apparently Li Qingzhao was urged to join them.  She declined.  Instead she wrote the following *ci*.

To the tune of "Spring in Wuling"

Wind subsides, blooms gone,
Fallen petals scenting the earth.
Too lazy to comb hair even though
It's late in the day.
Thing are the same but he is no more;
All is nothing.
Attempting to speak –
Tears flow first.
They say spring is superb on the Double Brook.
I would enjoy sailing there too,
But fear a light skiff on the Double Brook
Could not carry too much sorrow.

武陵春

風住塵香花已盡，日晚倦梳頭。物是人非事事休。欲語淚先流。聞說雙溪春尚好，也擬泛輕舟。只恐雙溪舴艋舟，載不動、許多愁。

This *ci* shows that several years after Zhao Mingcheng's death Li Qingzhao was still quite bereaved even though she was surrounded by her kinfolks.  Perhaps she had too fond a memory of outing experiences in her youth with which floating down a river or stream as a refugee in a strange place would not compare favourably.

While she appeared to have declined the invitation to picnic on the Double Brook, she did visit another famous place around Jinhua that was often frequented by tourists.  It was the Ba Yong Lou (八詠樓,

the Eight-Song Tower).  It was situated by a river.  From its upper levels the view was unobstructed for miles.  On the occasion of her visit there she wrote a *shi* in which she again expresses her deep attachment to the majestic land and her sorrow for the plight of her country.[7]

## Historical Record of Emperor Zhe Zong's Reign

The sorrow mentioned in the last quoted *ci* to the tune of *Spring in Wuling* was perhaps more than just about her lingering grief over Zhao Mingcheng's death, the loss of homeland, and the scattering of her cultural treasures.  It could have referred to vexation of another kind.  After Zhao Mingcheng's death, Li Qingzhao had on at least three occasions contact with the imperial court through documents.  While still in Jinhua she had the first such contact.  It was in the form of an edict commanding her to turn in the book *Zhe Zong Shi Lu* (哲宗實錄), that is, the *Historical Record of Emperor Zhe Zong's Reign*.  It was the culmination of a series of events.

Back in late 1132, about a month before the Chinese New Year, there was an edict from the imperial court to the family of the deceased prime minister Zhao Tingzhi in Quanzhou (泉州) in Fujian province to hand over the *Historical Record of Emperor Zhe Zong's Reign*.  This order was probably intended for Zhao Tingzhi's oldest son and Zhao Mingcheng's eldest brother Zhao Cuncheng (Huang 1974:175) but he died earlier that year in Guangdong province where he was the governor (Wang 1979:252-253; Xu 2009:487-488).  Over 30 years earlier, during the Northern Song period, the compilation of this book was ordered by Prime Minister Cai Jing after Emperor Song Hui Zong succeeded his brother Emperor Song Zhe Song and when Li Qingzhao's father-in-law Zhao Tingzhi was the deputy prime minister.  The book was not a public document but as the deputy prime minister Zhao Tingzhi kept a copy.

Emperor Song Gao Zong in 1132 wanted to collect all copies of the *Historical Record of Emperor Zhe Zong's Reign* in order to prevent any circulation of the book.  He was afraid that the book might contain criticisms of the two prominent Empress Dowagers Gao and Xiang of the Northern Song period.  Emperor Song Gao Zong knew that

---

[7] See Appendix A for the *shi* in Chinese.

these two empresses were staunch supporters of the Conservatives. Empress Dowager Gao was the mother of Emperor Song Shen Zong who, however, during his reign saw the need for reforms and appointed Wang Anshi as the prime minister to introduce changes (see Chapter 2). After Emperor Song Shen Zong's death while he was still in his 30s, his son Emperor Song Zhe Zong came to the throne. As the son was still a minor, his grandmother Empress Dowager Gao acted as the regent from 1086 to 1093 CE. During this time Emperor Song Zhe Zong had to abide by her decisions as she reinstated Conservatives in power and rolled back the reforms. The young emperor resented his grandmother's regency and policies. When he was old enough to exercise his authority as the emperor he tried to undo what the empress dowager had done. He reintroduced reforms, banished the Conservatives and reappointed Reformers to important positions. He died without an heir and was succeeded by his brother Emperor Song Hui Zong in 1100.

As the eleventh son of Emperor Song Shen Zong, Emperor Song Hui Zong had never expected to become an emperor and was not educated as a crown prince. Although Emperor Song Hui Zong was not a minor, in his first year as emperor he claimed that he was ignorant of statecraft and, therefore, asked the widow of his father Emperor Song Shen Zong, Empress Dowager Xiang (向皇太后), to act as the regent initially. The empress dowager also favoured the Conservatives and was instrumental in recalling some Conservatives back to key positions. She died in 1101 and Emperor Song Hui Zong reverted back to the reforms set out by his father and his elder brother, at least in name. While he was never serious about instituting political, economic or military changes, Emperor Song Hui Zong used Reformers such as Cai Jing and Zhao Tingzhi.

It was during Emperor Song Hui Zong's reign that the *Historical Record of Emperor Zhe Zong's Reign* was compiled and written. As it was a task undertaken by Reformers, Emperor Song Gao Zong, now the emperor of Southern Song, feared that the two Empress Dowagers would have been cast in an unfavourable light in that book while Wong Anshi the reformer would be exalted. Emperor Song Gao Zong was of the opinion that all empress dowagers of the Song dynasty were virtuous and capable, and wanted to stop circulation of the book. The decree to confiscate all copies of the *Historical Record of Emperor Zhe Zong's Reign* made it a crime to read the book let alone to keep a copy (Chen 2001:181-182).

In most families, such an important book would have been handed down from father to the eldest son. That was the thinking of Emperor Song Gao Zong's court. Hence the order to the Zhao family to turn in the *Historical Record of Emperor Zhe Zong's Reign* went to Quanzhou where the surviving sons of Zhao Tingzhi were thought to be living. But the Zhao family there did not have it. Apparently after their father Zhao Tingzhi's death, the book went to Zhao Mingcheng and in 1132 it was in Li Qingzhao's possession (Huang 1974:175-176). Consequently the emperor did not get a copy of *Historical Record of Emperor Zhe Zong's Reign* from the Zhao family in Quanzhou. Thus in 1135 the imperial edict went to Li Qingzhao to turn in the document (Ma 1971:72).

The edict that was conveyed to Li Qingzhao in Jinhua was significant in two respects (see Ma 1971:72). First, it was an official recognition that Li Qingzhao was still a widow of the Zhao family. This in turn meant that her second marriage was unequivocally over. Records from the Song dynasty do not indicate what formal process, if any, took place in the dissolution of Li Qingzhao's marriage to Zhang Ruzhou.

Second, the edict demanding the *Historical Record* gives a glimpse into Li Qingzhao's collection of art and cultural relics even after the many losses she had sustained in the years after Zhao Mingcheng's death. She described in the "Postscript" how the art and cultural treasures were robbed and stolen from her on several occasions. It was logistically necessary for her to say then that very little of the collection was left and that the remaining pieces were incomplete and of no great value. However, in presenting the *Historical Record* to the court in response to the edict revealed that at least during her sojourn in Jinhua she still retained not simply a few fragments of books and records, but complete records of great political, historical and cultural value. The *Historical Record* consisted of 100 chapters in the first volume and 94 chapters in the second.

Early in 1135, the invaders withdrew their soldiers. The emperor of Jin died in the summer (fifth month in the Chinese calendar). With the country in mourning, any attempt of the Jin to extend its territories to the south must be suspended for the time being. The puppet king Liu Yu of Greater Qi was unable to launch any military campaign without the Jin backing. Thus the pressures on the

Southern Song court eased considerably.  The people in the south were able to breathe a sigh of relief.  With other refugees Li Qingzhao returned to Hangzhou in 1135 or 1136, possibly following the move of the imperial court in case there was any further fallout related to the *Historical Record* (Chen 2001:295).

## Qin Hui

With the retreat of the Jin forces to the north, political decisions and military events in the next few years cemented the de facto division of China for about a century:  Jin in the north and Southern Song in the south.  It is difficult to say if the Southern Song government ever had a chance to rout the Jin from the north and re-establish a unified China.  But the years 1135 – 1137 CE afforded the best time for Southern Song to do so.  The more recent campaigns southward had not produced the total annihilation of Song as Jin had desired.  The puppet king Liu Yu had not proved useful or effectual.  The death of the Jin emperor and succession by a relatively inexperienced nephew created a situation of discontinuity and internal dissent.  Moreover, the Song army under capable generals such as Han Shizhong and the young Yue Fei had won some important battles, putting a check on the southward expansion of the Jin.  If there was political will at the very top to launch a northern expedition to recover the lost territories, this was the time to do it.

In 1137 Emperor Song Gao Zong sent another delegation to Jin, ostensibly to bring back the remains of Emperor Song Hui Zong who had died in exile in 1135.  But the emissary Wang Lun's (王綸) mission was to negotiate a peace settlement with Jin who seemed to be more willing to come to an agreement with Song.  After his return, Wang Lun was dispatched to Jin again later in the same year.  By that time, the Jin government had renounced and withdrawn its support of the puppet kingdom of Liu Yu and was more interested in a treaty, again signalling an inclination towards peace (Ma 1971:76).

In 1138 Hangzhou was formally named as the capital of the diminished Song empire.  It was also in 1138 that Qin Hui was reinstated as a co-prime minister by Emperor Song Gao Zong.  As the impact of Qing Kuai on the reign of Emperor Song Gao Zong was overwhelming, a brief sketch of his political role in the first three decades of Southern Song is essential to our understanding of the life of Li Qingzhao.

Qin Hui was related to Li Qingzhao by marriage if Li Qingzhao's mother was the granddaughter of Wang Zhun and daughter of Wang Gui. As discussed in Chapter 2, evidence supporting this lineage of Li Qingzhao's mother is stronger than that for her being the granddaughter of Wang Gongchen. This means that Li Qingzhao's mother and the father of Qin Hui's wife nee Wang were siblings, and that Li Qingzhao and Qin Hui's wife were cousins.

Towards the end of the Northern Song period when the capital Bianjing was attacked by the Jin, Qin Hui made a name for himself as a defender of the country and an advocate of active resistance against the invaders. After the occupation of Bianjing by the Jin army, Qin and his wife were among those taken into captivity to the Jin homeland in the northeast. While there he persuaded the retired Emperor Song Hui Zong to accept the rule of the Jin. Thus he came to the attention of the Jin leaders. Quite unexpectedly he and his wife returned to the diminished Song domains in the south in 1130, allegedly having escaped from the camp of a Jin general (Yu 1995:112; Xu 2009:481). Unknown to Emperor Song Gao Zong or the Southern Song court he was already a traitor secretly working for the Jin.

The officials who proposed a policy of military action against the Jin suspected Qin Hui's role as a traitor and a secret agent for the Jin. However, Qin Hui's arguments for letting the Jin keep the northern half of China and, therefore, co-existence of Song and Jin fell in line with Emperor Song Gao Zong's own inclinations. As early as 1131, the emperor appointed Qin Hui as a key advisor. In the autumn of that year, Qin Hui became a co-prime minister (Xu 2009:483). But his tenure in office lasted only a year. He was dismissed from that position in the autumn of 1132 mainly as a result of the advice provided by Qi Chongli who severely criticized Qin's proposal of letting Jin keep the northern half of China (Xu 2009:485). Qi Chongli's counsel was approved by the emperor.

A month later, Qi Chongli helped to obtain Li Qingzhao's release from prison. As has been mentioned earlier, given his close relationship with Emperor Song Gao Zong at that time, it would not be surprising if the emperor had heard of Li Qingzhao's plight.

Emperor Song Gao Zong essentially favoured Qin Hui's

proposal of acknowledging Jin Emperor as the overlord and letting the Jin keep the northern half of China. Early in 1137 Emperor Song Gao Zong reinstated Qin Hui as a member of the inner cabinet. A year later, Qin Hui was appointed a co-prime minister again. Then in 1140 he became the sole prime minister and remained in that powerful position till his death late in 1155 (Xu 2009:502-511).

Qin Hui had a long memory of those he perceived as having injured him. In 1153, more than 20 years after his dismissal from the high position at the instigation by Qi Chongli, he ordered the family of Xie Ji, who was the son of Zhao Mingcheng's cousin Xie Kejia and the father-in-law of Qi Chongli's daughter to surrender Qi's memorial advising the emperor to take such action.[8] By that time Qin Hui had been the sole prime minister for many years. He wanted to destroy any records that contained unfavourable remarks about him, especially one that bore the written approval of the emperor.

Throughout his years in office Qin Hui adamantly advocated the surrender and appeasement policy in dealing with the Jin which meant meeting the Jin demands for land, money and goods and thus achieving a peace by any means. As an under cover agent for the Jin, he always promoted the Jin interests by advocating coexistence with Jin and objecting to any suggestion of military action by Southern Song to recover the north. Furthermore, Qin Hui would ruthlessly put any opponents to death. Most of the officials simply acquiesced with his orders. Among the few who stood by their own principles and were not subservient to Qin Hui was Hu Songnian (Xu 2002:231-232).

In 1141 an agreement was reached between Jin and Song, and a formal treaty was signed between the two countries for a permanent peace. Despite fierce opposition by other ministers to his policy, Qin Hui negotiated the surrender of more territories in Henan and Shaanxi provinces to the Jin. In the treaty, Emperor Song Gao Zong acknowledged the Jin emperor as the overload and he the subject. He promised to pay yearly tribute of huge amounts of silk and silver to Jin. Such a peace was deeply humiliating to the Song people.

The traitor Qin Hui knew that the Song army under General Yue

---

[8] The reason for Xie Ji being in possession of the document was probably that Qi Chongli's daughter was an only child and she brought her deceased father's papers to her husband's house.

Fei had been successful in repelling the Jin and recovering some of the territories occupied by Jin and could be so again, if Emperor Song Gao Zong and the Song government had the will to fight. As the sole prime minister with supreme power, Qin Hui now convinced Emperor Song Gao Zong to kill Yue Fei as a token of gratitude to the Jin for their agreement to the terms of the treaty (Huang 1974:179). Yue Fei was executed without having been convicted of any crime. The possibility of Song recovering the northern part of their empire was lost forever.

In return, the Jin government promised to send Emperor Song Gao Zong's mother and her relatives to the south. Of all members of the imperial family, including Emperor Song Hui Zong and Emperor Song Qing Zong, taken captive by the Jin to their homeland in the northeast, she was the only one to return to Song alive. It took place in 1142. Accompanying her on her journey south were three coffins containing the alleged remains of Emperor Song Hui Zong, his empress, and Emperor Song Gao Zong's primary wife who was considered as his empress (Ma 1971:76; Huang 1974:179).

Qin Hui is one of the most villainous characters in Chinese history as he became a traitor and a secret agent of the Jin in captivity shortly after the end of the Northern Song period. He was said to be hen-pecked. According to folklore but not recorded in the official history of the Song dynasty, Qin Hui betrayed his own country at the instigation or at least with strong encouragement of his wife out of greed. Through the centuries since the Southern Song period, his wife and Li Qingzhao' cousin,[9] has been regarded as equally treacherous and responsible for the deaths of the patriotic military officers Yue Fei and his son Yue Yun (岳雲), and for the missed opportunity by the Song government to repel the Jin. Much later, in 1162, Emperor Song Gao Zong abdicated in favour of his adopted son who is known in

---

[9] The father of Mrs. Qin Hui nee Wang and Li Qingzhao's maternal uncle was Wang Zhongduan (王仲端 also known as Wang Zhongshan 王仲山). Late in 1129, as the governor of Fuzhou (撫州) he surrendered to the Jin army. So did his elder brother Wang Zhongyi (王仲嶷) in Yuanzhou (袁州) which was entrusted to him to defend (Xu 2009:475-476).

history as Emperor Song Xiao Zong (宋孝宗).[10] One of the new emperor's earliest edicts was to clear Yue Fei's name of any blemish and posthumously restore to him all titles and honours stripped from him by Qin Hui (Fang 2000:208; Bai 2002:255). The tombs of Yue Fei and Yue Yun were appropriately rebuilt. To this day, by their tombs, the statues of Mr. and Mrs. Qin Hui are in a kneeling position with their heads bent, thus for ever in acknowledgement of their guilt and in obeisance to those they murdered. Although Li Qingzhao and Qin Hui's wife nee Wang were kinswomen, their sentiments about their country were diametrically opposite. Li Qingzhao could not have picked her kinfolks and could not be held responsible in any way for their actions.

In 1142, Emperor Song Gao Zong's respected counsellor Qi Chongli who helped Li Qingzhao to gain release from prison and who engineered the removal of Qin Hui from the imperial court several years earlier died at the age of 60 *sui* (Wang 1984:369). Emperor Song Gao Zong was now complacently settled in Hangzhou and proceeded to enjoy his reign undisturbed.

## Back in Hangzhou

After her return to Hangzhou around 1135 and 1136, Li Qingzhao possibly established her own residence and began to lead a more active social life. She also re-connected with Zhao Mingcheng's family (Ma 1971:76).

As Emperor Song Gao Zong was eager to maintain the atmosphere and the reality of peace throughout the realm within the

---

[10] The founder and first emperor of the Song dynasty was Emperor Song Tai Zu (see Chapter 2). He died suddenly and under mysterious circumstances. He was succeeded not by his son but by his younger brother Emperor Song Tai Zong who was historians' prime suspect in causing the founder's death although it was said that Emperor Song Tai Zu had promised their mother that he would pass the throne to the younger brother. All the Song emperors up to and including Emperor Song Gao Zong were descended from the younger brother Emperor Song Tai Zong. As Emperor Song Gao Zong's only son died in childhood, he adopted a direct descendant of Emperor Song Tai Zu to be his son and heir. It was a gesture of returning the throne to the line of the founder of the dynasty.

context of concord with the Jin, he re-established some palace practices as if to hide the inescapable national shame. One of them he reinstituted in 1143 was the custom of having congratulatory poems written in honour of various members of the imperial family on major festivals. The verses were written by the scholar officials of the Imperial College (*hanlin xueshi* 翰林學士). As Li Qingzhao gained renown for her literary ability among the *shidafu* since her young adulthood she was asked to write some celebratory poems (*tiezi*帖子) and she did. Five of them are extant and were possibly written at the request of some palace ladies. She wrote two such poems in honour of the emperor and his Imperial Concubine Wu respectively at the beginning of spring in 1143. Later in the same year on the *Duanwu* festival (端午)[11] she composed three more in honour of the emperor, the same imperial concubine who had been recently installed as the Empress, and all the palace ladies respectively. These poems (included in Appendix A) are elegant but devoid of any deeper meaning or literary value. Nonetheless, they signify that she was at that time recognized as a *minfu*, retaining the position of the widow of the scholar-official Zhao Mingcheng. At least for a time, so it appears, Li Qingzhao moved in the highest social circles. This was the second time she had contact with the court through the written word.

Composing these celebratory poems did not end all that happily for Li Qingzhao. According to records by a Song dynasty writer, one scholar official of the Imperial College who did not like what Li Qingzhao did was Qin Zi, courtesy name Qin Chucai (秦梓, 字楚材), the elder brother of Qin Hui. As the official in charge, he dispensed some money to Li Qingzhao in recompense for her verses and dismissed her (Huang 1974:180). This possibly meant that Li

---

[11] The *Duanwu* festival occurs on the fifth day of the fifth month in the Chinese calendar. It is commonly known in the West as the Dragon Boat festival as races of dragon boats were, and still are, held all over China and beyond. The festival is to commemorate the patriotic poet of Chu kingdom, Que Yuan, who lived in the late Warring States period. Vilified by other nobles, exiled by the King Huai of Chu who would not heed Que Yuan's advice, and saddened by the sufferings of the people, he drowned himself in a river in Hunan province. People took to boats with the image of dragon painted on the brow and threw glutinous rice wrapped in bamboo leaves to prevent the mutilation of his body by the water creatures and to feed his spirit.

Qingzhao would not be called upon to render similar services in the future.   Neither would she have easy access to the imperial court, or ladies of the imperial family.

There is speculation as to why Qin Zi treated Li Qingzhao this way.   One opinion is that he detested Li Qingzhao's second marriage (Ma 1971:84).   Another view is that he possibly felt slighted as Li Qingzhao did not write any poems on his behalf which he would have submitted to the palace in his own name (Chen 1995:97).   However, an underlying reason could have well been the critical stance Li Qingzhao undoubtedly took regarding Qin Hui's perfidious machinations in bringing about a humiliating peace and, above all, in the execution of Yue Fei.   She would not have been totally silent in face of those developments even though Mrs. Qin Hui was her cousin. Her dissatisfaction with the ongoing political development would have reached the Qin brothers sooner or later.   It is said that Qin Zi was an upright gentleman who did not approve of his brother's wrongdoings and resigned from the Imperial College after a stint of only three months (Ma 1971:84).   However, in the absence of more details from the Song time, it is hard in the later centuries to determine the exact nature of the relationship and ties between the two Qin brothers.   Did Qin Hui exert pressure on his elder brother in the latter's action towards Li Qingzhao?   Did Qin Zi resent Li Qingzhao's critical attitude towards his younger brother even though he himself did not approve of Qin Hui's politics or policy?

Li Qingzhao's political attitude towards repelling the Jin was well known.   But with the peace treaty and the prevailing mood of "live and let live" now that there would be no more invasion by the Jin, Qin Hui's faction had achieved its goal.   People in the capital Hangzhou, and especially among the upper echelons, including the emperor himself, now turned their attention to settling down in Hangzhou and leading an easy and pleasurable life as they were used to in Bianjing before 1127.

Li Qingzhao seemed to avoid such company even though she was gregarious by nature and desperately nostalgic for the elegant and affluent lifestyle in Bianjing which she enjoyed in her young adulthood. The following *ci* was written most likely after the peace treaty had been signed with the Jin and, therefore, there was renewed interest in celebrating the festival of the lanterns on the first full moon, that is, the fifteenth day of the Chinese New Year.

To the tune of "Happiness of Everlasting Meeting" (*Yuanxiao*)[12]

Molten gold of the setting sun,
White jade of gathering clouds –
Where am I?
Dense mists dye the willow trees,
Mournful melody of "Plum Blossoms Falling" drifts from a flute.
Who discerns the hints of spring?
The delightful Lantern Festival,
A fine, calm day –
Could it not turn stormy in a flash?
They come on handsome horses and in grand carriages,
But I decline my drinking pals and poet friends' invitation.
Back in prosperous Bianjing on festive days,
Gentlewomen of leisure preferred the First Full Moon the most.
Splendidly adorned with green feather in their hats,
And gold filigree ornaments shimmering like the willow in snow,
They paraded their finery in rivalry.
Now the face haggard,
Fringed by wind-blown hair and frosted temples,
I dare not venture out of an evening.
Would rather hide behind the bamboo screen
Listening to laughter and chatter of passers-by.

### 永遇樂 – 元宵

落日鎔金，暮雲合璧，人在何處？染柳煙濃，吹梅笛怨，春意知幾許。元宵佳節，融和天氣，次第豈無風雨。來相召，香車寶馬，謝他酒朋詩侶。中州盛日，閨門多暇，記得偏重三五。鋪翠冠兒，撚金雪柳，簇帶爭濟楚。如今憔悴，風鬟霜鬢，怕見夜間出去。不如向，簾兒底下，聽人笑語。

Of the all the festivals, Li Qingzhao seemed to be most fond of the Lantern Festival.  It was a celebration of the first full moon in the

---

12 *Yuanxiao* is the fifteenth day of the first month in the Chinese calendar, that is, the day of full moon after the Chinese New Year.  It is usually rendered in English translations as the Lantern Festival or the First Full Moon, which are used in this *ci*.

Chinese calendar when lanterns of various colourful designs competed with the lustre of the moon. As the name suggests, the festivities took place at night. Revellers would wander through the streets admiring the lanterns, then stop at a restaurant or return home to drink wine and compose poetry. This *ci*, therefore, begins with the sunset. Li Qingzhao's comparison of the brilliance of the sinking sun to molten gold commands unending admiration by *ci* lovers generation after generation. Yet no doubt when she composed it as she watched the white clouds gathering around the golden sun she was feeling less than cheerful. The scene made her wonder where she was, intimating that she might wish to be somewhere else.

In the *ci*, the mists intensifying the greening of the willow leaves, and the tune about the plum blossoms herald the arrival of spring as Chinese New Year is commonly called the Spring Festival. Her friends call on her to join them in their merry-making. Composing poetry while drinking wine in the company of friends, to celebrate the return of spring, would normally be a very welcome pastime for her but she refuses their invitation. Could there be a reason? Perhaps her description of these friends suggests one. Those visitors are grandly attired and equipped. They are probably the officials with their families and other hangers-on; and some might even be relatives. But they gain money, power and social status because they curry favour with the traitor prime minister Qin Hui and his ilk. She would prefer her solitude to their company.

In the second part of the *ci* she recalls that celebrations of the Lantern Festival in Bianjing – where she would like to be – when ladies of the gentry were decked out in their finery and adorned with jewellery and flowers, vying with each other for being the most attractive. But that was then, and now half the country is lost and those in power have no inclination to change the situation. Thus alone she listens to the laughing voices of the party-goers.

## Final Years

The final years of Li Qingzhao's life were spent in obscurity. A few events are mentioned in extant records, mostly memoirs, of Song scholars. It could be surmised that she spent much time revising and editing her own works and the manuscript about bronze and stone inscriptions on which she and Zhao Mingcheng spent so much of their energy and time.  In any case, as a literatus she would continue to fill her days with reading, writing, art and music.


## Visit to Mi Youren

As has been indicated earlier, although the collection of art treasures had been greatly depleted in the early years after her arrival in southern China (~1128 – 1135 CE), she nevertheless retained some important and invaluable articles.  One of them was a work of calligraphy by the famous artist Mi Fei (米芾) of the Northern Song period.  She brought this piece along on a visit to his son Mi Youren (米友仁) who by that time was also a renowned calligrapher.  She asked the younger Mi to inscribe a colophon on the father's masterpiece.  Mi's colophon states that Yi'an Jushi brought the father's calligraphy and he was much moved.

Whether it was on the same occasion or on a different visit, Mi Youren wrote a colophon on another calligraphy piece by his father. In that inscription he mentions that Yi'an Jushi asked for his colophon and that it had been 40 years since he last saw his father's writing.  Mi Youren died in early 1150.  The two colophons were most likely written in the preceding year (Huang 1974:181; Zhuge 2004: 196).  Her visit to Mi Youren shows that even in old age she sought and enjoyed the company of artists and scholars.  It also illustrates her abiding love for art.  Her request for the son's colophons on the father's works of calligraphy also demonstrates Li Qingzhao's recognition of the historical nature of art and her unwavering passion for the historical continuity of art collection.


## "A Slow Sad Melody"

While Li Qingzhao amused herself with art objects and scholarly work, she was alone and lonely.  The best known of her *ci* was most likely composed in those final years.  It is a song of utter desolation and deep sadness that could not be shaken off.

## To the tune of "A Slow Sad Melody"

Seek, seek, search, search,
Cold, cold, desolate, desolate,
Grieving, grieving, wretched, wretched, forlorn, forlorn.
With days fluctuating between warm and cold,
'Tis most difficult to be at ease.
How could two or three cups of weak wine
Defend against the fierce evening wind?
Wild geese flying past
Find my heart dejected;
Yet they are old acquaintances from bygone days.
Yellow chrysanthemums scattered all over ground,
Faded, withered,
Who will pick them now?
Gazing, solitary by the window,
How to bide time till the nightfall?
A fine rain falls on the sycamore tree
In the dusk – drop (by) drop, dripping, dripping.
With all this,
How could a single word "sorrow" convey all the feelings of woe?

聲聲慢

尋尋覓覓，冷冷清清，悽悽慘慘戚戚。乍暖還寒時候，最難將息。三杯兩盞淡酒，怎敵他、晚來風急。雁過也，正傷心，却是舊時相識。滿地黃花堆積，憔悴損，如今有誰堪摘？守著窗兒，獨自怎生得黑。梧桐更兼細雨，到黃昏，點點滴滴。這次第、怎一個愁字了得！

This *ci* is undoubtedly the most widely read and the most admired piece of all Li Qingzhao's works. Its originality is staggering. As has been mentioned in Chapter 5, Li Qingzhao was fond of using repetitive words and she used them adroitly.  She begins this masterpiece with fourteen repetitive words, a feat that had never been attempted by anyone before, nor could anyone match this extraordinary skill since. Fourteen repetitive words without a break is a daring move, yet it only accentuates her misery. The seven sets of repeated words appear most naturally and find immediate resonance in the hearts and minds of readers.  Then later in the ci, Li Qingzhao uses four more repetitive words about the rain.

Since this *ci* came into public circulation, it has won critical acclaim, right from the Southern Song period, in which Li Qingzhao died, to the present.  Here are only two examples of the accolades heaped on this piece.

The Southern Song dynasty scholar Zhang Duanyi (張端義) compared the first fourteen repetitive words to the sword dance by Mistress Gongsun (公孫大娘) who was the most famous dancer in the Tang dynasty (Xu 2002:164).  She was most renowned for her sword dance.  The poet Du Fu allegedly saw it and was affected by it till his old age.  Mistress Gongsun's sword dance also enchanted the calligrapher Zhang Xu (張旭) who was so inspired by it that his cursive style of writing began to take on the life and vigour shown in her dance.  Thus one form of art often inspires and nourishes other forms (Cai 1994:139).  Zhang Duanyi in bringing up Mistress Gongsun's sword dance in his praise of Li Qingzhao was indeed anticipating that Li Qingzhao would influence generations of poets and other artists to come.

In the Qing dynasty, Xu Qiu (徐釚) likened the initial fourteen repetitive words in Li Qingzhao's *ci* to big and small pearls falling on a jade platter (Xu 2002:166).  This simile is rather unusual, but reading her words aloud and hearing them do convey the fluid beauty and a sense of delicate asymmetry, as occasioned by the falling of big and small pearls, whereas repetition of words could otherwise deliver a very dull evenness.

This *ci* to the tune of "A Slow Sad Melody" bears all the characteristics for which Li Qingzhao is best known, admired and loved.  Besides the repetition of words at the beginning of the poem, she skilfully uses four more repeated words later about the fine rain. She uses simple and easy to understand language, mixed with a few colloquial phrases.  Yet the words she chooses are anything but vulgar. They are graphic and the phrasing most original.  For example, she fascinates readers with her use of the single word "black" to denote night time which creeps in after interminable gazing and sitting alone by the window.  The word "nightfall" is used in the translation to make her meaning clear.  The blackness that arrives could also signify the end of her life.  She seems to be waiting for it but cannot pierce through the black shroud that slowly envelopes her.

Another hallmark of Li Qingzhao's *ci* is the way she infuses the objects around her with human understanding to reflect her own mood and emotions. The wild geese are old friends; they could carry letters to loved ones far away according to Chinese folklores. For Li Qingzhao they bring no missives from anyone and neither does she have anyone to whom she cares to write. Her loved ones, perhaps including her brother, were possibly all deceased by the time she wrote this *ci*. So the wild geese simply fly by even though she and they were formerly acquainted.

In this *ci*, we see familiar motifs that have appeared in other pieces by Li Qingzhao: the yellow chrysanthemums, sitting and gazing by the window, and the rain. Yet none of them is staid. Each scene and all the metaphors are used to depict her state of mind, and they appear poignantly and yet in all appearance so naturally.

In her old age, Li Qingzhao no longer seemed to heed her own instructions laid down in her essay on the theory of *ci*. In this *ci*, there is no allusion to any historical event. Nor are there references to words or works by previous poets, except perhaps the one reference to the *Book of Poetry* that will be mentioned below. This is simply her own song.

There are different opinions as to when the *ci* to the tune of "A Slow Sad Melody" was written. Most literary critics date this piece as one of her later works. According to Xu (2002:163) it could not have been written before 1147 as an anthology of *ci*, entitled *Yuefu Yaci*[13] (樂府雅詞 meaning Elegant Lyrics of *Yuefu*), was compiled by Zeng Zao (曾慥) in 1146. It contains 22 *ci* by Li Qingzhao but not this one. As this is such a masterpiece, and recognized as such since the Southern Song time, the only plausible reason for Zeng Zao not including it in his anthology would be that either it had not been composed by 1146, or had only been recently composed but not yet circulated by 1146.

Some literary critics think that this *ci* was composed early in her life. Chen Zumei in the late 20th and early 21st centuries is the foremost proponent of this view. According to Chen (1995:22-23; 68-69) there is a misprint in the current popular version of this *ci*: the character *wan* (晚 meaning evening or night) in line seven should have been *xiao* (曉 meaning the dawn). Thus the fierce wind mentioned in that line would not just be in the dark night, but from morning to night. Chen (1995:68-69) finds support for the character *xiao* as the

---

[13] See explanation of *yuefu* in the section on *ci* in Chapter 1.

original word used by Li Qingzhao in the writings of Liang Qichao (梁啓超), a most prominent man of letters in the early 20th century.

Chen, however, goes further. She alleges that with the purported description of the blustery wind throughout the day in the *ci*, Li Qingzhao is alluding to the poem "Zhong Feng" ("终風") in the *Book of Poetry*. This poem and another entitled "Shi Ren" ("碩人") are about the Duchess Zhuang Jiang of Wei (衛莊姜). She was married to Duke Zhuang of Wei (衛莊公) who reigned in 757 – 735 BCE during what is known as the Spring and Autumn period in Chinese history. Despite her great beauty the duchess was neglected and perhaps even abused by her husband who favoured his concubines. She bore no children. The stormy day in the poem "Zhong Feng" is about her plight. The people of Wei sang of her great beauty in the poem "Shi Ren" to show the Duke their sympathy for her. Chen argues that Li Qingzhao wrote this *ci* towards the end of her stay in Qingzhou when she, well past the age of 30 *sui*, had not produced an heir for Zhao Mingcheng and when Zhao Mingcheng most likely became attached to one or more other women. The *ci* was meant to remind Zhao Mingcheng of her pitiful circumstances (Chen 1995:68-69).

As Liang Qizhao describes the pain and sorrow in this *ci*, Li Qingzhao wrote every character with tears and, with her teeth clenched, swallowed each tear-soaked character (Chen 1995:68). This one is indeed the most woeful of all her *ci*. Pain and desolation engulf the writer relentlessly and totally. Even if we follow Liang Qichao's interpretation of her sorrows lasting from morning to night, it does not necessarily mean that the sorrow in this *ci* was due to Zhao Mingcheng's desertion. The pain, sorrow and loneliness expressed in the *ci* to the tune of "A Slow Sad Melody" seem to express even greater depths of despondency than that in her earlier works, if the intensity of emotions could in fact be measured or compared. Indeed the word *xiao* for the dawn would make better sense in this *ci* as it is about the composer's various experiences throughout the day, e.g., observation of the wild geese flying by, empathizing with the chrysanthemums, and watching by the window and dreading the slow passing of time till the nightfall. It is this deep pain expressed here that would be more in line with her life situation and feelings in her later years and, therefore, support the claim that this *ci* was written in her old age. The circumstances in her final years were in fact far more pitiful than her loss of Zhao Mingcheng's affection in her younger days.

In the earlier period, it must have been heart-wrenching for Li Qingzhao when Zhao Mingcheng bestowed his affection and attention on other women and she wrote several *ci* at that time about her sad situation (see Chapter 4). But even when Zhao Mingcheng was romantically involved with other women, she and Zhao Mingcheng seemed to continue scholarly work and appreciate their art collection together.  In her old age, she was left alone in many different ways.  She unquestionably carried on her literary and artistic works and found solace in them.  She edited and completed the *Jin Shi Lu* for which she named Zhao Mingcheng as the sole author although her input was considerable at various stages of production of the book. Moreover, she also compiled and edited her own writings such that shortly after her death 12 or 13 volumes of her essays, *shi*, and *ci* were in circulation.  Despite all this meaningful and interesting work, which would occupy some of her time, she was solitary and lonely without relief.

There were several layers of her solitude and most of them were not self-imposed.  Even when the rift between her and Zhao Mingcheng was most devastating to her, there was perhaps some slim hope that there would yet be rapprochement.  As things turned out, towards the end of his life, they seemed to be reconciled.  But his passing made her solitude impenetrable; it was the absolute silence of the other that only death could impose.  The fiasco of a second marriage made the situation ever worse for her:  it accentuated the immense wealth of happiness she did enjoy in the early years of her first marriage on the one hand, and led to the contempt and ostracism by many hypocritical scholars and officials on the other.  Then on top of the loss of Zhao Mingcheng as a husband and a companion in scholarly work, she also lost her home and homeland in the north, and the greater portion of her art collection through pressure from high places, theft and plunder.  Although there is no mention whether or not Zhao Mingcheng had any daughters, we know for certain that he did not have any sons.  In Chinese society at that time it was mainly the sons who were expected to provide for and look after their aged parents.  Li Qingzhao was without emotional or economic support from any adult children which was so important to a person's welfare in old age.  Lastly, she was alone because of her political views: either she was shunned by those literati who agreed with the traitor Qin

Hui's policy, or she avoided them by choice as discussed above in relation to the *ci* to the tune of "Happiness of Everlasting Meeting." It was against this backdrop that Li Qingzhao composed the *ci* to the tune of "A Slow Sad Melody."

## Wine and Inebriation

Any casual reader of Li Qingzhao's *ci* would have noticed the frequent mention of wine and getting inebriated with it. Of the forty-some *ci* that Zhuge (2004:191) considers to be genuine works by Li Qingzhao,[14] he finds that about half of them have some reference to imbibing alcoholic beverages. This is far more than that in the extant *ci* of other female writers of the Song dynasty.[15]   Moreover, Li Qingzhao describes drinking wine in a variety of contexts and ways: a light repast, golden cups of wine, drinking companions, dregs of wine, heavy drunkenness, fine wine, weak wine, signs of getting drunk, and so forth.   It is far more than sipping wine at some festivals as described by other women *ci* writers.

According Zhuge (2004:290-192), the way Li Qingzhao took to drinking was more the style of the male scholars rather than the well bred ladies of the gentry class.   There is some truth to this assertion. Li Qingzhao was concerned about political events and developments in her days as a *shidafu* would.   She wrote about them and sometimes satirized them. She was competitive and risk-taking, as shown in her writings about the gambling game *dama*.   These were largely traits exhibited by men during her life time.

Furthermore, Li Qingzhao's drinking and writing about it are in ways reminiscent of the most famous Chinese poet of all time, Li Bai

---

[14] As has been pointed out in Chapter 1, there is no agreement among literary critics on the authenticity of *ci* attributed to Li Qingzhao.

[15] According to Zhuge (2004:190-192), the well known Zhu Shuzhen mentions wine in seven out of her extant 26 *ci*, that is, 27 percent.   Drinking wine comes up in only two out of the 13 *ci* (15 percent) by Madam Wei. About 25 percent of Zhang Yuniang's (張玉娘) *ci*, that is four out of 16 *ci*, has reference to drinking.   There were 84 other known women writers of the Song dynasty whose extant works total 108 *ci*.   Of these only 30 *ci*, that is 27 percent, has anything to do with drinking alcoholic beverages.

of the Tang dynasty. He was far better known for being a prodigious drinker than for his immeasurable talent. Li Bai was not a conformist, shunning fame and riches other scholars sought in officialdom as he adopted the attitude of a free spirit. We can see traces of this attitude in Li Qingzhao's *ci* as she quite certainly was a kindred spirit of Li Bai, enjoying nature and being her own person. In the words of Song writers, she was a drifter in her old age, meaning that she did not abide by the prescribed norms for a widow's behaviour which had by the Southern Song period become very oppressive (Chao Gongwu as quoted in Wang 1979:267; see also Wang 1979:10, 319).

While it is true that she wrote and drank like a male scholar, the comparison has its limitations. In addition to those topics, issues, sentiments and styles that are typically characterized as masculine, her *ci* also give voice to other sentiments and issues that do not typically or genuinely come from a man's brush. In her *ci*, there is the inescapable pain that only a woman neglected by her husband could put into words. Then there is the sorrow of childless widowhood. A male counterpart of her day when deserted by his wife for another man or bereft by her death would be able to find consolation in other women without recrimination; in fact, he would be expected and encouraged to do so. For a similar turn of events in Li Qingzhao's life, she received derision, contempt and ostracism from at least some of the male scholars. Throughout her life she drank wine in the company of friends and relatives on festive occasions and composed poetry for amusement. But she also drank alone and imbibed stronger liquor that would intoxicate quickly and induce slumber. Ultimately she could not dull her pain with alcohol. As she puts it, how could two or three cups of wine defend against the fierce wind or overcome desolation?

## Final Events

Around the year 1150 when she was 68 *sui*, Li Qingzhao completed editing Zhao Mingcheng's manuscript *Jin Shi Lu*. The year is so fixed because in one commentary about a particular metal pot in the *Jin Shi Lu* she states that she saw the article with her own eyes in 1150. All other commentaries in the *Jin Shi Lu* appear as if written by Zhao Mingcheng. This is the only commentary that is in Li Qingzhao's voice (Huang 1974:181-182). Thus she could not have completed the editorial work before 1150. She presented a copy of the magnum opus to the imperial court as mentioned by the Song dynasty writer Hong Gua (quoted in Wang 1979:266) who, however, did not provide the exact year. The event most likely took place in 1151 or later. From extant records, this was her last known contact with the imperial court and it again involved a document.

Zhu Xi, the Southern Song philosopher, wrote in 1156 that he had read the *Jin Shi Lu* written by Zhao Mingcheng. This is the earliest recorded mention of the *Jin Shi Lu* other than by Li Qingzhao. It would mean that *Jin Shi Lu* would have been available to readers outside of Zhao Mingcheng's immediate family in or before 1156 and that Li Qingzhao would have presented the tome to the imperial court before its availability to the general public (Wang 1979:266).

The last recorded event of her life was her offer to teach the young Madam Sun and the latter's rejection of the proposition. The incident, described in Chapter 6, could have taken place between 1151 and 1159. The prevailing view among critics is that it most likely happened around 1155 as Madam Sun would not have been so indoctrinated with the neo-Confucian ideology of suppressing women's ability and talent as to comprehend its meaning and intent at an earlier age, say, at 11 *sui* in 1151 (Wang 1979:267).

Although Madam Sun refused a priceless opportunity to be tutored by Li Qingzhao, one could imagine that many others, young and old, male and female, did come to her in her old age who was a renowned scholar, *ci* composer and art connoisseur. They would have come to learn from her and to admire the art works that she still possessed.

Like other aspects or period in Li Qingzhao's life when little or nothing is known, several writers after her death out of their fondness and respect for Li Qingzhao, created touching anecdotes. A few of them, such as the Zhao Mingcheng's dream that he would marry a female *ci* composer, have been presented in earlier chapters. Perhaps out of displeasure with Madam Sun's rebuff of Li Qingzhao's kindness and generosity, writers came up with a story that has come down through the dynasties. It is about one young woman by the name of Zhang Yufu (張玉夫). However, neither the authenticity of the story nor its alleged Song dynasty author could be verified (Wang 1979:267).

The story goes something like this (see Chen 2001:207-209).

Zhang Yufu was a granddaughter of some minor official in the Northern Song dynasty. Her family moved south to Hangzhou after the Jin invaders occupied the north. Li Qingzhao taught her the classics and how to write poetry. When Zhang Yufu came of age, she was betrothed to a graduate of the Imperial University, Lin Zijian (林子建) who very soon gained an appointment in his native province Fujian. One fine summer day, he set out for a home visit and then to his new position, and Miss Zhang gave him all her savings to defray his travelling expenses. He promised her that he would return for their wedding in the autumn or at the latest in early winter. She waited through autumn and winter till the following spring but there was no word from Lin Zijian. She then decided to go to Fujian in search of her betrothed. Accompanied by a maid servant, she travelled all over the province but could not find him. It was a difficult journey and she endured many hardships. It was obvious that Lin Zijian did not keep his word and that she was abandoned. At last resting in one inn, Zhang Yufu wrote a *shi* about her tribulations and journey on the wall of her room. In the preface to the poem, she claimed that Li Qingzhao taught her to compose poetry.

The story of Zhang Yufu was also repeated by writers in the Ming and Qing dynasties. Critics generally believe that it is a touching story but fictitious. On the other hand, Li Qingzhao probably did have students in her old age, perhaps to earn some income but more likely to share her enthusiasm for learning, knowledge and poetry with a younger generation.

## Date of Death

Like many other important details of her life, the date of Li Qingzhao's death is not known. From Madam Sun's tombstone inscription composed by Lu Lou mentioned above, Madam Sun was born in 1141. The earliest she could have refused Li Qingzhao' instruction would be when she was 11 *sui*, which would be in the year 1151. Thus Li Qingzhao was still alive in 1151.

Previously some biographers put the year of her death as 1151, based on Chao Gongwu's memoirs. He was the nephew of Li Qingzhao's mentor Chao Buzhi and would probably have known about her life and death. There are three extant versions of Chao Gongwu's memoirs. They all mention that Li Qingzhao "drifted around in her old age and died" (quoted in Wang 1979:267). An identical preface appears in all three versions. However, a year (which would be the equivalent of 1151) was inserted in the preface of one version of the memoir whereas there is no year of writing in the two other versions. Nevertheless, the same preface in all three versions includes events that took place over 10 years after 1151, so the preface could not have been written in that year. The year included in that one version was added erroneously by a later editor.

Zhu Xi's reading of the Inscriptions in 1156 helps to date Li Qingzhao's death. He lived in the present province of Fujian where Zhao Mingcheng's brothers and their families eventually settled. Zhu Xi could have read the hand-written manuscript while in contact with the Zhao family. If it was a printed copy that he read, it could only be after the *Jin Shi Lu* had been presented to the Imperial Court around 1151 as mentioned above. Whether he read a printed copy or the original manuscript, it would signify that Li Qingzhao was no longer living. Printing of the *Jin Shi Lu* would not be likely until after Li Qingzhao's death. Most certainly she would not have parted with the hand-written manuscript in her life time and it could only have been passed on to Zhao Mingcheng's family members after her death (Huang 1974:183).

Given the events described above Li Qingzhao's death would have occurred sometime after 1151 and before 1156 when she was between 68 and 73 *sui*. The best estimate by the Li Qingzhao scholars is that she lived to at least 73 *sui* (Huang 1974:182-183; Wang 1979:267-269; Yu 1995:138; Xu 2009:512).

While during her life time and in the years immediately after her death, Li Qingzhao was better known for her *shi* and essays, it was her *ci* that have endeared her to generations of Chinese readers. Some of the accolades given by critics in the different dynasties have been presented in this book. The most poignant and definitive critical acclaim came from a scholar named Li Tiaoyuan of the Qing dynasty when the ideology of suppressing women's position and ability had become pervasive and almost unassailable throughout Chinese society. His praise of Li Qingzhao is lavish: she alone among all the female writers of the Song dynasty created a unique style; she could be compared to the best male *ci* writers; and every *ci* of hers was superior. "She was not only head and shoulders above the women, but simply decided to surpass the men" (quoted in Wang 1979:323).

# 8 Legacy of Li Qingzhao

As has been shown in previous chapters, even those who criticized Li Qingzhao's personal life had praise for her writings. Recognition of her literary excellence began during her life time and became more widespread after her death. At that time in the Southern Song period, the repressive ideology of restricting women to the inner quarters had already been well established and was becoming increasingly influential, seeping from the upper scholar-official circles and the gentry social class to the general populace. Yet Li Qingzhao's *ci* gained ever more critical acclaim. Through the centuries, she speaks to generations of Chinese through her *ci*, beguiling them with her incomparable use of words and pulling their heartstrings with the exquisite genuineness of her feelings. This concluding Chapter is an open letter in her own voice to the author of the book.

## Her Legacy:  An Open Letter from Li Qingzhao

Djao Wei, Greetings!

It is gratifying and humbling to have a book written in a foreign language about me over so many centuries after my death. There are undoubtedly some details in this book that do not correspond to the actual events. But there are no gross inaccuracies or fabrications, and I myself have forgotten some details. Humility was not my strong suit but I know enough modesty to appreciate accolades. I could do no less than responding to the care with which you wrote the book by sharing with you and all readers how I see my life. In the process I might suggest a few answers to the question you pose at the beginning of your book:  Why should anyone read about Li Qingzhao in the 21st century?

## My Character

In all modesty I acknowledge that I was endowed with talents. I was quick in learning and had a prodigious memory. It was easy for me to play music, paint pictures, excel in calligraphy, write essays and compose poetry, and do all of these things exceedingly well. However, I did not have any special talents that other people did not possess either, granted perhaps I had them to a greater extent. What made me a very unique case was the set of circumstances surrounding my birth that nurtured my abilities. I was born of parents who valued learning, writing and the arts. Although I lost my mother fairly early in life, my stepmother was also fond of learning and writing. Above all, I was fortunate to have a father who in the best Confucian tradition emphasized learning and was an excellent teacher. When I was growing up it was not uncommon for daughters of the gentry to be educated and accomplished. But my father from my earliest memory encouraged me to explore and think on my own, and then to express concisely what I found or thought. Little wonder then that I was never reluctant to say or write how I saw or felt about things.

Given my upbringing, the comfortable home and the learned environment my parents provided for my brother and me, I enjoyed privileges that those who were more gifted than I did not have. We took the classics and history, painting and poetry, calligraphy and music, *weiqi* and all the arts for granted. They were as natural to us as the air we breathed. Posterity perhaps should not praise me for what I accomplished, but should certainly have denounced me shamelessly if I did not. I could not have done any less.

My education was rigorous and I must admit that I always worked hard. I excelled in many areas because I utilized my talents and my time. If I was exemplary in any way it was that I was courageous – or foolhardy in the eyes of those wiser in the ways of the world – to write, say and do the things that I did. Dying as I did in lonely and much more straitened circumstances than those in which I grew up, I nevertheless could in all honesty say that I did not waste my time and that I kept my integrity.

You have described quite correctly that I was playful and wilful in life. I loved life and lived to the fullest although the poetry composed in later life, especially after moving south, did not contain much joy. But if I had any less zest for life I could not have endured for so long. I was bereft of the people I loved, of the home I cherished, of the art and cultural relics my husband Zhao Mingcheng and I treasured, and in my final years deserted by many acquaintances who judged people by their material wealth or by some hypocritical ethical code. As you know, you in the 21$^{st}$ century are still debating whether or not I remarried. It was not a shame to remarry. My regret was that in my second marriage I was united with a scoundrel. In the Southern Song period, the oppressive ideology forbidding widows to remarry as proposed by the neo-Confucian ideologues was already getting widespread support and acceptance among the scholars.    Some ridiculed me. But I endured, trying to overcome difficulties till old age because life as given to us by our parents was precious.

It was quite certainly this tenacious embrace of life, wrapped in the elegance of speech shown in my poetry that attracted Zhao Mingcheng to me.  I was not afraid to make decisions. I was a doer and took care of things.  Above all, I saw the value of his hobby of collecting inscriptions on stones and metal vessels. When we first got married, it was only a hobby and a costly one.  Again, in all modesty, with my support and assistance he was able to make it the central activity of his life for which he is now immortalized. We had such fun together!  As I put it in the autobiographical essay "Postscript," we wished that we would grow old together enjoying the charmed life of scholars and working on the *Jin Shi Lu* . But that was not to be our lot.


## The Collection

No material things quite consumed us as the collection we amassed. From early childhood I delighted in objects of beauty as I tried to create them myself.  Working with Zhao Mingcheng I learned to be a steward in authenticating and compiling texts, and thus verifying or refuting historical events.  It was meaningful scholarship.  We also came into contact if not possession of many exquisite art works. Each piece invariably made me gasp as I saw it for the first time. As I held each object in my hands or with my gaze, I would have the unmistakable sensation that through it I was connected with the ancients of thousands of years ago.

I did not exaggerate that we were poor in the early years of our marriage when Zhao Mingcheng was still a university student.  Of course, given our family background, it was a temporary poverty as are many college students in the 21$^{st}$ century.  We came into some money from the Zhao family land holdings while we lived in seclusion in Qingzhou. In the "Postscript" I was truthful in saying that we were frugal. We economized willingly and wholeheartedly in order to enrich our collection.

While the scholarly work on the items in the collection continued to engross and fascinate us, over time imperceptibly the possession and retention of those objects themselves came to dominate our attention. As I mentioned a couple of times in the "Postscript," watching over the collection and enjoying the articles were an addiction. The tumultuous time we lived in made us feel how insecure our lives were, let alone material objects outside of us. The fear of losing them consumed me. While I did everything to keep them, I always held to the notion that we were safeguarding an ancient legacy of the entire Chinese people. Perhaps that was self-deception. But it gratifies me to know that some of the cultural treasures and art works that went into the imperial collection of Southern Song court are still held in the Palace Museum collections in Beijing or Taibei.

In the end, except for a couple of pieces, I lost them all. Yet I held each piece of art and cultural relic in my heart. No bandits or soldiers, no thieves or conniving officials could take them away from me. Thus I could echo the wisdom of Lao Zi by saying that as there is "having," there is always "not having." I certainly was less worried when there was nothing to worry about. But the sense of history that became solidified through having handled those ancient objects was something that I could not have learned from the books alone. By admiring art works, bronze vessels and stone inscriptions with my different senses, I learned the deeper meaning of history. Knowing that I was part of history enabled me to live more fully as a person. Perhaps I never reached the state of "not having" although the words of Lao Zi were my constant companion in my final years.

I understand that some billionaires have been acquiring art works in your time. I wonder whether they understand the worth of art besides the price. Do they understand the meaning of the art they have locked up in their vaults? Do they develop a sense of history through the art they possess? Do the art works they acquire teach them how precious all human existence is and that it hangs by a thin thread in the universe? Perhaps my life in the Song dynasty could teach the art collectors of the 21st century something yet.

In my life, I also savoured the key tenet in the *ru* tradition, the other philosophical foundation in the Chinese legacy that is traced to Kong Fuzi. Materials possessions could be gained and lost. The only true treasure besides life lies in the web of human relationships.

The ancient philosophers, Kong Fuzi and Meng Zi in the *ru* tradition and Lao Zi and Zhuang Zi in the daoist tradition, all influenced my thinking and the way I conducted my life. That said, I could never subscribe to some of the interpretations of their philosophy offered by the scholars of my day. Many of them, like the Cheng brothers and then later Zhu Xi, bastardized the teachings of Kong Fuzi and Meng Zi and devised their own ideology in order to prop up the ruler of the country and the patriarch of the family by suppressing and oppressing women. Some of the ceremonies or customs the later *ru* ideologues promoted were meaningless. I was too much a free spirit to be bound by such nonsense. But women in the later dynasties often had no choice. The beautiful and talented character Lin Daiyu (林黛玉) in Cao Xueqin's wonderful novel *Dream of the Red Mansions* with her love of learning and ability to write rather reminds me of myself; I tend to think that there was a real person who was Cao's model. But due to the pervasive influence of the oppressive neo-Confucian ideology by the Qing dynasty, the fictional character or a real woman with Lin Daiyu's ability and sensibility could not have been able to do in that later age what I was able to accomplish in the earlier historical period.

The ideas of Lao Zi and Zhuang Zi were profound and in my solitude I sometimes mused over them. In their own days, their ideas were not even called daoist. Their philosophy came to be known as daoist philosophy much later, but it was very different from what had come to be known as the daoist religion. I could only see faint traces of Masters Lao and Zhuang in the preaching of the daoist priests or religious masters. Emperor Song Hui Zong was such a devotee of the daoist religion. As he became increasingly immersed in a host of myths and nonsensical practices he assuredly hastened the extinction of the Northern Song dynasty which caused so much grief to all the people I knew and loved. No, I had no use for the daoist religion. Neither did I follow the Buddhist religion. Although in my writings I on some occasions alluded to deities and mythical places prominent in the daoist and Buddhist religions as they fed my imagination, I could never be their adherent.

Other thinkers like Han Feizi and Mo Zi were all fascinating to me. But I could not subscribe to any one tradition of thought. I could not be constrained to any one school.

In my long life I certainly met some mean-spirited *xiaoren*. Some of them tried to use a philosophical or religious tradition, or their high positions, to intimidate me or to rationalize their actions for their dishonesty and greed. But I was also fortunate to have many stoically loyal friends. They offered advice and assistance when I was in difficult straits. With others I spent much time composing poetry or discussing current events. Some of them, like my *jiemei* in Qingzhou, I never saw again after moving south. How I missed them!

Of course my closest friend and confidante was my husband Zhao Mingcheng. We spent so much delightful time together admiring a scroll of painting or calligraphy, getting excited over a new found stone or vessel inscription, or playing music. How we cherished our collection of art and antiques! Those were the good times. But then those we loved the most could hurt us the most. The women he flirted with caused me pain. His untimely death ripped me apart and almost brought me to an early end. It was a good thing that I could bring my tears and some laughter into the verses and essays I wrote. This leads to my greatest passion: writing.

## *Ci* and Other Writings

It was true that during my life time and for a few decades afterwards, I was best known among the scholars for my *shi* and essays. It was so mostly because I made sharp and cogent criticisms of the regime in my *shi* and essays. Some critics in the later centuries thought that I did not go far enough in my objections to Emperor Song Gao Zong's policy of appeasement and capitulation to the Jin. Many scholars in my own time on the other hand praised me, as some still do today, for voicing the dissatisfaction with the policy felt by the populace. They thought that I was brave in writing those verses in the years immediately after moving south.

As you have pointed out, I was not slow with words or with expressing my views. Although I often chafed under the yoke of being a woman and, therefore, must be excluded from officialdom and participation in politics, in the case of criticizing Emperor Song Gao Zong's policy I actually had the advantage as a woman over the male scholars.  Zhao Mingcheng, his brothers, his cousins and other relations, and my own brother were all officials and some of them in fairly senior positions.  Given the intrigues and internecine conflicts within the court, they could not express the views as I did without losing their positions or even their heads.  I was able to write with impunity or without causing too much embarrassment or vexation to Zhao Mingcheng for another reason.  I must point out that although the cowardly Emperor Song Gao Zong sought peace and security from the Jin instead of resisting them, he was not entirely incorrigible. While he did not tolerate critics and opponents to his policy within his government, he did not ban freedom of expression totally, nor did he institute vast networks of spies who arrested scholars on the flimsiest evidence of sedition in their writings.  These things of course happened later in the Ming and Qing dynasties.  The rulers of the Song dynasty, even in the Southern Song period, by and large respected scholarship and honoured scholars.  My relatives and I were very fortunate in this regard.

Even in my lifetime when the scholars admired my *shi* and essays, my *ci* was gaining increasing recognition, especially among those not in official positions.  People loved my *ci* because I spoke from the heart.  With my knowledge of history, the classics and a large body of literature, I was able to allude to antecedents and incorporate words or phrases from literary giants in my *ci* as well as in my essays and *shi*.  I wrote in the essay on the theory of *ci* that allusions and using borrowed words were fundamental requirements in composing *ci*.  But in my mature years I only used them if they added to the musicality or the expressiveness of the *ci*.  What made my *ci* so poignantly refreshing and so greatly loved by the readers was the way I used simple, everyday language.  As you have pointed out in the book, I had a knack of turning a phrase and I did that with simplicity and genuine feelings.  In that regard, the use of repetitive words or phrases, for which I have been so widely praised even to this day, was quite plainly an imitation of how people spoke and still speak today. Haven't you noticed how most people repeat words or phrases in their everyday language?

After moving south, as you have pointed out in the book, my *ci* was more than expressing my personal feelings, a stipulation about the nature of *ci* that I had earlier put in the essay on *ci*.  In the south the *ci* became politicized because the national disaster I was living through was part of my emotions, part of me. I was unable to separate "public problems and private troubles" into neat compartments. I am glad that you learned something from the American sociologist C. Wright Mills who coined the phrase in connecting individual biographies with the history of a society. Knowledge is without borders and people should learn from whatever sources they encounter in their lifetime. I never ceased to learn even in poverty in my old age.

In the final analysis, I wrote because I loved the use of language. As a sociologist you would know that oral language is a cultural universal, something that is found in all human cultures. I understand that scientists are trying to decode "languages" used by other animals such as dolphins, etc. But to the best of their knowledge, it is only human beings who have developed incredibly complex systems of communication known as language. If you listen to the different languages, you would find how musical every language is. I only knew Chinese and of course to me it was superbly beautiful. Then when it was rendered into a song, as the *ci* were still sung in my days, it was simply enchanting. It was always a moving experience as I wrote each *ci*.

What made composing *ci* even more exhilarating for me was the written Chinese language. Each character was a picture of something or a representation of an idea. As I wrote each character, I was putting the sound of a word into a visual image. Furthermore, the use of the gentle yet strong brush on the soft paper made the process so much more tactile. People in your 21$^{st}$ century are always dealing in multimedia presentations. Writing *ci* was every bit an experience in multimedia to me.

I think that Chinese is the only pictorial script that is still in use in the world today. I feel heartened that readers are still able to read my *ci* in the original language. On the other hand, if I were living in your day and age, I would most certainly want to learn as many other languages as I could so that I might appreciate the literary works produced in those languages.

So there is another book about me. I think that the book will introduce an old woman like me to the English reading public who do not read Chinese so that more people could enjoy my *ci* and other writings. In the larger picture, I always had a strong sense of history and the place of individuals, including myself, in it. If this book could refresh or add to their knowledge of Chinese women, literature and civilization, or if it could dispel some misconceptions of Chinese women, history and civilization, and if it could strengthen the appreciation of all human literary legacy and human history, then I would have illumined with clarity as my name dictated and I would not have walked on this planet in vain 900 years ago.

With the folly of youth, I compared myself to the flower above all flowers, the plum blossom. I am not ashamed to have done so as throughout my life I tried my best to live up to the ideals of integrity and endurance symbolized by this small but exquisite flower. You, all other women and all Chinese should do no less.

With best wishes for good health,

Yi'an Jushi

# Appendix A

# Selected Writings of Li Qingzhao

## *Ci* 詞

### <浣溪沙> - 閨情
### Washing Brook Sand – Sentiments from the Boudoir (Page 56)

繡面芙蓉一笑開，斜飛寶鴨襯香腮。眼波纔動被人猜。一面風情深有韻，半牋嬌恨寄幽懷。月移花影約重來。

### <多麗> – 詠白菊 Many Beauties – in Praise of White Chrysanthemums (Page 79)

小樓寒，夜長簾幕低垂，恨蕭蕭，無情風雨，夜來揉損瓊肌。也不似、貴妃醉臉，也不似、孫壽愁眉。韓令偷香，徐娘傅粉，莫將比擬未新奇。細看取，屈平陶令，風韻正相宜。微風起，清芬醞藉，不減荼蘼。漸秋闌、雪清玉瘦，向人無限依依。似愁凝、漢皋解佩；似淚灑、紈扇題詩。明月清風，濃煙暗雨，天教憔悴度芳姿。縱愛惜，不知從此，留得幾多時。人情好，何須更憶，澤畔東籬？

## *Shi* 詩

### 上樞密韓公工部尚書胡公 並序
### Two Poems in Honour of Envoys to Jin Lord Hand Lord Hu (Pages 178-81)

紹興癸丑五月，樞密韓公、工部尚書胡公使虜，通兩宮也。有易安室者，父祖皆出韓公門下，今家世淪替，子姓寒微，不敢望公之車塵。又貧病，但神明未衰落，見此大號令，不能忘言，作古、律詩各一章，以寄區區之意，以待採詩者云。

三年夏六月，天子視朝久。凝旒望南雲，垂依思北狩。如聞帝若曰，岳牧與群后。賢寧無半千？運已遇陽九。勿勒燕然銘，勿種金城柳。豈無純孝臣，識此霜露悲？何必羹捨肉，便可車載脂。土地非所惜，玉帛如塵泥。誰當可將命？幣厚辭益卑。四岳僉曰俞，臣下帝所知。中朝第一人，春官有昌黎。身為百夫特，行足萬人師。嘉祐與建中，為政有皋夔。匈奴畏王商，吐蕃尊子儀。夷狄已破膽，將命公所宜。公拜手稽首，受命白玉墀。曰臣敢辭難，此亦何等時！家人安足謀，妻子不必辭。願奉天地靈，願奉宗廟威。徑持紫泥詔，直入黃龍城。單于定稽顙，侍子當來迎。仁君方恃信，狂生休請纓。或取犬馬血，與結天日盟。

胡公清德人所難，謀同德協必志安。脫衣已被漢恩暖，離歌不道易水寒。
皇天久陰后土淫，雨勢未回風勢急。車聲轔轔馬蕭蕭，壯士懦夫俱感泣。
閭閻嫠婦亦何知，瀝血投書干記室。夷虜從來性虎狼，不虞預備庸何傷。
衰甲昔時聞楚幕，乘城前日記平涼。葵丘踐土非苴城，勿輕談士棄儒生。
露布詞成馬猶倚，崤函關出雞未鳴。
巧匠何曾棄樗櫟，芻蕘之言或有益。不乞隋珠與和壁，只乞鄉關新消息。
靈光雖在應蕭蕭，草中翁仲今何若？遺氓豈尚種桑麻，殘虜如聞保城郭。
嫠家父祖生齊魯，位下名高人比數。當年稷下縱談時，猶記人揮汗成雨。
子孫南渡今幾年，飄流遂與流人伍。欲將血淚寄山河，去灑東山一抔土。

## 題八詠樓　On Eight-Song Tower (Page 191)

千古風流八詠樓，江山留與後人愁。水通南國三千里，氣壓江誠十四州。

## 帖子　Celebratory Poems (Page 199)

### 皇帝閣春帖子
莫進黃金簟，新除玉局床。春風送庭燎，不復用沉香。

### 貴妃閣春帖子
金環半后禮，鉤弋比昭陽。春生百子帳，喜入萬年觴。

### 皇帝閣端午帖子
日月堯天大，璿璣舜曆長。側聞行殿帳，多集上書囊。

### 皇后閣端午帖子
意帖初宜夏，金駒已過蠶。至尊千萬壽，行見百斯男。

### 夫人閣端午帖子
三宮催解稯，妝罷未天明。便面天題字，歌頭御賜名。

## Couplet mocking Zhang Jiucheng (Page 156)
露花倒影柳三變，桂子飄香張九成。

# Essays 文

## 詞論 *Ci* Lun (Pages 92-95)

樂府聲詩並著，最盛於唐。開元天寶間，有李八郎者，能歌擅天下。時新及第進士開宴曲江，榜中一名士先召李，使易服隱名姓，衣冠故敝，精神慘沮，與同之宴所，曰：表弟願與座末。眾皆不顧。既酒行樂作，歌者進。時曹元謙、念奴為冠，歌罷，眾皆咨嗟稱賞。名士忽指李曰：請表弟歌。眾皆晒，或有怒者。及轉喉發聲，歌一曲，眾皆泣下，羅拜，曰：此李八郎也。自後鄭、衛之聲日熾，流靡之變日煩，已有<菩薩蠻>、<春光好>、<莎雞子>、<更漏子>、<浣溪沙>、<夢江南>、<漁父>等詞，不可遍舉。五代干戈，四海瓜分豆剖，斯文道熄，獨江南李氏君臣尚文雅，故有 "小樓吹徹玉笙寒"、"吹皺一池春水" 之詞。語雖奇甚，所謂 "亡國之音哀以思" 也。

逮至本朝，禮樂文武大備，又涵養百餘年，始有柳屯田永者，變舊聲，作新聲，出<樂章集>，大得聲於世，雖協音律，而詞語塵下。又有張子野、宋子京兄弟，沈唐、元絳、晁次膺輩繼出，雖時時有妙語，而破碎何足名家。至晏元獻、歐陽永叔、蘇子瞻，學際天人，作為小歌詞，直如酌蠡水於大海，然皆句讀不葺之詩爾，又往往不協音律者。何耶？蓋詩文分平側，而歌詞分五音，又分五聲，又分六律，又分清濁輕重。且如近世所謂<聲聲慢>、<雨中花>、<喜遷鶯>，既押平聲韻，又押入聲韻；<玉樓春>本押平聲韻，又押上去聲韻，又押入聲韻。本押仄聲韻，如押上聲則協，如押入聲，則不可歌矣。王介甫、曾子固，文章似西漢，若作一小歌詞，則人必絕倒，不可讀也。乃知別是一家，知之者少。後晏叔原、賀方回、秦少游、黃魯直出，始能知之。又晏苦無鋪敘，賀苦少典重。秦即專主情致，而少故實，譬如貧家美女，雖極妍麗豐逸，而終乏富貴態。黃即尚故實，而多疵病，譬如良玉有瑕，價自減半矣。

## 祭趙湖州文(斷句) In Memory of Zhao Huzhou (Fragment) (Page 137)

白日正中，嘆龐翁之機捷；堅城自墮，憐杞婦之悲深。

## 投翰林學士綦崈禮啓 Letter to Hanlin Scholar Qi Chongli (Page 158)

清照啓：素習義方，粗明詩禮。近因疾病，欲至膏肓，牛蟻不分，灰釘已具。嘗藥雖存弱弟，應門惟有老兵。既爾蒼皇，因成造次。信彼如簧之舌，惑茲似錦之言。弟既可欺，持官文書來輒信；身幾欲死，非玉鏡架亦安知。僶俛難言，優柔莫決。呻吟未定，強以同歸；視聽才分，實難共處。忍以桑榆之晚節，配茲駔儈之下才。

身既懷臭之可嫌，惟求脫去；彼素抱璧之將往，決欲殺之。遂肆侵凌，日加毆擊。可念劉伶之肋，難勝石勒之拳。局天扣地，敢效談娘之善訴；升堂入室，素非李赤之甘心。外援難求，自陳何害？豈期末事，乃得上聞。取自宸衷，付之廷尉。被桎梏而置對，同凶醜以陳詞。豈惟賈生羞絳灌為伍，何啻老子與韓非同傳。但祈脫死，莫望賞金。友凶橫者十旬，蓋非天降；居囹圄者九日，豈是人為！抵雀捐金，利當安往？將頭碎璧，失固可知。實自謬愚，分知獄市。此蓋伏遇內翰承旨，搢紳望族，冠蓋清流，日下無雙，人間第一。奉天克復，本原陸贄之詞；淮蔡底平，實以會昌之詔。哀憐無告，雖未解驂；感戴鴻恩，如真出己。故茲白首，得免丹書。清照敢不省過知慚，捫心識媿、責全責智，已難逃萬世之譏；敗德敗名，何以見中朝之士！雖南山之竹，豈能窮多口之談？惟智者之言，可以止無根之謗。

高鵬尺鷃，本異升沉；火鼠冰蠶，難同嗜好。達人共悉，童子皆知。願賜品題，與加湔洗。誓當布衣蔬食，温故知新。再見江山，依舊一瓶一鉢；重歸畎畝，更須三沐三薰。忝在葭莩，敢茲塵瀆。

## 金石錄後序 Postscript to *Jin Shi Lu*

右<金石錄>三十卷者何？趙侯德父所著書也。取上自三代，下迄五季，鐘、鼎、甗、鬲、盤、匜、尊、敦之款識，豐碑大碣、顯人晦士之事蹟，凡見於金石刻者二千卷，皆是正譌謬，去取褒貶，上足以合聖人之道，下足以訂史氏之失者皆載之，可謂多矣。嗚呼！自王涯、元載之禍，書畫與胡椒無異；長輿、元凱之病，錢癖與傳癖何殊。名雖不同，其惑一也。

余建中辛巳，始歸趙氏。時先君作禮部員外郎，丞相時作吏部侍郎，侯年二十一，在太學作學生。趙、李寒族，素貧儉。每朔望謁告出，質依取半千錢，步入相國寺，市碑文果實歸，相對展玩咀嚼，自謂葛天氏之民也。後二年，出仕宦，便有飯疏衣練，窮遐方絕域，盡天下古文奇字之志，日就月將，漸益堆積。丞相居政府，親舊或在館閣，多有亡詩、逸史、魯壁、汲冢所未見之書，遂盡力傳寫，浸覺有味，不能自己。後或見古今名人書畫、三代奇器，亦復脫衣市易。嘗記崇寧間，有人持徐熙<牡丹圖>，求錢二十萬。當時雖貴家子弟，求二十萬錢，豈易得邪？留信宿，計無所出而還之。夫婦相向惋悵者數日。

後屏居鄉里十年，仰取俯拾，衣食有餘。連守兩郡，竭其俸入，以事鉛槧。每獲一書，即同共校勘，整集籤題。得書畫彝鼎，亦摩玩舒卷，指摘疵病，夜盡一燭為率。故能紙札精緻，字畫完整，冠諸收書家。余性偶強記，每飯罷，坐歸來堂烹茶，指堆積書史，言某事在某書某卷、第幾頁第幾行，以中否角勝負，為飲茶先後。中即舉杯大笑，至茶傾覆懷中，反不得飲而起。甘心老是鄉矣，雖處憂患貧窮，而志不屈。收書既成，歸來堂起書庫大櫥，簿甲乙，置書冊。如要講讀，即請鑰上簿，關出卷帙。或少損污，必懲責揩完塗改，不復向時之坦夷也。是欲求適意而反取懰慄。余性不耐，始謀食去重肉，衣去重采，首無明珠翡翠之飾，室無塗金刺繡之具。遇書史百家字不刓闕、本不譌謬者，輒市之儲作副本。自來家傳<周易>、<左氏傳>，故兩家者流，文字最備。於是几案羅列，枕席枕藉，意會心謀，目往神授，樂在聲色狗馬之上。

至靖康丙午歲，侯守淄川，聞金人犯京師，四顧茫然，盈箱溢篋，且戀戀，且悵悵，知其必不為己物矣。建炎丁未春三日，奔太夫人喪南來，既長物不能盡載，乃先去書之重大印本者，又去畫之多幅者，又去古器之無款識者，後又去書之監本者，畫之平常者，器之重大者，凡屢減去，尚載書十五車。至東海，連艫渡淮，又渡江，至建康。青州故第尚鎖書冊什物，用屋十餘間，期明年春再具舟載之。十二月，金人陷青州，凡所謂十餘屋者，已皆為煨燼矣。

建炎戊申秋九月，侯起復知建康府。己酉春三月罷，具舟上蕪湖，入姑孰，將卜居贛水上。夏五月、至池陽，被旨知湖州，過闕上殿。遂駐家池陽，獨赴召。六月十三日，始負擔，捨舟坐岸上，葛衣岸巾，精神如虎，目光爛爛射人，望舟中告別。余意甚惡，呼曰：“如傳聞城中緩急，奈何？”戟手遙應曰：“從眾。必不得已，先棄輜重，次衣被，次書冊卷軸，次古器；獨所謂宗器者，可自負抱，與身俱存亡，勿忘也。”遂馳馬去。途中奔馳，冒大暑，感疾。至行在，病痁。七月末，書報臥病。余驚怛，念侯性素急，奈何！病痁或熱，必服寒藥，疾可憂。遂解舟下，一日夜行三百里。比至，果大服柴胡、黃芩藥，瘧且痢，病危在膏肓。余悲泣，倉皇不忍問後事。八月十八日，遂不起。取筆作詩，絕筆而終，殊無分香賣履之意。

葬畢，余無所之。朝廷已分遣六宮，又傳江當禁渡。時猶有書二萬卷，金石刻二千卷，器皿、茵褥，可待百客，他長物稱是。余又大病，僅存喘息。事勢日迫，念侯有妹婿任兵部侍郎，從衛在洪州，遂遣二故吏，先部送行李往投之。冬十二月，金人陷洪州，遂盡委棄。所謂連艫渡江之書，又散為雲煙矣。獨餘少輕小卷軸書帖，寫本李、杜、韓、柳集，<世說>，<鹽鐵論>，漢、唐石刻副本數十軸，三代鼎鼐十數事，南唐寫本書數篋，偶病中把玩，搬在臥內者，巋然獨存。

上江既不可往，又虜勢叵側，有弟迒任勅局刪定官，遂往依之。到臺，臺守已遁。之剡，出睦，又棄衣被，走黃巖，雇舟入海，奔行朝，時駐蹕章安。從御舟海道之溫，又之越。庚戌十二月，放散百官，遂之衢。紹興辛亥春三月，復赴越。壬子，又赴杭。先侯疾亟時，有張飛卿學士，攜玉壺過視侯，便攜去，其實珉也。不知何人傳道，遂妄言有頒金之語，或傳亦有密論列者。余大惶怖，不敢言，亦不敢遂已，盡將家中所有銅器等物，欲赴外廷投進。到越，已移幸四明。不敢留家中，並寫本書寄剡。後官軍收叛卒，取去，聞盡入故李將軍家。所謂巋然獨存者，無慮十去五六矣。惟有書畫硯墨可五七簏，更不忍置他所，常在臥榻下，手自開闔。在會稽，卜居土民鍾氏舍，忽一夕，穴壁負五簏去。余悲慟不得活，重立賞收贖。後二日，鄰人鍾復皓出十八軸求賞，故知其盜不遠矣。萬計求之，其餘遂牢不可出。今知盡為吳說運使賤價得之。所謂歸然獨存者，乃十去其七八。所有一二殘零不成部帙書冊，三數種平平書帖，猶愛惜如護頭且，何愚也邪！

今日忽閱此書，如見故人。因憶侯在東萊靜治堂，裝卷初就，芸籤縹帶，束十卷作一帙。每日晚吏散，輒校勘二卷，跋題一卷。此二千卷，有題跋者五百二卷耳。今手澤如新，而墓木已拱，悲夫！昔蕭繹江陵陷沒，不惜國亡而毀裂書畫；楊廣江都傾覆，不悲身死而復取圖書。豈人性之所著，生死不能忘歟？或者天意以余菲薄，不足以享此尤物邪？抑亦死者有知，猶斤斤愛惜，不肯留人間邪？何得之艱而失之易也！

嗚呼！余自少陸機作賦之二年，至過蘧瑗知非之兩歲，三十四年之間，憂患得失，何其多也！然有有必有無，有聚必有散，乃理之常。人亡弓，人得之，又胡足道。所以區區記其終始者，亦欲為後世好古博雅者之戒云。紹興四年玄黓歲壯月朔甲寅，易安室題。

## 打馬圖經序 Preface to *Dama Tujing* (Pages 186-190)

慧則通，通即無所不達；專則精，精即無所不妙。故庖丁之解牛，郢人之運斤，師曠之聽，離婁之視，大至於堯舜之仁，桀紂之惡，小至於擲豆起蠅，巾角拂棋，皆臻至理者何？妙而已。後世之人，不惟學聖人之道不到聖處，雖嬉戲之事，亦不得其依稀彷彿而遂止者多矣。夫博者，無他，爭先術耳，故專者能之。予性喜博，凡所謂博者皆耽之，晝夜每忘寢食。且平生多寡未嘗不進者何？精而已。

自南渡來，流離遷徙，盡散博具，故罕為之，然實未嘗忘於胸中也。今年冬十月朔，聞淮上警報，江浙之人，自東走西，自南走北，居山林者謀入城市，居城市者謀入山林，旁午絡繹，莫不失所。易安居士亦自臨安泝流，涉嚴灘之險，抵金華，卜居陳氏第。乍釋舟楫而見軒窗，意頗適然。更長燭明，奈此良夜何。於是博弈之事講矣。

且長行、葉子、博塞、彈棋，近世無傳。若打揭、大小豬窩、族鬼、胡畫、數倉、賭快之類，皆鄙俚不經見。藏酒、摴蒱、雙蹙融，近漸廢絕。選仙、加減、插關火，質魯任命，無所施人智巧。大小象戲、弈棋，又惟可容二人。獨采選、打馬，特為閨房雅戲。嘗恨采選叢繁，勞於檢閱，故能通者少，難遇勍敵；打馬簡要，而苦無文采。

按打馬世有二種：一種一將十馬者，謂之 "關西馬"；一種無將二十馬者，謂之 "依經馬"。流行既久，各有圖經凡列可考；行移賞罰，互有同異。又宣和間人取二種馬，參雜加減，大約交加僥倖，古意盡矣。所謂 "宣和馬"者是也。予獨愛 "依經馬"，因取其賞罰互度，每事作數語，隨事附見，使兒輩圖之。不獨施之博徒，實足貽諸好事，使千萬世後知命辭打馬，始自易安居士也。時紹興四年十一月二十四日，易安室序。

## 打馬賦 *Dama Fu*

予性專博，晝夜每忘食事。南渡金華，僑居陳氏，講博弈之事，遂作
<依經打馬賦>曰：

歲令云徂，盧或可呼。千金一擲，百萬十都。樽俎具陳，已行揖讓之禮；
主賓既醉，不有博弈者乎？打馬爰興，摴蒲遂廢。實小道之上流，乃閨房
之雅戲。齊驅驥騄，疑穆王萬里之行；間列玄黃，類楊氏五家之隊。珊珊
珮響，方驚玉鐙之敲；落落星羅，忽見連錢之碎。
若乃吳江楓冷，胡山葉飛；玉門關閉，沙苑草肥。臨波不渡，似惜障泥。
或出入用奇，有類昆陽之戰；或優游仗義，正如涿鹿之師。或聞望久高，
脫復庚郎之失；或聲名素昧，便同癡叔之奇。亦有緩緩而歸，昂昂而出。
鳥道驚馳，蟻封安步。崎嶇峻坂，未遇王良；蹢躅鹽車，難逢造父。且夫
邱陵云遠，白雲在天，心存戀豆，志在著鞭。止蹄黃葉，何異金錢。用五
十六采之間，行九十一路之內。明以賞罰，覈其殿最。運指麾於方寸之
中，決勝負於幾微之外。
且好勝者人之常情，游藝者士之末技。說梅止渴，稍疏奔競之心；畫餅充
饑，少謝騰驤之志。將圖實效，故臨難而不迴；欲報厚恩，故知礙而先
退。或銜枚緩進，已踰關塞之艱；或賈勇爭先，莫悟穽塹之墜。皆由不知
止足，自貽尤悔。當知範我之馳驅，勿忘君子之箴佩。況為之賢已，事實
見於正經；用之以誠，義必合於天德。牝乃叶地類之貞，反亦記魯姬之
式。鑒髻墮於梁家，溯滸循於岐國。故遶床大叫，五木皆盧；瀝酒一呼，
六子盡赤。平生不負，遂成劍閣之師；別墅未輸，已破淮淝之賊。今日豈
無元子，明時不乏安石。又何必陶長沙博局之投，正當師袁彥道布帽之擲
也。
辭曰：佛貍定見卯年死，貴賤紛紛尚流徙。滿眼驊騮雜騄駬，時危安得真
致此？木蘭橫戈好女子！老矣誰能志千里，但願相將過淮水。

## 打馬圖經命詞 *Dama Tujing Mingci*

打馬世有二種：一種一將十馬者謂之 "關西馬"；一種無將二十馬者，謂之
"依經馬"。流行既久，各有圖經凡例可考。行移賞罰，互有異同。李易安
獨取為閨房雅戲，乃因依經馬，取其賞罰互度，每事作數語，精妍工麗，
世罕其儔，不僅施之博徒，實足貽諸同好，韻事奇人，兩垂不朽矣。

### 鋪盆

凡置局，二人至五人，鈞聚錢置盆中，臨時商量，多寡從眾；然不可
過四五人之數，多則本采交錯，多至喧鬧矣。詞曰：

既先設席，豈憚攫金，便請著鞭，謹令編垿。罪而必罰，已從約法之三
章；賞必有功，勿效遶床之大叫。凡不從眾議喧鬧者，罰十帖入盆。

## 本采

凡第一擲，謂之本采。如擲賞罰色，即不得認作本采。詞曰：

公車射策之初，記其甲乙；神武掛冠之日，定彼去留。汝其有始有終，我
則無偏無黨。

## 下馬

凡馬每二十匹用犀象刻成，或鑄銅為之如大錢樣，刻其文為馬，文各
以馬名別之；或只用錢，各以錢文為別，仍雜采染其文。詞曰：

夫勞多者賞必厚，施重者報必深。或再見而取十官，或一門而列三戟。又
昔人君每有賜，臣下必先乘馬焉。秦穆公悔赦孟明，解左驂而贈之是也。
豐功重錫，爾自取之，予何厚薄焉？

## 行馬 之一

凡馬局十一窩，遇入窩不打，賞一擲。詞曰：

九，陽數也，故數九而立窩；窩，險途也，故入窩而必賞。既能據險，以
一當千；便可成功，寡能敵眾。請回後騎，以避先登。

## 行馬 之二

凡疊成十馬，方許過函谷關。十馬先過，然後餘馬隨多少得過。自至
函谷關，則少馬不許踰別人多馬。詞曰：

行百里者半九十，汝其知乎？方茲萬物勒爭先，千羈競轡，得其中道，止
以半途。如能疊騎先馳，方許後來繼進。既施薄效，須稍旌甄，可倒半
盆。

## 行馬 之三

凡疊足二十馬到飛龍院，散采不得行，直待自擲真本采，堂印、碧
油、雁行兒、拍板兒、滿盆星諸賞采等，及別人擲自家真本采，上次
擲罰采，方許過。詞曰：

萬馬無聲，恐是銜枚之後；千蹄不動，疑乎立仗之時。如能翠幕張油，黃
扉啟印；雁歸沙漠，花發武陵。歌筵之小板初齊，天際之流星暫聚。或受
彼罰，或旌己勞。或當謝事之時，復過出身之數。語曰：鄰之薄，家之厚
也。以此始者，以此終乎？皆得成功，俱無後悔。

## 打馬 之一

凡多馬遇少馬，點數相及，即打去馬。馬數同，亦許打去，任便再
下。詞曰：

眾寡不敵，其誰可當？成敗有時，夫復何恨？或往而旋返，有同虞國之
留；或去亦無傷，有類塞翁之失。欲刷孟明五敗之恥，好求曹劌一旦之
功。其勉後圖，我亦不棄汝。

## 打馬 之二

凡打去人全垜馬，倒半盆。被打人出局，如願下者亦許。詞曰：

趙幟皆張，楚歌盡起。取功定霸，一舉而成。方西鄰責言，豈可蟻封共處？既南風不競，固難金垺同居。便請回鞭，不須戀廄。

### 打馬 之三

被打去全馬，人願再下。詞曰：

虧於一簣，敗此垂成。久伏鹽車，方登峻坂，豈期一蹶，遂失長塗。恨群馬之皆空，忿前功之盡棄。但素蒙剪拂，不棄駑駘；願守門闌，再從驅策。溯風驤首，已傷今日之障泥；戀主銜恩，更待明年之春草。

### 倒行

凡遇打馬，過疊馬，遇入窩，許倒行。詞曰：

唯敵是求，唯險是據。後騎欲來，前馬反顧。既將有為，退亦何害。語不云乎：日暮途遠，故倒行而逆施之也。

### 入夾

凡遇飛龍院，下三路，散采不許行。遇諸夾采，方許行。詞曰：

昔晉襄公以二陵而勝者，李亞子以夾寨而興者，禍福倚伏，其何可知？汝其勉力，當取大捷。

### 落塹

凡尚乘局，下一路謂之塹，不行不打，雖後有馬到亦同。落塹謂之同處患難，直待自擲諸渾花賞采、真本采、傍本采；別人擲自家真本采，傍本采，上次擲罰采，下次擲真傍撞方，許依元初下馬之數飛出。飛盡為倒盆，每飛一匹，賞一帖。詞曰：

凜凜臨危，正欲騰驤而去；駸駸遇伏，忽驚穿塹之投。項羽之騅，方悲不逝；玄德之驥，已出如飛。既勝以奇，當旌其異。請同凡例，亦倒金盆。

### 倒盆

凡十馬先到函谷關，倒半盆；打去人全馬，倒半盆。全馬先到尚乘局為細滿，倒倍盆，遇尚乘局為驫滿，倒一盆。落塹馬飛盡，同驫滿，倒一盆。詞曰：

瑤池宴罷，騏驥皆歸；大宛凱旋，龍媒並入。已窮長路，安用揮鞭。未賜弊帷，尤宜報主。驥雖伏櫪，萬里之志常存；國正求賢，千金之骨不棄。定收老馬，欲取奇駒。既以解驂，請拜三年之賜；如圖再戰，願成他日之功。

### 漢巴官鐵量銘跋尾注 Commentary in *Jin Shi Lu* (Page 211)

此盆色類丹砂。魯直石刻云："其一曰秦刀，巴官三百五十戊，永平七年第二十七酉。"余紹興庚午歲親見之。今在巫山縣治。韓暉仲云。

# Appendix B

# Chronology of Chinese History

Late Neolithic Cultures 新石器時代晚期
(archaeological evidence ):
      Yanhshao 仰韶文化          8,000-5,000 yrs ago
      Longshan 龍山文化         7,000-4,000 yrs ago
      (and other neolithic cultures
      in various parts of China)

Tribal Societies 部落聯盟時期     27$^{th}$ – 21 centuries **BCE**
(Chinese traditions 傳說時代)
      legendary model rules such as
      Yellow Emperor, Yao, Shun & others

Xia 夏                          21$^{st}$ – 16$^{th}$ centuries

Shang 商 or Yin 殷           16$^{th}$ – 12$^{th}$ centuries

Zhou 周                 12$^{th}$ century - 256
      Western Zhou 西周  ~1122 - 771
      Eastern Zhou 東周 771 - 256
        - Spring and Autumn period 春秋 770 - 476
        - Warring States period 戰國 475 - 221

Qin 秦                      221 - 207

Han 漢                 202 BCE - 220 **CE**
      Western Han 西漢   202 BCE - 9 CE
      Eastern Han 東漢  25 - 220 CE

*Period of Disunity*           220 - 591 CE
      Three Kingdoms 三國 220 - 280
      Western Jin 西晉 266 - 316
      Eastern Jin 東晉 317 - 420
      Southern Dynasties 南朝  420 - 589
      Northern Dynasties 北朝  386 – 581

Sui  隋                                                      581 – 618

Tang      唐                                                 618 - 907

Five Dynasties and Ten Kingdoms Era  五代十國      907 - 979

Song  宋
    Northern Song  北宋                       960 – 1127
    Southern Song  南宋                       1127 - 1279

      Liao  遼    916 - 1125
      Western Liao  西遼  1124 - 1211
      Xixia  西夏  1038 - 1227
      Jin  金  1115 - 1234

Yuan (Mongol)  元                                           1271 - 1368

Ming  明                                                     1368 - 1644

Qing (Manchu)  清                                           1644 - 1911

Republican of China (Nationalist)      中華民國      1911 - 1949
    Taiwan 1945 to present

People's Republic of China (Communist)                1949 to present
    中華人民共和國

# References

Ayling, Alan and Duncan Mackintosh. 1969. *A Further Collection of Chinese Lyrics*. London: Routledge and Kegan Paul.

Bai Shouyi. 2002. *An Outline History of China*. Rev. ed. Beijing: Foreign Languages Press.

Cai, Zhuozhi. 1994. "Gongsum Daniang." P. 139 in *100 Celebrated Chinese Women*. Translated by Kate Foster. Singapore: Asiapac Books Ptd. Ltd.

Chen Youbing 陳友冰 and Wang Deshou 王德壽. 2001. *Song Ci Qing Shang II: Nan Song Pian 宋詞清賞: 南宋篇*. Taibei: Zheng Zhong Shu Ju Gu Fen You Xian Gong Si.

Chen Zumei 陳祖美. 1995. *Li Qingzhao Ping Zhuan 李清照評傳*. Nanjing: Nanjing Da Xue Chu Ban She.

_____. 2001. *Li Qingzhao Xin Zhuan 李清照新傳*. Beijing: Beijing Da Xue Chu Ban She.

*Chinese History*. 1988. Beijing: China Reconstructs Press.

Chu Binjie 褚斌杰, Sun Chong'en 孫崇恩 and Rong Xianbin 榮憲賓, ed. 1984. *Li Qingzhao Zi Liao Hui Bian 李清照資料彙編*. Beijing: Zhong Hua Shu Ju.

*Concise English-Chinese Chinese-English Dictionary 精選英漢-漢英詞典*. 2001. 2nd ed. (Orthodox Chinese 繁體字本). Hong Kong: Oxford University Press (China) Ltd.

Deng Hongmei 鄧紅梅. 2005. *Li Qingzhao Xin Zhuan 李清照新傳*. Shanghai: Shanghai Gu Ji Chu Ban She.

Djao, Wei. 2003. *Being Chinese: Voices from the Diaspora*. Tucson: University of Arizona Press.

Ebrey, Patricia. 1993. *The Inner Quarters: Marriage and the Lives of Chinese Women in the Sung Period*. Berkeley: University of California Press.

Fan Ru 樊茹. 1996. *Zhong Wai Li Shi Da Shi Nian Biao 中外歷史大事年表*. Hong Kong: Zhong Hua Shu Ju (Hong Kong) Ltd.

Fan Wenlan 范文瀾. 1965. *Zhongguo Tong Zhi Jian Bian 中國通史簡編*. Book 3, volume 2. Rev. ed. Beijing: Ren Min Chu Ban She.

Fang Hao 方豪. 2000. *Song Shi 宋史*. 2nd ed. Taibei: Wen Hua Da Xue Chu Ban Bu.

Fung Yu-lan. 1964. *A Short History of Chinese Philosophy*, edited by Derk Bodde. New York: The MacMillan Co.

_____. 1991. *Selected Philosophical Writings of Fung Yu-lan*. Beijing: Foreign Languages Press.

Gao Hongxing 高洪興, Xu Jinjun 徐錦鈞 and Zhang Qiang 張強 (Eds.). 1991. *Fu Nü Feng Su Kao 婦女風俗考*. Shanghai: Shang Hai Wen Yi Chu Ban She.

Gould, J. and Kolb W.L. (Eds.). 1964. *A Dictionary of the Social Sciences*. Compiled under the auspices of the United Nations Educational, Scientific and Cultural Organization. London: Tavistock.

Hou Jian 侯建 and Lü Zhimin 呂智敏. 1985. *Li Qingzhao Shi Ci Ping Zhu 李清照詩詞評註*. Taiyuan: Shanxi Ren Min Chu Ban She.

Hu, Pinqing. 1966. *Li Ch'ing-chao*. New York: Twayne Publishers.

Huang Mugu 黃墨谷. [1980] 1984. "翁方綱<金石錄>本讀後 – 兼評黃盛漳<李清照事蹟考辨>中'改嫁新考' Weng Fanggang *Jin Shi Lu* Ben Du Hou – Jian Ping Huang Shengzhang 'Li Qingzhao Shi Ji Kou Bian" Zhong 'Gai Jia Xin Kou'." Pp. 392 – 401 in *Li Qingzhao Yan Jiu Lun Wen Ji 李清照研究論文集*, edited by Jinan Shi She Hui Ke Xue Yan Jiu Suo 濟南市社會科學研究所編. Reprint, Beijing: Zhonghua Shu Ju: Xin Hua Shu Dian Beijing Fa Xing Suo.

Huang Shengzhang 黃盛璋. [1957] 1984. "Li Qingzhao Shi Ji Kou Bian 李清照事蹟考辨." Pp. 311 – 357 in *Li Qingzhao Yan Jiu Lun Wen Ji 李清照研究論文集*, edited by Jinan Shi She Hui Ke Xue Yan Jiu Suo 濟南市社會科學研究所編. Reprint, Beijing: Zhonghua Shu Ju: Xin Hua Shu Dian Beijing Fa Xing Suo.

————. [1962] 1974. "Zhao Mingcheng Li Qingzhao Fu Fu Nian Pu 趙明诚李清照夫婦年譜." Pp. 132 – 187 in *Li Qingzhao Yan Jiu Hui Bian 李清照研究彙編*, edited by Zhou Kangxie 周康燮. Reprint, Hong Kong: Chong Wen Shu Dian.

Huang, Ray. 1992. *China: A Macro History*. Rev. ed. Armonk, NY: M.E. Sharpe, Inc.

Huo Ran 霍然. 1997. *Song Dai Mei Xue Si Chao 宋代美学思潮*. Changchun: Changchun Chu Ban She.

Jiang Hanchun 姜漢椿 and Jiang Hansen 姜漢森. 2008. *Xin Yi Li Qingzhao Ji 新譯李清照集*. Taibei: San Min Shu Ju You Xian Gong Si.

Jin Wenming 金文明. (Ed.) 1985. *Jin Shi Lu Jian Zhen 金石錄校證*. Shanghai: Shanghai Shu Hua Chu Ban She.

Ko, Dorothy. 1994. *Teachers of the Inner Chambers: Women and Culture in Seventeenth-century China*. Stanford, CA: Stanford University Press.

*Lao Zi 老子*. (Also known as *Dao De Jing 道德經*, or the *Book of Lao Zi*). Any edition or translation.

Lau, D.C. 1967. "Introduction." Pp. vii – xlv in *Lao Tzu: Tao Te Ching*. Translated by D.C. Lau. London: Penguin Books.

Lee, Godfrey 李夢軒. 2008. "Ci Xue Shi Yi 詞學釋義." Unpublished manuscript.

Li Xinchuan 李心傳. [Southern Song dynasty] 1975a. *Jianyan Yi Lai Xi Nian Yao Lu 建炎以來繫年要錄*. Vol. 20. Taibei: Taiwan Shang Wu Yin Shu Guan.

_____. [Southern Song dynasty] 1975b. *Jianyan Yi Lai Xi Nian Yao Lu* 建炎以來繫年要錄. Vol. 27. Taibei: Taiwan Shang Wu Yin Shu Guan.

_____. [Southern Song dynasty] 1975c. *Jianyan Yi Lai Xi Nian Yao Lu* 建炎以來繫年要錄. Vol. 58. Taibei: Taiwan Shang Wu Yin Shu Guan.

Lin Jiaying 林家英 and Qing Zhenxuan 慶振軒. 1986. "Chun Si Mian Mian Shi Chun Cao: *Xiao Chongshan* Shang Xi" 春思綿綿似春草: <小重山>賞析. Pp 1 – 8 in *Li Qingzhao Ci Jian Shang* 李清照詞鑒賞, edited by Lin Jiaying 林家英, Yan Zhaodian 閻昭典 and Liu Haijun 劉海軍. Jinan: Qi Lu Shu She.

Lin Wenzhao. 1987. "Magnetism and the Compass." Pp. 152 – 165 in *Ancient China's Technology and Science,* compiled by the Institute of the History of Natural Sciences, Chinese Academy of Sciences. Beijing: Foreign Languages Press.

Liu Qi 劉跂. [Song dynasty] 1985. "*Jin Shi Lu* Hou Xu 金石錄後序." Pp. 558-559 in *Jin Shi Lu Jian Zhen* 金石錄校證, edited by Jin Wenming 金文明. Shanghai: Shanghai Shu Hua Chu Ban She.

Liu Ruilian 劉瑞蓮. 1990. *Li Qingzhao Xin Lun* 李清照新論. Taiyuan: Shanxi Ren Min Chu Ban She.

Liu Yixuan 劉憶萱. 1981. *Li Qingzhao Shi Ci Xuan Zhu* 李清照詩詞選註. Shanghai: Shanghai Gu Ji Chu Ban She.

*Lun Yu* 論語. (Also known as the *Analects of Confucius*, or the *Sayings of Kong Fuzi*). Any edition or translation.

Ma Bin 馬彬 [Nan Gongbo 南宮博]. 1971. *Nan Du Yi Hou De Li Qingzhao* 南渡以後的李清照. Taibei: Taiwan Shang Wu Yin Shu Guan.

Marx, Karl and Frederick Engels. 1970. *The German Ideology.* Edited with introduction by C.J. Arthur. New York: International Publishers.

Mills, C. Wright. 1961. *The Sociological Imagination.* New York: Grove Press.

Owen, Stephen. 1986. *Remembrances: the Experience of the Past in Classical Chinese Literature.* Cambridge, MA: Harvard University Press.

National Palace Museum 國立故宮博物院. 2000. *Qian Xi Nian Song Dai Wen Wu Da Zhan Dao Du Shou Ce* 千禧年宋代文物大展導讀手冊. Taibei: National Palace Museum.

Rexroth, Kenneth and Ling Chung. 1979. *Li Ch'ing-chao Complete Poems.* New York: New Directions Publishing Corporation.

Sima Qian. [Western Han dynasty] 1996. *Shi Ji* 史記. Reprint, Beijing: Tuan Jie Chu Ban She.

*Song Shi* 宋史. [Yuan dynasty] 1986. *Er Shi Wu Shi* 二十五史. Vol. 7. Shanghai: Shanghai Gu Ji Chu Ban She.

Sun Yanwen 孫燕文. 2004. *Li Qingzhao Ci Xin Shang* 李清照詞欣賞. Tainan: Wen Guo Shu Ju.

Tang Guizhang 唐圭璋 and Pan Junzhao 潘君昭. 1984. "Lun Li Qingzhao Di Hou Qi *Ci* 論李清照的後期詞." Pp. 73 – 84 in *Li Qingzhao Yan Jiu Lun Wen Ji* 李清照研究論文集, edited by Jinan Shi She Hui Ke Xue Yan Jiu Suo 濟南市社會科學研究所編. Reprint, Beijing: Zhonghua Shu Ju, Xin Hua Shu Dian Beijing Fa Xing Suo.

Tao Yuanming 陶淵明. [Eastern Jin dynasty] (1989). "Gui Qü Lai Ci 歸去來 辭." Pp. 364-365 in *Xin Yi Gu Wen Kuan Zhi* 新譯古文觀止, edited by Xie Bingying 謝冰瑩, Qiu Xieyou 邱燮友, Zuo Songchao 左松超, Ying Yukang 應裕康, Huang Junlang 黃俊郎, and Fu Wuguang 傅武光. New ed. Taibei: San Min Shu Ju You Xian Gong Si.

Wang Xuechu 王學初. 1979. *Li Qingzhao Ji Jiao Zhu* 李清照集校註. Being: Renmin Wenxue Chu Ban She.

Wang Zhongwen 王仲聞. [1963] 1984. "Li Qingzhao Shi Ji Zuo Pin Za Kao 李清照事蹟作品雜考." Pp. 359 – 391 in *Li Qingzhao Yan Jiu Lun Wen Ji* 李清照研究論文集, edited by Jinan Shi She Hui Ke Xue Yan Jiu Suo 濟南市社會科學研究所編. Reprint, Beijing: Zhonghua Shu Ju: Xin Hua Shu Dian Beijing Fa Xing Suo.

Wen Shaokun 溫紹堃 and Qian Guangpei 錢光培. 1987. *Li Qingzhao Ming Pian Shang Xi* 李清照名篇賞析. Beijing: Beijing Shi Yue Wen Yi Chu Ban She.

Xia Chengtao 夏承燾. 1974. " 'Yi'an Ju Shi Shi Ji' Hou Yu '易安居士事輯'後 語." Pp. 269 – 272 in *Li Qingzhao Yan Jiu Hui Bian* 李清照研究彙編, edited by Zhou Kangxie 周康燮. Hong Kong: Chong Wen Shu Dian.

————. [1961] 1984. "Li Qingzhao *Ci* Di Yi Shu Te Se 李清照詞的藝術特 色." Pp. 65 – 72 in *Li Qingzhao Yan Jiu Lun Wen Ji* 李清照研究論文集, edited by Jinan Shi She Hui Ke Xue Yan Jiu Suo 濟南市社會科學研究 所編. Reprint, Beijing: Zhonghua Shu Ju, Xin Hua Shu Dian Beijing Fa Xing Suo.

Xie Xueqin 謝學欽. 2009. *Li Qingzhao Zheng Zhuan* 李清照正傳. Beijing: Zhong Guo Wen Shi Chu Ban She.

Xing Runchuan. 1987. "The Invention and Development of Printing and Its Dissemination Abroad." Pp. 383 – 391 in *Ancient China's Technology and Science,* compiled by the Institute of the History of Natural Sciences, Chinese Academy of Sciences. Beijing: Foreign Languages Press.

Xu Beiwen 徐北文. 1990. *Li Qingzhao Quan Ji Ping Zhu* 李清照全集評註. Jinan: Jinan Chu Ban She.

Xu Peijun 徐培均. 2002. *Li Qingzhao Ji Jian Zhu* 李清照集箋註. Shanghai: Shanghai Gu Ji Chu Ban She.

————. 2009. *Li Qingzhao Ji Jian Zhu* 李清照集箋註. 2nd printing with new Afterword. Shanghai: Shanghai Gu Ji Chu Ban She.

Yu Zhifang 余茝芳 and Shu Jing 舒静. 1999. *Li Qingzhao De Ren Sheng Zhe Xu 李清照的人生哲學 (Life Philosophy of Li Ching-chao)*. Taibei: Yang Zhi Wen Hua Shi Ye You Xian Gong Si. (Title in English provided by the publisher).

Yu Zhonghang 于中航. 1986. "Li Qingzhao Sheng Ping Za Kao San Ti 李清照生年雜考三题." Pp. 381 – 391 in *Li Qingzhao Yan Jiu Lun Wen Xuan 李清照研究論文選*, ed. by Jinan Shi She Hui Ke Xue Yan Jiu Suo 濟南市社會科學研究所編. Shanghai: Shanghai Gu Ji Chu Ban She.

_____. 1995. *Li Qingzhao Nian Pu 李清照年譜*. Taibei: Taiwan Shang Wu Yin Shu Guan Gu Fen You Xian Gong Si.

Yu Ziliu 余紫榴. 1988. *Zhongguo Shi Hua Wu Qian Nian: Long De Gen 中國史話五千年: 龍的根*. Hong Kong: Shang Wu Yin Shu Guan Xianggang Fen Guan.

Zha Liangyong 查良鏞 [Jin Yong 金庸]. 1984. *Da Mo Ying Xiong Zhuan 大漠英雄傳*. Taibei: Yuan Jing Chu Ban Shi Ye Gong Si. (First published as a serialized novel on *Hong Kong Commercial Daily* in 1957 under the title of *She DiaoYing Xiong Zhuan 射鵰英雄傳*).

Zhao Dongyu 趙東玉 and Li Jiansheng 李健勝. 2003. *Zhongguo Li Dai Fu Nü Sheng Huo Lüe Ying 中國歷代婦女生活畧影 (The Glimpse of Women's Life in Past Dynasties of China)*. Shenyang: Shenyang Chu Ban She. (Title in English provided by the publisher).

Zhao Mingcheng 趙明誠. [Song dynasty] 1985. "*Jin Shi Lu* Xu 金石錄序." Pp. 1-3 in *Jin Shi Lu Jian Zhen 金石錄校證*, edited by Jin Wenming 金文明. Shanghai: Shanghai Shu Hua Chu Ban She.

_____. [Song dynasty] 1991. *Song Ben Jin Shi Lu 宋本金石錄*. Reprint, Beijing: Zhonghua Shu Ju, Xin Hua Shu Dian Beijing Fa Xing Suo.

Zhou Baozhu 周寶珠, Yang Qianmiao 楊倩描, and Wang Zengyu 王曾瑜. 2002. *Er Shi Wu Shi Xin Bian: Bei Song Shi, Nan Song Shi 二十五史新編: 北宋史, 南宋史*. Shanghai: Shanghai Gu Ji Chu Ban She.

Zhou Zhide. 1987. "Shipbuilding." Pp. 479-493 in *Ancient China's Technology and Science,* compiled by the Institute of the History of Natural Sciences, Chinese Academy of Sciences. Beijing: Foreign Languages Press.

Zhuge Yibing 諸葛憶兵. 2004. *Li Qingzhao Yu Zhao Mingcheng 李清照與趙明誠*. Beijing: Zhong Hua Shu Ju.

# Index

An Lushan 安禄山, 42, 43
ancestral town, 30–31

Bai Juyi 白居易, 39, 41, 97, 109, 119
Bi Sheng 毕升, 27
Bianjing 汴京, 20, 22, 24, 26, 31, 32,
    35, 39, 51, 53, 65, 69, 71, 82, 86,
    97, 113, 115, 118, 119, 122, 196,
    201–03
Bianliang 汴梁. *See* Bianjing
*Book of Poetry* 诗经, 7, 207, 208

Cai Jing 蔡京, 49, 64, 65, 68, 74, 76,
    94, 98, 114, 115, 192, 193
calligraphy, xv, 14, 25, 33, 43, 52, 54,
    71, 83, 84, 89, 97, 104, 109, 115,
    117–20, 146, 149, 150, 151, 154,
    169, 204, 216, 220
    "Jin Xie Yu Ci Shi Quan 進谢御赐
        诗卷", 150
    *Leng Yan Jing* 楞严经, 97, 119
    "Zhao Shi Shen Miao Tie 赵氏神妙
        帖", 117
Cao Cao 曹操, 111
Cao Xueqin 曹雪芹, xvi, 102, 219
Chang'an 长安, 42, 43, 49, 121
Changjiang 长江, 23, 31, 44, 116, 120,
    122, 124, 130, 132, 134, 143, 144,
    158
Chao Buzhi 晁补之, 13, 32, 61, 67, 80,
    90–92, 94, 168, 213
Chao Gongwu 晁公武, 65, 211, 213
character, her, 215–17
Chen Dong 陈东, 126
Chen Shidao 陈师道 (Chen Wuji 陈无
    己), 52, 53, 61, 62
Chen Zhensun 陈振孙, 169
Chen Zumei 陈祖美, 29, 69, 81, 107,
    207
Chi You 蚩尤, 189
Chinese calendar and *sui*, 5–6
Chinese names, 3–4
*Chongyang* 重阳, 32, 85, 86

*Chronological Record of Important
Events Since the Jianyan Years*
建炎以来系年要录, 130, 131, 142,
    150, 159, 160, 162, 169
Chu, Irene, xviii

*ci* 词 by Li Qingzhao
    "A Cutting of the Plum Blossoms
        一剪梅", 87, 108
    "A Slow Sad Melody 声声慢", 2,
        204–09
    "As in a Dream 如梦令", 35, 57
    "Blossoms on the Hill 山花子", 181,
        182
    "Bodhisattvas' Headdress 菩萨蛮",
        10, 156
    "Butterflies Love Flowers 蝶恋花",
        13, 99, 112, 121, 128
    "Chang Shou Le 长寿乐", 183
    "Clear Peaceful Joy 清平乐", 139
    "Fairies by the River 临江仙", 128
    "Grievance Against the Lord 怨王
        孙", 40, 72
    "Happiness of Everlasting Meeting
        永遇乐", 202
    "Inebriated in the Shadow of
        Flowers 醉花阴", 2, 85, 86
    "New Version of Silk Washing
        Brook Sand 摊破浣溪沙", 181
    "Painted Lips 点绛唇", 36
    "Reminiscence of Flute Playing on
        the Phoenix Terrace 凤凰台上忆吹
        箫", 105, 108
    "Small Overlapping Hills 小重山",
        80
    "Spring in the Jade Tower 玉楼春",
        73, 108
    "Spring in Wuling 武陵春", 191
    "Telling Heartfelt Sentiments 诉衷
        情", 2, 127
    "The Abridged Version of
        Magnolia Blossom 减字木兰花",
        2, 55

"The Expanded Plucking the
Mulberries 添字采桑子", 122
"The Fisherman's Pride 渔家傲", 3,
38, 146
"Walking in Fragrance 行香子", 68,
124
"Washing Brook Sand 浣溪沙", 88,
108
*ci* poetry, 6–13
*haofang* 豪放 and *wanyue* 婉约,
148–49
civil service examinations, 23, 29, 42,
43, 63, 76, 92
provincial examination, 160
collected works of Li Qingzhao, 13–
15
collection of art and antiques, 82–84,
142–55
donate to court, 144–48
legacy, 217–20

Dali 大理, 22
*Dao De Jing* 道德经. *See* Lao Zi
daoist philosophy, 24, 79, 147, 219
daoist religion, 24, 99, 147, 148, 219
death, date of, 213–14
*Diamond Sutra* 金刚经, 27
divorce, 159–65
Djao Sing-Ming, xvi
Dragon Boat Festival. *See Duanwu*
*Dream of the Red Mansions* 红楼梦,
xvi, 102, 219
Du Fu 杜甫, 39, 66, 144, 206
*Duanwu* 端午, 200
Dawenkou culture 大汶口文化, 170

Emperor Song Du Zong 宋度宗, 172
Emperor Song Gao Zong 宋高宗, 5, 6,
23, 120, 124, 125, 130, 131, 133,
134, 139, 143, 144, 146, 147, 152,
154, 156, 158, 161, 169, 178, 179,
185, 186, 188, 192, 193, 195–98,
199, 220
Emperor Song Hui Zong 宋徽宗, xv,
22, 48, 51, 64, 74, 90, 92, 98, 102,
114, 115, 119, 143, 154, 172, 178,
192, 193, 195, 196, 198, 219

Emperor Song Li Zong 宋理宗, 172
Emperor Song Qin Zong 宋钦宗, 22,
114, 179
Emperor Song Ren Zong 宋仁宗, 29
Emperor Song Shen Zong 宋神宗, 18,
23, 29, 59, 60, 63, 171, 192, 193
Emperor Song Tai Zong 宋太宗, 172,
198
Emperor Song Tai Zu 宋太祖, 20, 21,
27, 28, 58, 109, 171, 198
Emperor Song Xiao Zong 宋孝宗, 198
Emperor Song Ying Zong 宋英宗, 173
Emperor Song Zhe Zong 宋哲宗, 24,
63, 64, 143, 192
Emperor Tang Su Zong 唐肃宗, 43, 46,
47
Emperor Tang Xuan Zong 唐玄宗, 39,
41–49, 92
Emperor Zhou Tai Zu 周太祖, 171
Empress Chen 陈皇后, 81
Empress Dowager Gao 高太皇太后, 63,
192
Empress Dowager Meng 孟皇太后,
143, 145
Empress Dowager Xiang 向皇太后,
193
Empress Zhang 张皇后, 47, 49
Empress Zhen 甄皇后, 171
essays by Li Qingzhao
*Ci Lun* 词论, 92–95
"Postscript to the *Jin Shi Lu* 金石录
后序", 31, 32, 54, 67, 70, 71, 75–
78, 82–84, 89, 95, 96, 108, 111,
116, 118, 120, 126, 131–34, 136,
137, 143–45, 149, 151–55, 158,
166, 182, 183, 194, 217, 218
letter to Qi Chongli 投翰林学士綦崇
礼启, 160–65
Preface to *Dama Tujing* 打马图经序,
*Dama Tujing Mingci* 打马图经命
词, *Dama Fu* 打马赋, 186–90
ethnicity in China, 6, 22, 42, 115, 125,
190

Fa Hui Si 法慧寺, 150
Fan Zhongyan 范仲淹, 171
*fantizi* 繁体字, 16, 17

*fen xiang mai lü* 分香卖履, 111, 137
Five Dynasties and Ten Kingdoms
    period 五代十国, 11, 20, 22, 171,
    174
foot binding, 174
*fu* 赋, 23, 186
Fu Cha 傅察, 114, 179
Fung, Yvonne, xviii

Gao Lishi 高力士, 42, 47, 49
Gong Yi 龚一, 88
Gongsun, Mistress 公孙大娘, 206
Gui Lai Tang 归来堂. *See* Return
    Home Hall
Guo Ziyi 郭子仪, 43–45, 48, 50
Guo, Madam 郭夫人, 51, 74, 76, 77,
    82, 98, 118, 119, 161, 172

Han dynasty 汉朝, 8, 9, 16, 18, 24, 52,
    81, 96, 103, 107, 111, 125, 171,
    184, 189
    Eastern Han 东汉, 8, 103, 111, 140,
        184, 189
    Western Han 西汉, 8, 18, 24, 103,
        107, 140, 171
Han Wo 韓偓, 37
Han Xiaozhou 韓肖胄, 178–80, 183
Han Yu 韓愈, 144
Hangzhou 杭州, 23, 140, 145, 150,
    156, 158, 159, 161, 178, 181, 183,
    184, 186, 194, 195, 199, 201, 212
*hanlin xueshi* 翰林学士, 199
heavenly emperor, 147
*Historical Record of Emperor Zhe
    Zong's Reign* 哲宗实录, 167, 192–
    94
Hong Gua 洪适, 168, 211
*Honglou Meng* 红楼梦. *See Dream of
    the Red Mansions*
Hu people 胡人, 42
Hu Songnian 胡松年, 178, 180, 181,
    197
Hu Zi 胡仔, 92, 94, 168, 169
Hua Mulan 花木兰, 190
Huang Di 黄帝. *See* Yellow Emperor
Huang Shengzhang 黄盛璋, 41

Huang Tingjian 黄庭坚, 52, 60, 61, 62,
    65, 67, 114
Huanghe (Yellow River) 黄河, 124
Huzhou 湖州, 131, 132, 135, 137

ideology, 14, 61, 94, 141, 170, 172,
    173, 175, 212, 214, 215, 217, 219
Imperial Concubine Yang Yuhuan 杨
    玉环贵妃, 39, 41–44, 49, 50, 66
*Inscriptions on Bronzes and Stones.
    See Jin Shi Lu*
intercalary month, 142, 144

Jiang Kui 姜夔, 10, 110
*jiantizi* 简体字, 16, 17
*Jianyan* 建炎 reign period, 5, 6, 131,
    168
*Jianyan Yi Lai Xi Nian Yao Lu* 建炎以
    来系年要录. *See Chronological
    Record of Important Events Since
    the Jianyan Years*
*jicai* 荠菜, 49
*jie* 节, 173–77
*jiemei* 姊妹, 100–02, 110, 112, 220
Jin 金, 22, 23, 54, 68, 88, 113–20, 123,
    125–27, 132, 133, 136, 139, 140,
    143–46, 149, 150, 158, 161, 165,
    168, 175, 176, 178–81, 184–88,
    190, 194–99, 201, 212, 220, 221
Jin dynasty 晋朝, Western and Eastern,
    125
*Jin Shi Lu* 金石录, 31, 51, 52, 54, 95–
    98, 108, 113, 114, 119, 144, 151,
    154, 155, 167, 169, 183, 209, 211,
    212, 214, 217
*Jin Shi Lu* Hou Xu. *See* essays by Li
    Qingzhao "Postscript to the *Jin Shi
    Lu*"
Jingzhi Hall 静治堂, 108
Jinhua 金华, 184–87, 190–92, 194
*jinshi* 进士, 23, 31, 51, 63, 92, 126,
    156, 171
*junzi* 君子, 166

King Xiang of Wei 魏襄王, 71
Kong Fuzi 孔夫子, 8, 23–25, 71, 76,
    83, 166, 188, 189, 219

Kublai Khan 忽必烈, 23, 159, 173

Laizhou 莱州, 98, 99, 102, 104, 108,
    112, 113, 119
Lantern Festival. *See Yuanxiao*
Lao Zi or *Lao Zi* 老子, 19, 24, 25, 79,
    148, 153–55, 189, 218, 219
Lee, Godfrey, xviii, 7
Li Bai 李白, 19, 39, 107, 144, 210
Li Fuguo 李辅国, 43, 47, 49
Li Gang 李钢, 116
Li Gefei 李格非 (Li Wenshu 李文叔),
    18, 19, 23–25, 29, 30, 33, 34, 44,
    51, 53, 54, 57, 60, 61, 65, 67, 69,
    74, 90, 94, 168, 169
Li Guangbi 李光弼, 43, 45, 48, 50
Li Hang 李远, 29, 121, 144, 159, 178
Li Linfu 李林甫, 42, 43
Li Mi 李泌, 43
Li Mo 李谟, 131
Li Qingzhao's name, 19–20
Li Si 李斯, 96
Li Tiaoyuan 李调元, 177, 214
Li Xinchuan 李心传, 130, 131, 132,
    142, 150, 160, 169
Li Yi'an 李易安. *See* Yi'an Jushi
Li Zhuo 李擢, 121, 143
Liang Qichao 梁启超, 208
Liao 辽, 22, 26, 58, 64, 115, 119
Liu Bang 刘邦, 134, 140
Liu Gongquan 柳公权, 52
Liu Kun 刘琨, 124, 125
Liu Qi 刘跂, 96
Liu Xiang 刘向, 107
Liu Xiu 刘秀, 184, 189
Liu Yiqing 刘义庆, 107
Liu Yong 刘永, 10
Liu Yu 刘豫, 140, 180, 181, 184, 185,
    187, 190, 194, 195
Liu Zongyuan 柳宗元, 144
*lizhi* 荔枝, 42
Longshan 龙山, 31, 170
Lu Defu 陆德夫, 86
Luoyang 洛阳, 23

Ma Bin 马彬 (Nan Gongbo 南宫博),
    133, 157

Manchu, 6, 174
Mao Jin 毛晋, 14, 56
McTyeire School 中西女子中学, xv, xvi
Meng Zi 孟子, 25, 219
Mi Fei 米芾, 204
Mi Youren 米友仁, 204
Ming dynasty 明朝, 14, 90, 165, 173,
    174
*mingfu* 命妇, 161, 162, 165, 167
mother, Li Qingshao's, 27–30

Nanjing 南京, 23, 81, 88, 97, 113,
    116–20, 124, 126–37, 144, 145
    Leaving Nanjing, 130–33
    Nanjing sojourn, 120–30
New Laws, 57–60
*niangjia* 娘家, 66, 69, 77
Ningbo 宁波, 145, 146
Northern Qi dynasty 北齐朝, 54
Nüzhen 女真, 22, 115

Ouyang Che 欧阳澈, 126
Ouyang Xiu 欧阳修, 93, 95, 128–30

patriarchy, 28, 174
*pianti* style 骈体, 166, 188
*pinyin* 拼音, 4
political factional strife, 57–68
portrait in Zhucheng, 89–90
printing press, 26–27

Qi Chongli 綦密礼, 158, 160–69, 196,
    197, 199
Qidan 契丹, 22, 42
Qijia culture 齐家文化, 170
Qin dynasty 秦朝, 8, 97
Qin Guan 秦观, 41, 61, 93
Qin Hui 秦桧, 126, 195–201, 203, 209
Qin Hui's wife nee Wang 秦桧妻王氏,
    195–99
Qin Shihuang 秦始皇, 96, 134
Qin Zi 秦梓, 200
Qing dynasty 清朝, 14, 15, 76, 89, 95,
    165, 173–175, 183, 187, 206, 214,
    219
*Qingming* 清明, 32, 72, 190
Qingxian 清宪, 74

Qingzhou 青州, 16, 76, 77, 80, 81, 82, 87–92, 94, 97–100, 104, 105, 108, 112, 117, 118, 132, 133, 136, 140, 146, 156, 208, 218, 220

Qu Yuan 屈原, 39, 80

Qujialing culture 屈家岭文化, 170

Reformers and Conservatives, 60–65

Return Home Hall 归来堂, 78, 83, 84, 89

*Romance of the Western Chamber* 西厢记, xv

Romanization, 1, 4

*ru* school 儒家, 25. *See also* Kong Fuzi

scholar-official class, 22, 27, 29, 30, 101

second marriage, 157–59
    controversy, 165–77

settlements on concubines. *See fen xiang mai lü*

Shang dynasty 商朝, 7, 45

Shangguan Wan'er 上官婉兒, 91

Shanghai 上海, xv, xvi, xvii, 15

Shaoxing 绍兴, 145, 146, 149, 150, 152, 158, 159, 169

*shi* 诗 by Li Qingzhao
    "By Chance 偶成", 139, 156
    celebratory poems (*tiezi* 帖子), 199
    "Crossing the Yan Sandbar at Night 夜发严滩", 185
    "*Ganhuai* 感怀", 102–04, 112
    "On History 咏史", 141
    Two poems honouring Envoys, 178–81
    "Two poems on 'The Wuxi Ode in Praise of the Restoration' to Rhyme with Zhang Wenqian 浯溪中兴颂诗和张文潜二首", 40–50
    "Wujiang 乌江", 134, 135

*shi* fragments, 65, 66, 124, 168

*Shi Ji* 史记, 18, 96

*shi* poetry 诗, 7–9

Shi Siming 史思明, 42, 43

*shidafu* 士大夫, 13, 17, 32, 91, 109, 168, 177, 199, 210

*shou jin shu* 瘦金书, xv, 115

*Shu Yu Ci* 漱玉词, 14, 15, 56, 89

*Shu Yu Ji* 漱玉集, 14, 169

Sima Qian 司马迁, 18, 24, 96

Sima Tan 司马谈, 24

Song dynasty 宋朝, 4, 5, 9, 10, 13, 15, 16, 18, 21–23, 25–27, 29, 30, 33, 58, 60, 72, 93, 94, 96, 109, 110, 112, 113, 119, 120, 126, 130, 131, 141, 160, 162, 167, 170–77, 186, 193, 194, 198, 200, 206, 210, 211, 212, 214, 218, 219, 221
    Northern Song 北宋, 9, 12, 16, 22, 23, 26, 27, 28, 43, 54, 56, 61, 63, 67, 68, 77, 91, 92, 93, 96, 110, 114, 115, 117, 119, 121, 122, 125, 128, 148, 167, 170–73, 175, 176, 179, 192, 196, 198, 204, 212, 219
    Southern Song 南宋, 9, 10, 14, 22, 23, 37, 56, 61, 92–94, 110, 113, 117, 120, 125, 126, 130, 131, 136, 141, 148, 158, 160, 167, 172–77, 181, 183, 188, 189, 193–98, 205–07, 211, 212, 215, 217, 218, 221

*Song Shi* 宋史, 13, 18, 19, 24, 25, 29, 62, 78, 179

Southern and Northern Dynasties 南北朝, 107, 125, 151, 152, 190

Spring and Autumn period 春秋时代, 72, 208

Su Shi 苏轼, 44, 53, 60–63, 65, 77, 80, 90, 94, 109, 110, 114, 148, 177

*sui* 岁. *See* Chinese Calendar and *sui*

Sui dynasty 隋朝, 26, 52, 151

Sun, Madam 孙夫人, 175–76, 212–13

Tang dynasty 唐朝, 8, 9, 19–21, 23, 27, 37, 39, 41, 43, 44, 50, 54, 64, 66, 68, 71, 91, 96, 97, 99, 121, 144, 154, 166, 171, 174, 206, 210

Three Heavenly Mountains, 146, 147

Three Kingdoms period 三国时代, 125, 140, 171

tones in Chinese language, 11

Tong Guan 童贯, 49, 115

Wang Anshi 王安石, 59, 60, 63, 93, 171, 177, 192
Wang Dao 王导, 124
Wang Gongchen 王拱辰, 29, 30, 195
Wang Gui 王珪, 29, 33, 195
Wang Jixian 王继先, 142–43, 150, 161
Wang Lun 王纶, 195
Wang Mang 王莽, 140–41, 184, 189
Wang Peng Yun 王鹏运, 89
Wang Xuechu 王学初, 15, 29, 30, 56
Wang Yi 王亦, 131
Wang Zhongwen 王仲闻. *See* Wang Xuechu
Wang Zhun 王准, 29, 195
Wang Zhuo 王灼, 33, 50, 56, 168, 169
Wanli Emperor 万历皇帝, 165
Warring States period 战国时代, 24, 26, 39, 71, 79, 97, 107, 147, 180, 200
Weaving Maid and the Cowherd, 69
Wei, Madam 魏夫人, 14, 141, 210
*weiqi* 围棋, 25, 33, 216
Wen, Madam 文夫人, 179, 183
Wenzhou 温州, 145, 146
wine and inebriation, 210–11
writings, assessment of, 220–23
*wu si* 无嗣, 112
*wu yin* 五音, 10
Wu Zetian 武则天, 91, 171
Wuling Creek 武陵溪, 106

Xiang Guo Temple 相国寺, 54
Xiang Yu 项羽, 134, 135, 140
Xiao Yi 萧绎, 151, 154
*xiaoren* 小人, 166, 220
Xie Ji 谢伋, 121, 137, 161, 162, 197
Xie Kejia 谢克家, 121, 137, 142, 143, 150, 161, 197
Xie Xueqin 谢学钦, 177
Xin Qiji 辛弃疾, 110, 148
Xiongnu 匈奴 (Hun), 125
Xixia 西夏, 22, 58
Xu Bo 徐渤, 165
Xu Peijun 徐培均, 15, 35, 81
Xu Qiu 徐釚, 206
Xu Xi 徐熙, 71

Yan Guang 严光, 184, 185
Yan Rui 严蕊, 110
Yan Xin Life Science and Technology, xviii
Yan Zhenqing 颜真卿, 43
Yang Guang 杨广, 151, 154
Yang Guozhong 杨国忠, 42, 66
*Yang Pass*, 99, 106
Yang Shen 扬慎, 14
Yellow Emperor 黄帝, 19, 24, 189
Yen Shu-Jen, xv
Yi Shizhen 伊世珍, 53, 85, 86, 90
Yi'an Jushi 易安居士, 4, 13–15, 18, 37, 56, 78, 86, 92, 126, 160, 168, 169, 188, 204, 223
Yi'an Room 易安室, 78, 152
Yu Zhengji 俞正己, 168, 169
Yu Zhengxie 俞正燮, 166, 167, 175
Yuan dynasty 元朝, 53, 85, 173, 174
Yuan Jie 元结, 43, 44, 48
Yuan You Party 元祐党, 63, 65, 67, 69, 70, 74, 90, 92, 94
*Yuanfeng* reign period 元丰, 18, 29
*Yuanxiao* 元宵, 129, 201
Yue Fei 岳飞, 126, 184, 195, 197, 198, 201
Yue Yun 岳云, 198
*yuefu* 乐府, 8, 9, 207

Zeng Zao 曾慥, 207
Zhang Duanyi 张端义, 206
Zhang Feiqing 张飞卿, 145
Zhang Jiucheng 张九成, 156
Zhang Ruzhou 张汝舟, 158–69, 178, 194
Zhang Wenqian 张文潜 (Zhang Lei 张耒), 41, 43, 44, 48, 49, 61, 68
Zhang Xu 张旭, 206
Zhang Yufu 张玉夫, 212, 213
Zhao Cuncheng 赵存诚, 76, 119, 121, 192
Zhao Defu 赵德甫. *See* Zhao Mingcheng
Zhao Kuangyin 赵匡胤. *See* Emperor Song Tai Zu
Zhao Lingren Li 赵令人李, 162

Zhao Mingcheng 赵明诚 (Zhao Defu
    赵德甫), 16, 30, 31, 37, 51–56, 61,
    62, 65, 69–71, 74–78, 80–91, 95–
    100, 104, 105, 107–09, 111–14,
    116–20, 126, 127, 130–40, 142–45,
    148–60, 162, 165, 167–69, 175,
    178, 179, 182, 183, 191–94, 197,
    199, 200, 203, 208, 209, 211, 212,
    214, 216, 217, 220, 221
    death, 136–38
Zhao Sicheng 赵思诚, 76, 119, 121
Zhao Tingzhi 赵挺之, 18, 19, 51–54,
    57, 60–67, 70, 71, 74–77, 95, 98,
    160, 192, 193
Zhao Yanwei 赵彦卫, 14, 37, 169
Zhe Zong Shi Lu 哲宗实录. See
    Historical Record of Emperor Zhe
    Zong's Reign
Zhou dynasty 周朝, 8, 26, 77, 171

Zhou Hui 周煇, 126, 130
Zhou Yi 周易, 83
Zhu Bian 朱弁, 13
Zhu Shuzhen 朱淑贞, 113, 210
Zhu Xi 朱熹, 14, 61, 141, 142, 212,
    214, 219
Zhuang Chuo 庄绰, 29
Zhuang Zi 庄子, 24, 25, 39, 79, 147,
    219
zhuangyuan 状元, 29
Zhuge Yibing 诸葛忆兵, 29
Zizhou 淄州, 97, 108, 109, 113, 114,
    116–18, 119
Zuo Zhuan 左传, 83, 154

# About the Author

Born in China, Wei Djao grew up in Shanghai and Hong Kong. She has a Ph.D. in sociology from the University of Toronto, specializing in China. She was a tenured associate professor of sociology at the University of Saskatchewan, and a tenured professor of Global/Asian Studies at North Seattle Community College. She also taught in California, Hong Kong, and Alberta, Canada.

Dr. Djao has written three other books: *Being Chinese: Voices from the Diaspora* (Tucson: University of Arizona Press, 2003) which is about the Chinese overseas, that is, people of Chinese ancestry who live in non-Chinese societies; *Inequality and Social Policy: The Sociology of Welfare* (Toronto: John Wiley & Sons, 1983), and *Choices and Chances: Sociology for Everyday Life* (San Diego, CA: Harcourt Brace Jovanovich, 1990, co-author: Lorne Tepperman).

Wei's articles have appeared in scholarly journals, such as *Canadian Ethnic Studies, Journal of Contemporary Asia, Journal of Sociology and Social Welfare, Canadian Review of Social Policy, Service Social,* and *Social Praxis,* as well as in edited books published in Canada, China, and the United States. Professor Djao's research and teaching interests included the global society, China, women of colour, Pacific Rim studies, and the Chinese overseas.

Professor Djao is currently on the faculty of the College of Education (Ph.D. Programs), Walden University, Minneapolis, MN.

In 2009 Wei helped to establish the online magazine *Ginger Post* www.gingerpost.com where Chinese Canadians and other Chinese overseas can exchange news and information, and where they can also learn about their heritage culture.

She was the interviewer, narrator, writer, or researcher in the production of three television documentaries: *American Nurse* (an award-winning thirty-minute program about the experiences of New York-born Chinese American veteran of the Vietnam War Lily Lee Adams); *Another Day in America* (a documentary on Japanese American women artists in the San Francisco Bay area); and *Chinese Cafes in Rural Saskatchewan.* These documentaries are in the video collections of libraries in the United States, Canada, Hong Kong and Singapore.

Wei Djao and her family live in Toronto. She enjoys hiking and cross-country skiing. She also does botanical illustration with Chinese brushes. She can be contacted at: editor@gingerpost.com.